*f***P**

THINKING BEYOND LEAN

How Multi-Project Management Is Transforming Product Development at Toyota and Other Companies

MICHAEL A. CUSUMANO

KENTARO NOBEOKA

THE FREE PRESS

New York   London   Toronto   Sydney   Singapore

*f*P

THE FREE PRESS
A Division of Simon & Schuster Inc.
1230 Avenue of the Americas
New York, NY 10020

Manufactured in the United States of America

10 9 8 7 6 5 4 3 2 1

Library of Congress Cataloging-in-Publication Data

Cusumano, Michael A.
    Thinking beyond lean: how multi-project management is
transforming product development at Toyota and other companies/
Michael A. Cusumano, Kentaro Nobeoka.
        p. cm.
    Includes bibliographical references and index.
    1. Automobiles—Design and construction. 2. Industrial project
management. 3. Concurrent engineering.   I. Nobeoka, Kentarō.
II. Title.
TL278.C87   1998   98-3545
629.2'068'5—dc21   CIP

ISBN: 978-1-439-10177-3
ISBN: 1-439-10177-9

This book is dedicated to the memory of

RAMCHANDRAN "JAI" JAIKUMAR

Jai was a pioneer in the study of flexible manufacturing systems, a world-class mountaineer, a cherished friend and colleague of many people, and a devoted husband and father. He inspired everyone who knew him to think more deeply, to see more clearly, and to enjoy life more fully. We are fortunate that he left us with so many wonderful ideas and moments to ponder and celebrate. Thanks, Jai, for everything. Always.

Contents

Preface   *ix*
Acknowledgments   *xi*

1: Introduction: Beyond "Lean" in Product Development   1

2: The Toyota Benchmark:
   Multi-Project Development Centers   19

3: Organizing Product Development in the
   World Auto Industry   51

4: Strategies for Product Development and Multiple Projects   101

5: Multi-Project Strategies and Project Performance   115

6: Multi-Project Strategies and Company Performance   137

7: Organizational Requirements for
   Effective Multi-Project Management   157

8: Implications and Lessons for Managers   183

   Appendices   199

   Endnotes   219
   References   227
   Index   239
   About the Authors   247

Preface

This book began in 1991 as a study sponsored by MIT's International Motor Vehicle Program (IMVP), the multi-million dollar research effort on the automobile industry funded by the Sloan Foundation as well as most of the world's auto makers. At this time, Michael Cusumano, a professor at the MIT Sloan School of Management who specializes in strategy and technology management, took on the responsibility of overseeing product development research. Kentaro Nobeoka later joined him in this role. Nobeoka had worked in product planning at Mazda before coming to MIT as a graduate student and a researcher for IMVP. Their goal was to continue the study of best practices in product development among world auto makers chronicled in IMVP's international best-seller, *The Machine That Changed the World*, published in 1990 by James Womack, Daniel Jones, and Daniel Roos, as well as in *Product Development Performance*, published in 1991 by our colleagues Kim Clark at the Harvard Business School and Takahiro Fujimoto at the University of Tokyo.

One of the first milestones we reached in our effort came in 1992. We wrote an article ("Strategy, Structure, and Performance in Product Development") that reviewed what we know and did not know about product development in the auto industry. We concluded that we knew a lot about how the best companies managed individual projects to reduce engineering costs, cut development lead time, and improve product quality. *The Machine That Changed the World* and *Product Development Performance* had discussed these principles of "lean" thinking in great detail as they applied to individual projects. But we realized how little we knew about how companies might design products from shared components and then coordinate projects that they linked strategically, technically, and organizationally. Therefore, we decided to make "multi-project management" of product development the focus of our research. This emphasis contrasted with benchmarking the performance of companies on individual projects, which Clark, Fujimoto, and other colleagues have continued to do. We also decided to explore how auto companies were streamlining product development to improve their performance in the highly competitive environment of the 1990s and in preparation for the year 2000.

We began by creating a database on 210 automobile products from public information. This enabled us to determine which cars shared "platforms," the underbody to an automobile and an expensive, critical subsystem that defines the performance of the product. We then launched a survey of several hundred project managers and engineers. The survey data enabled us to analyze project performance as well as organizational issues such as coordination within and across projects and functional engineering areas within a firm. Other graduate students sponsored by IMVP and working under Cusumano at the time took up related studies. In particular, Greg Scott focused on writing case studies on product development at the U.S. auto companies, and Yaichi Aoshima focused on knowledge transfer across different product generations in Japanese auto companies. In October 1996, Nobeoka also published a preliminary version of the data analyses and case studies in Japanese.

This book is the culmination of our six-year study. Overall, we interviewed 335 managers and engineers at 17 auto makers between 1994 and 1997. It is our conclusion that Toyota and other leading auto makers have discovered a better way to develop products by moving beyond recent thinking about project management, including the lean principles proposed in *The Machine That Changed the World*. In the chapters that follow, we explain what we mean.

Acknowledgments

This book represents six years of research sponsored by the International Motor Vehicle Program at MIT. The Sloan Foundation, most auto companies, many auto suppliers, and several industry and government organizations have all contributed financially to this program and deserve our many thanks. Since the research has a long history, there also have been many individuals to whom we need to express our gratitude.

Both authors would like to thank the directors of IMVP at the Massachusetts Institute of Technology (Dan Roos and Charley Fine) as well as executives from the Sloan Foundation (Ralph Gomery and Hirsh Cohen) for their support over many years. They made this book possible and helped to fund Nobeoka's doctoral studies at MIT, along with support from the MIT Sloan School of Management doctoral program. We also offer our deepest thanks to the hundreds of managers and engineers who allowed us to visit and provided us with project and survey data; we list their names in Appendix 5. The Japan Automobile Manufacturers Association also provided assistance with access to Japanese companies. In addition, Nancy Staudenmayer of Duke University, John Paul MacDuffie of the Wharton School at the University of Pennsylvania, and Scott Stern and Greg Scott of MIT read the final manuscript and provided many useful suggestions.

Within IMVP, we would like to thank Donna Carty, Ann Rowbotham, and Agnes Chow for administrative support. Our European director, Andrew Graves, helped arrange visits to European companies. Fiat was an especially gracious host for a key meeting we held with other European companies in 1993 and another meeting in 1996. In addition, many colleagues and students affiliated with IMVP have been extraordinarily helpful and encouraging over the years. In particular, we need to thank several of our fellow researchers in product development: Greg Scott of MIT, Takahiro Fujimoto of the University of Tokyo, Yaichi Aoshima of Hitotsubashi University, and David Ellison of the Wharton School, University of Pennsylvania. Kim Clark of the Harvard Business School and Ed Roberts of the MIT Sloan School also served on Kentaro Nobeoka's doctoral thesis committee and provided many useful suggestions in an earlier stage of this study.

Also closely associated with this project were several MIT master's students working under Cusumano after 1990. They examined topics such as component sharing and productivity in engine development (Douglas Doi), the impact of product variations on manufacturing performance (Jane Boon and Jan Klatten), development of software for electronic components at Ford (Vladimir Otchere), and changes in the product development organization at GM (Dantar Oosterwal).

Michael Cusumano would like to thank the Institute of Innovation Research at Hitotsubashi University for hosting him for several months during mid-1997, when he completed work on this book. He would like to thank the MIT Sloan School administration (Dean Glen Urban and Associate Deans Richard Schmalensee and Tom Allen) for their flexible approach to his schedule. In addition, he would like to acknowledge the MIT Sloan School's International Center for Research on the Management of Technology (ICRMOT), which has supported much of his research in past years, as well as the new MIT Center for Innovation in Product Development, which is currently supporting his work on rapid product development techniques.

Kentaro Nobeoka would like to thank Ken Kusunoki of Hitotsubashi University, Susumu Ogawa and Shinichi Ishii of Kobe University, Hiroshi Okano of Osaka City University, and Shinsuke Itoh of Yuhikaku for their useful comments on his earlier manuscripts in Japanese. He also would like to acknowledge his senior colleagues, Hideki Yoshihara, Tadao Kagono, Kenji Kojima, and Toshihiro

Kanai of Kobe University, for their stimulating suggestions on his research work. In addition, he thanks Tsutomu Kagawa and Mamoru Hoshino from the Japan Automobile Manufacturers Association for their assistance in gaining access to Japanese firms. He also thanks Antony Sheriff, a former classmate at the MIT Sloan School, who was a co-researcher at the very early stages of this research.

Michael A. Cusumano   *Kentaro Nobeoka*
Cambridge, MA   *Kobe, Japan*

September 1997

THINKING
BEYOND
LEAN

Chapter 1

Introduction:

Beyond "Lean" in
Product Development

This book is about how to manage product development more strategically and efficiently. We talk about *multi-project management* and the benefits this kind of thinking can bring to projects and to companies. The basic idea is to create new products that share key components but to utilize separate development teams that ensure each product will differ enough to attract different customers. If possible, projects that share components and engineering teams should overlap in time so that a firm can deliver many products quickly and utilize very new technologies. The evidence we have suggests that, if they follow these principles, firms can achieve dramatic improvements in performance—huge savings in development costs (engineering hours) as well as remarkable growth in sales and market share. The examples and data we present are mainly from the automobile industry. The ideas, however, apply to many companies that have more than one product and want to expand the number of new products rapidly and efficiently.

Managers, in our view, have a simple choice: They can manage

FIGURE 1–1

A Simple Model of Multi-Project Product Development

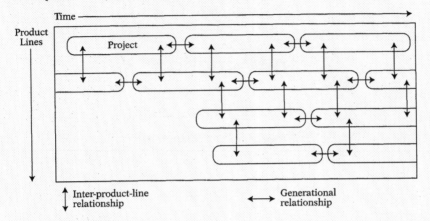

new product development as if each project and product exists in isolation—and possibly maximize their chances of delivering something fast and producing a "hit." Or, they can view each development project as part of a broader portfolio of projects—existing in the past, present, and future (Figure 1–1). If they follow *multi-project thinking,* then they can try to maximize the chances that the organization will produce *a stream of new products* that cover a range of market segments and make the best possible use of R&D investments.

KEY QUESTIONS

How to manage more than one project at a time is no simple matter, especially for companies that have many product lines, many projects to coordinate, and complex products with many components. Automobile manufacturers provide particularly excellent cases to study because of the challenges they face. They generally have numerous product lines and lots of projects ongoing simultaneously. Their products contain 30,000 or so components and usually take a million or more engineering hours per project to develop. The actual time and cost needed to create an automobile depend on how fast companies go through the different steps required. This speed, in turn, depends at least in part on how much they overlap functional activities such as concept generation (deciding what to design), product planning (determining product specifications and how a new product fits with other products), advanced engineering (coordinating the development of major components such as engines or transmissions with particular projects), product engineering (creating detailed designs for components and subsystems), process engineering (designing equipment and techniques for manufacturing), and pilot production (low-volume experimental manufacturing).

A critical decision for automobile companies, or any company building a complex product with many components or subsystems, is whether or not to organize groups around functional activities or around projects that bring together people from the different functions or component areas. Most auto makers have moved toward a mixture of functional groups and projects (or clusters of projects, which we refer to as "development centers"). In doing so, all companies have debated *how to balance what is optimal for the individual project versus what is optimal for the organization* as a whole. In our discussions, we break down this problem into several issues, such as:

- Which functions should companies keep centralized to take advantage of scale and scope economies by providing engineering services and components (such as body design or engine technology) to more than one project?
- Which functions should companies disperse among projects in order to maximize the distinctiveness and innovativeness of the individual products?
- How much authority over budgets and personnel should a project manager have versus managers of functional departments?
- To what extent should companies seek a balance of functional with project management by grouping related projects together and then sharing some technologies as well as functions at least for clusters of similar projects?

We try to provide answers to these and other questions. We base our arguments on detailed case studies and interviews with managers and engineers, as well as extensive analyses of data we have collected on automobile development projects and company performance. Before we discuss our results, however, we need to explain the background behind our concern for *multi-project* as opposed to *single-project* management in product development.

LEAN PRINCIPLES AND SINGLE PROJECTS

Most writings on best-practice in product development refer to single projects. This is true of *Product Development Performance* (1991) by Clark and Fujimoto, who first collected quantitative data from auto makers at the individual project level.[1] This is also true of *The Machine That Changed the World* (1990) by Womack, Jones, and Roos, which summarized concepts that leading auto makers use to manage product development as well as manufacturing more efficiently. To characterize these "best practices," *The Machine That Changed the World* also used the word *lean,* a term coined by John Krafcik, who was a master's student at MIT in the mid-1980s.[2] A more recent book, *Lean Thinking* (1996) by Womack and Jones, has extended some of these ideas about efficiency and eliminating waste to the organization of companies and operations more generally.[3]

Lean refers to a general way of thinking and specific practices that emphasize less of everything—fewer people, less time, lower costs. In product development, firms around the world in many industries now follow many of the lean concepts discussed in the books we have just cited (Table 1–1). Two especially important principles, which Clark and Fujimoto highlighted in particular, are the following: (1) overlapping different functional activities or development phases, such as concept generation, product engineering, and process engineering; and (2) using relatively independent product teams led by "heavyweight" project managers. The product teams usually bring together people from different engineering functions as well as marketing, and in this sense are *cross-functional* in organization. In addition, the heavyweight project managers generally have extensive control over product concepts as well as the people and budgets involved in component engineering, production preparations, and marketing. As a result, they have the ability to create distinctive new designs and then

TABLE 1–1

Lean Versus Functional Product Development

Lean Thinking	Functional Management
Rapid model replacement	Slow model replacement
Frequent model-line expansion	Infrequent model-line expansion
More incremental product improvements	More radical product improvements
Heavyweight project managers	Lightweight project coordinators
Overlapping, compressed phases	Sequential, long phases
High levels of supplier engineering	High levels of in-house engineering
Design team and project-manager continuity	Department member continuity
Good communication mechanisms	Walls between departments
Cross-functional teams	Narrow skills in specialized departments

Source: Adapted from Cusumano, 1994. Also see Clark and Fujimoto, 1991, and Womack and Jones, 1996.

quickly move product concepts through the development process and into manufacturing.

Other lean principles also contrast with the use of more traditional functional management practices in product development. In more traditional functional companies, for example, each engineering department tends to have a strong manager who hands off work to other departments, often in a sequential manner. This approach contrasts with relatively short, overlapping phases and cross-functional teams guided by a strong project manager.

There is no doubt that lean thinking has significantly improved project performance. During the 1980s, for example, many Japanese auto makers used heavyweight project managers, overlapping phases, and other techniques when they replaced and expanded their product lines nearly twice as often as U.S. and European companies.[4] As seen in Table 1–2, the Japanese required only about two-thirds of the lead or calendar time required for the average project (about 45 months compared to 60 months or so for U.S. and European producers). They also needed approximately half the engineering effort (1.7 million compared to 3.4 million in the United States and 2.9 million in Europe). This efficient and rapid model change or expansion allowed Japanese auto makers to introduce many new features and quality improvements into their products as well as expand their sales.

More important, we have learned that these practices and high R&D performance levels are not unique to Japanese firms. Table 1–2

TABLE 1–2

Lead Time and Engineering Hours Comparison

	Japan	United States	Europe
NUMBER OF PROJECTS			
1980s	12	6	11
1990s	8	5	12
ADJUSTED LEAD TIME (MONTHS)			
1980s	45	61	59
1990s	54	52	56
ADJUSTED ENGINEERING HOURS (MILLIONS)			
1980s	1.7	3.4	2.9
1990s	2.1	2.3	2.8
% OF HEAVYWEIGHT PROJECT MANAGERS			
1980s	17	0	0
1990s	25	20	0
% OF MIDDLE TO HEAVYWEIGHT PROJECT MANAGERS			
1980s	83	17	36
1990s	100	100	83
% COMMON PARTS			
1980s	19	38	30
1990s	28	25	32

Source: Ellison, Clark, Fujimoto, and Hyun, 1995, p. 11.

Notes: Adjusted Lead Time is the number of months required to develop a new product adjusted for average product complexity. *Adjusted Engineering Hours* is the number of hours required to develop a new product adjusted for average complexity. See the source of this table for additional explanation of the measures and adjustments.

includes data from a 1995 update of the Clark and Fujimoto survey. This indicates that auto makers around the world are adopting heavyweight or at least "middleweight" project management systems. We also can see companies moving toward comparable levels of performance in the time required for new product development (although U.S. auto makers tend to trail in product quality measures).[5]

BEYOND LEAN: MANAGING MULTIPLE PROJECTS

We are not saying that heavyweight project management and other lean principles are now outdated. Tightly organized cross-functional teams are usually nimble and fast, especially if they overlap phases and give lots of authority to project managers and creative engineers. In addition, companies often can improve their chances of producing distinctive individual products by organizing autonomous product teams that focus on new designs or technologies.

We are saying that, for managers, multi-project thinking usually fits reality much better than focusing on single projects, which lean practices in product development emphasize. Most companies have more than one product, and many companies have more than one new product under development at the same time. Companies may not deliberately link projects by sharing components. Nonetheless, any firm requires some sort of multi-project management if its projects compete for key engineers or financial resources, or target similar customers in the marketplace. Moreover, the evidence we have suggests that, over the long term, aiming simply for new designs or hit products in isolated projects is not enough: The best companies today view projects as part of a portfolio and make the most of their investments by introducing new technologies in as many products as possible as frequently as possible.

In past years, Japanese companies such as Toyota and Honda, and then other firms such as Chrysler in the United States, decided to become leaner in product development by focusing on one project at a time and getting better products out the door faster. Their goal was to increase market share almost at any cost. Since the mid-1980s, however, growth for many auto makers has slowed or stopped, and profits have fallen dangerously low in many years. The key problem has since become how to replace products and occasionally expand product lines with innovative, high-quality models that *minimize development and production costs.*

Not surprisingly, leading companies have already shifted their attention beyond simply the efficient management of individual projects. We can see some evidence of this in Table 1–2. In the early 1990s, Japanese firms slowed down many of their development projects. Though they still required fewer engineering hours than U.S. or European projects, compared to the 1980s, the Japanese took an extra nine months per project in this sample. Our interviews suggest that this is because they were taking more time in planning and focusing more on how to create innovative designs and avoid low-value features and unnecessary unique parts. Indeed, the data indicates that Japanese projects in the 1990s did increase their usage of common parts. This contrasts with the United States, where some companies reduced their emphasis on common parts in the early 1990s (see Table 1.2). The reverse trend now seems to be occurring, however, as U.S. companies move more toward platform sharing and what we call multi-project management.

This rethinking of product development in Japan and elsewhere occurred because there is at least one drawback to an exclusive focus on single projects: Heavyweight project managers can become *too heavy.* At leading Japanese companies, for example, projects accumulated so much autonomy that they produced "fat" designs—too few common components and too many unnecessary features and options.[6] As a result, however well they managed individual projects, these companies fell into the trap of optimizing product development for the good of each project rather than for the good of the firm as a whole.

Six years of research have convinced us that the best way to work for the good of the firm and create a portfolio of products at low cost is to shift the company mindset and organization into a *multi-project* mode. This means that a firm will develop some totally new products but focus an equal amount of attention on developing common core components and quickly sharing these across multiple projects. Moreover, we have observed that *companies can coordinate projects deliberately or in an ad hoc manner.* The best companies, such as Toyota, follow a deliberate approach and leave little to chance. They create families of well-integrated products that share design concepts as well as key components and basic technologies. Multi-project management, as we describe it in this book, thus requires conscious, planned efforts to link a set of projects *strategically*, through product portfolio planning, *technologically*, through the design of common core components, and *organizationally*, through overlapping the responsibilities and work of project managers and individual engineers.

STRATEGIES AND ORGANIZATIONS FOR MULTIPLE PROJECTS

Once companies establish a clear strategy for linking multiple projects, they need to create an appropriate organization and management processes to make this strategy work. In this book, we do not suggest to managers what specific products to build or what components to share, or how to manage the details of engineering work. Rather, we give many examples of good practice. We also present frameworks and data analyses that should help managers form their own multi-project strategies as well as find better ways of organizing product development in their own companies.

A useful start to explain our thinking is Figure 1–2, which presents our framework for project strategies. This focuses on how companies can link projects in order to share platform technologies that define the basic structure and performance of a new automobile product. The typology categorizes new projects into four types, depending on the extent of new technology or changes in a platform, how projects use the platform technology, and how fast or slow a company transfers a platform from one project to another. These four types cover all kinds of development projects and are mutually exclusive. The analysis in this book focuses on the design strategy for vehicle platforms in new cars, although the same framework can apply to major components for other products as well.

FIGURE 1–2

Typology of Project Strategies and Inter-Project Linkages

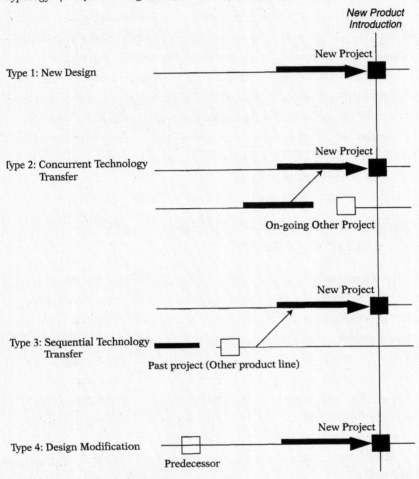

Source: Nobeoka and Cusumano, 1995, p. 398.

Projects that develop platforms primarily from scratch we categorize as the first type, *new design.* This strategy is most appropriate for incorporating the latest technology or totally new designs into a product without placing many restrictions on the development team. The distinction between new design and the other three types is conceptually similar to the difference between radical and incremental innovations.[7] Our framework, however, breaks down incremental changes into three types, depending on the strategy for leveraging technology.

Our next two strategies require projects to share a platform with other projects in the firm. In the second type, *concurrent technology transfer*, a new project begins to borrow a platform from a base or preceding project before the base project has completed its design work. Generally, this transfer occurs within two years after the introduction of the original or base platform. Because some of the development phases overlap chronologically, engineers in the new project and the base project can discuss adjustments in the platform and other component designs. This overlap, therefore, provides opportunities for effective and efficient technology sharing. In order to make this sharing work, however, the two interdependent projects often require extensive coordination and thus some form of multi-project management.

In the third type, *sequential technology transfer*, a project inherits a platform from a base project that has finished its design work. In other words, the second project reuses a platform design that already exists. It is "off-the-shelf." The reused platform is already relatively old compared to designs transferred while a base model is being developed, as in concurrent technology transfer. In addition, design constraints may be very high in sequential technology transfer because engineers from the two projects cannot make adjustments in the platform to suit the different products. In other words, the following project may have to force changes to accommodate elements of the core design and other components from the preceding project. This may result in too many design compromises and poor integration of product features and subsystems. Thus, sequential transfers may not be as efficient or effective as concurrent technology transfers.[8]

The last type, *design modification*, refers to a project that replaces an existing product but without creating a new platform or borrowing a platform from another product line. The modification project simply inherits or reuses the platform from the predecessor model in the same product line, perhaps with some minor changes. Design modification and sequential technology transfer are similar in that both inherit an existing platform from a predecessor product, although, in design modification, there is no transfer from another project. This type of project also can have no ongoing coordination with a base project. Therefore, engineers have to live with any constraints imposed by the platform of the predecessor (i.e., the current) model.

We can see these four strategies at work in Figure 1–3, which maps out a decade of product histories at three auto makers. Each horizontal line represents a distinct model line, such as the Honda Accord or the Acura Integra. The circles indicate when the com-

FIGURE 1–3

Multi-Project Strategic Map of Three Auto Makers

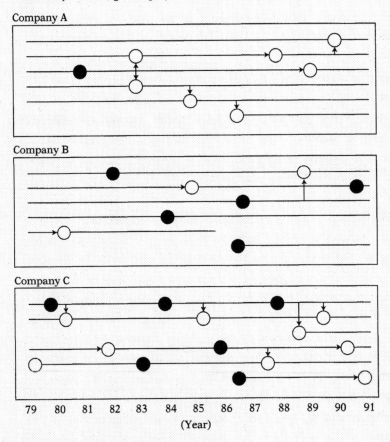

Company A

Company B

Company C

79   80   81   82   83   84   85   86   87   88   89   90   91

(Year)

● A new product developing a new platform.

○ A new product based on an existing platform.

→ Indicates platform technology transfer.

pany introduced a model change. The dark circles indicate the introduction of a new platform. The open circles indicate a new product based on the transfer or utilization of an existing platform from another model line or the previous model in the same line. The arrows indicate the direction of the platform technology transfers.

Company A (which is Chrysler) developed a new platform only once during this period, in 1980. Over the next decade, it utilized this same platform with some modifications in a series of new model lines and new generations of models. This reuse strategy was extremely economical and no doubt reflected the company's financial difficulties during these years. (It faced bankruptcy and the U.S. government bailed it out with a loan guarantee.) Given the circumstances, reusing the same platform for many years was a successful strategy. Nevertheless, one platform cannot usually meet changing market needs and technology evolution over a long time period. Indeed, by the early 1990s, this company faced another crisis due to negative customer reactions to its old products. It then encountered the daunting problem of creating new platforms for most of its existing models within a very short period of time.

Company B (which is Renault) on one occasion transferred a platform from one model line to another. Usually, however, it developed new platforms each time it replaced a product or added a new product line. This approach represented an attempt to optimize the performance of each new product or product replacement.[9] It was an expensive strategy, however, due to the costs of developing so many new platforms. No doubt this approach limited the number of new products and replacements the company introduced.

Company C (which is Honda) followed a different strategy. In particular, in the later 1980s, we can see that it developed a new platform for one product line and then, in parallel projects, quickly transferred this platform to other product lines. It also developed another new platform and transferred this to a second product line. Both Company A and Company C exhibit aggressive multi-project strategies in that they frequently transferred platforms across different projects. Compared to Company A, however, Company C mixed new development (the new platforms) with incremental development (products with platforms derived from other products). More-over, Company C transferred relatively new technologies even to projects that inherited an existing platform. Compared to Company B, we think that Company C made more effective use of its new plat-form investments.

Using the terminology of Figure 1–2, we would say that Company B (Renault) is a good illustration of the new design strategy (Type 1). All three companies at some point created new platform designs, although they did not rely so heavily on this strategy when introduc-ing new products or replacing existing products. Company C (Honda) presents the clearest case of concurrent technology trans-fer (Type 2). In the 1980s, this company developed a new platform for the Civic. The design included all-wheel double-wishbone sus-pension technology, which was highly innovative for cars of this class. Before completing the development of the Civic, however, Honda transferred this platform to two other independent projects (the Integra and the Concerto) that it was managing concurrently. Honda, therefore, quickly leveraged a new technology in more than one product line.

Company A (Chrysler) presents the best illustration of sequential technology transfer (Type 3). In 1980, it developed an innovative front-wheel-drive platform for small cars in its K-car project, and in-troduced this into the Aries/Reliant model. Over the next 11 years, it reused this platform in nearly every other new car product that it in-troduced, transferring this platform sequentially from one project to another. Chrysler also modified at least one product without chang-ing the platform (Type 4). If we extended the time period under analy-sis, we would see nearly all companies simply modifying some products without changing the platform. Not all products require fre-quent changes (for example, economy cars such as the Toyota Corolla and the Nissan Sentra, as well as luxury cars such as Porsche, Mer-cedes, and BMW models, change platforms relatively infrequently). In addition, carrying over components from one product generation to another is an important strategy for reducing costs.[10]

We demonstrate that projects and companies that rely more heavily on concurrent technology transfer perform better than companies that rely more on the other strategies we have identified. We summarize our findings in Table 1–3 and discuss the analysis in chapters 5 and 6. According to our research, auto makers that followed concurrent technology transfer more often (that is, they tended to create a second product quickly after each new platform design) would grow between 37 and 68 percent more over three years compared to firms that followed one of the other three strategies. Moreover, companies that quickly transferred platform technologies saved between 33 and 64 percent in engineering hours compared to firms following the other strategies. They also saved between 12 and 17 percent in lead time over projects that relied on new platform designs.

Even companies that are excellent already can improve their performance by thinking about how to manage multiple projects. For example, Toyota, which many companies use as a benchmark for excellence in manufacturing and engineering, introduced a new organizational structure in 1992–1993 specifically to support what we would call the concurrent technology transfer strategy. It then reduced its engineering costs for new models by 30 percent as well as

TABLE 1–3

Performance of the Concurrent Technology Transfer Strategy

Metric	Comparison Strategy	Performance
Sales growth (over three-year period)	New design	42% more
	Sequential technology transfer	37% more
	Design modification	68% more
Engineering hours (per average project)	New design	45–62% less
	Sequential technology transfers	33-64% less
	Design modification	40–63% less
Lead time (per average project)	New design	12–17% less

Source: See Tables 5–1, 6–2, 6–5, and Figure 5–3.

Note: The ranges for engineering hours and lead time depend on whether one uses raw data or data adjusted for factors such as project complexity.

cut lead time by several months. These results are especially remarkable given that Toyota was already a highly efficient user as well as the originator of heavyweight project managers and other lean practices.

The Toyota case also demonstrates the importance of linking product strategies and organizational strategies in product development. Figure 1–4 summarizes our framework for thinking about the range of organizational options available to managers. Of course, these are ideal organizational types that exist more as a spectrum than as a set of fixed practices. The spectrum varies, for example, by how much companies overlap or integrate phases, or how much authority they give to project managers versus functional department managers.

Although it is beyond the scope of this study to treat the topic in detail, we also believe that the most complex form of multi-project management involves multiple projects at more than one firm. This multi-firm multi-project strategy occurs, for example, when two companies cooperate to develop one platform and then each partner uses this platform to create distinct products in separate projects. The cases are few but increasing among automobile companies as well as in other industries. The benefits of multi-project management also should apply to a firm that shares platforms and other technologies

FIGURE 1–4

Organizational Strategies for Product Development

STRATEGY 1	STRATEGY 2	STRATEGY 3	STRATEGY 4
Functional Management	*Single Project Management (Lean)*	*Multi-Project Product Development*	*Multi-Firm Multi-Project Management*
Functional departments and sequential phases	Overlapped integrated functions and phases	Overlapping integration across multiple projects	Integration across multiple projects at multiple firms
Spectrum:	*Spectrum:*	*Spectrum:*	*Spectrum:*
In-house division	Lightweight (coordinator)	Multi-project coordinators	OEM sales (marketing)
↓	↓	↓	↓
Cross-divisions	Heavyweight project manager	Multi-project (platform) managers	Joint project management

with another company, although coordinating this technology transfer across firms can be more difficult than within a firm.

As suggested in the Honda case that we just cited, however, multi-project management can be complex to implement and requires a certain level of organizational sophistication. It requires extensive planning and physical coordination among various component technologies, project teams, and the work of individual engineers and managers. Therefore, we consider companies that succeed in multi-project management to be more advanced in strategic thinking as well as organizational capabilities compared to firms that simply manage projects one at a time or utilize traditional functional departments or even traditional matrix structures.

We also recognize that, while multi-project management may be a new term, it is not a new concept. Fundamentally, it deals with the age-old problem of how to meet a variety of customer needs as efficiently as possible. This is a problem common to managers in many industries. Recent ideas in the management literature that deal with this problem include "mass customization," which addresses how to accommodate different customer needs with products that mix standardized and customized components.[11] Similar notions include "product families"[12] and "platform management,"[13] as well as component "reuse" and object technologies, such as in software engineering.[14] If a firm is particularly skilled in technology creation, moreover, multi-project management makes it possible to leverage another popular notion—a "core competence." For example, a company can use either concurrent or sequential technology transfer to develop product platforms and then quickly diversify into related markets at minimal cost.[15]

PLAN OF THE BOOK

We have organized our study into eight chapters. We begin with company discussions that lay out the basic strategic, organizational, and managerial issues. We then probe more deeply into how different strategies and organizational forms affect performance at the project level and at the company level.

Chapter 2 begins by detailing recent changes at Japan's leading auto maker, Toyota. This company moved beyond lean thinking and heavyweight project managers in the early 1990s when it reorganized its product development groups around platform centers. Toyota did this specifically to facilitate a new multi-project strategy, with the excellent results we noted above. Chapter 3 then compares the strategies and structures for product development at nine leading auto makers in Japan, the United States, and Europe. All of these companies try to leverage technology across projects, although we discuss how some continue to focus mainly on single projects, while others manage multiple projects but in different ways.

Chapter 4 discusses different strategies for product development and multi-project management, such as radical versus incremental innovation, and platform sharing, and then relates these ideas to our four multi-project strategy types. Chapter 5 then analyzes the impact of our four strategies on project performance, measured by lead time and engineering hours in a sample of 103 projects. This discussion highlights the cost savings possible by overlapping development work across multiple projects. Chapter 6 examines the impact of our four multi-project strategies on company performance, measured by market share and sales growth at all the world's leading auto makers, based on an analysis of 210 projects. This discussion highlights how sales and market share can grow faster if firms rapidly transfer platform technologies across different projects. This sharing enables firms to increase their productivity in new product development—again, as long as companies ensure that individual products do not end up looking too much alike. Chapter 7 returns to the subject of organizational issues and focuses on requirements for effective multi-project management and concurrent technology transfer, such as matrix management and the need for especially good communication and knowledge transfer skills among engineers and project managers. Chapter 8 concludes with implications and lessons for managers.

Chapter 2

The Toyota Benchmark:

Multi-Project Development Centers

For several decades, Toyota has been a leader in adopting new organizational structures and processes in both manufacturing and product development.[1] For firms in many different industries, it has served as a benchmark for performance in these areas. In manufacturing, Toyota's "lean production system," symbolized by the JIT or Just-in-Time techniques, has revolutionized inventory management and manufacturing practices in a variety of industries.[2] In product development, Toyota led the auto industry in establishing project-based management that streamlined product development and effectively coordinated activities in different functional areas.[3] We noted in Chapter 1 that Clark and Fujimoto described Toyota's type of organization as a heavyweight project management system (originally referred to as the *shusa* system in Japanese). This features powerful project managers (*shusa*) with extensive authority over different functions such as design, manufacturing, and marketing.

Toyota performed remarkably well with its project-centered management system, and has set new standards for the auto industry in manufacturing as well as product development performance.[4] During the past 15 years, the company more than doubled the number of passenger car lines it offers (8 to 18). It also has maintained a four-year product life cycle for most of these product lines—shorter than most auto companies in the United States and Europe. In recent years, however, all Japanese manufacturers, including Toyota, have become much more concerned with efficiency in new product development. In most of their major markets, demand has slowed or even declined, while their cost competitiveness has decreased because of the appreciation of the yen and improvements by Western competitors.

In this chapter, we discuss how Toyota has again led the auto industry by introducing the most radical changes in its product development organization during the last 30 years. We examine how, during 1992–1993, Toyota adopted a strategy and structure specifically for multi-project management of product development. The new organization features three vehicle development centers that group similar projects together, based on common platforms. A fourth center provides common components to the different development centers. This structure differs from Toyota's former project-centered organization as well as from traditional functional and matrix organizations. We also review the results of this reorganization. Toyota seems to have significantly improved its ability to coordinate across projects as well as to integrate different engineering functions within projects and related sets of projects.

PROBLEMS WITH HEAVYWEIGHT PROJECT MANAGEMENT

In 1953, Toyota assigned the first shusa, or heavyweight project manager, to a new vehicle project.[5] When Toyota started product development for the 1955 Crown, Kenya Nakamura became the first shusa to head a project from the beginning. At that time, he was a member of Toyota's engineering management division. Toyota strengthened the shusa organization in February 1965 by formally establishing a product planning division to organize and support shusas. At that time, there were already 10 shusas in the company.[6] Each shusa had 5 or 6 staff members, which totaled about 50 members in the division. Toyota did not change the product planning division and shusa system until 1992, when it introduced the center organization. (As a minor change in 1989, instead of shusa, Toyota adopted the term *chief engineer* for its project managers. To avoid any confusion, we use the new term, chief engineer, to refer to this position, rather than shusa or project manager or product manager.)

The changes at Toyota began in 1990. Company executives decided to reevaluate their entire product and technology development organization. They were willing to change if necessary so that the organization would be better able to compete in the year 2000. Toyota thus launched an initiative, called the Future Project 21 (FP21), to study any problems in its product development organizational structure and processes. The leader of the project became Yoshiro Kinbara, an executive vice-president in charge of product and technology development. A manager at Toyota explained to us that no specific threats triggered this initiative. At that time, Toyota was actually doing better than most of its competitors. Toyota executives recognized, however, that organizations sometimes need review and overhauling to continue to be competitive in a changing environment. A consulting firm, the Nomura Research Institute, which Toyota hired for this project, evaluated Toyota's organization performance as a starting point for the FP21 initiative.

Soon after the FP21 started, the consulting team identified two important problems that led Toyota managers to conclude that they would need to rethink their strategy and structure. First, there appeared to be an organizational problem. In particular, Toyota had become less efficient in internal communications and had come to need more coordination tasks than before to manage new product development. Second, the competitive advantages of Japanese auto makers decreased significantly after around 1990. The rising yen made Japanese products more expensive at the same time that foreign competitors were improving their skills in product development as well as manufacturing. The following sections discuss these two problems in more detail.

FIGURE 2–1

Toyota's Product Development Organization in 1991

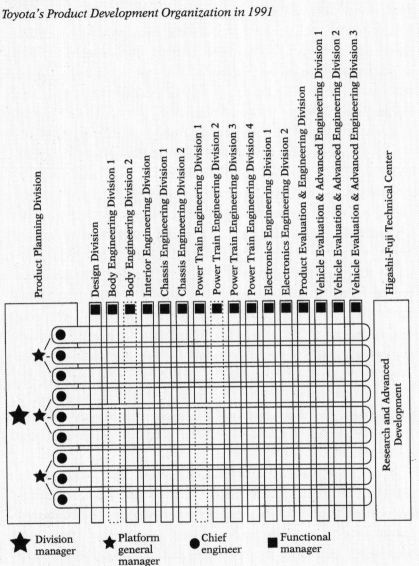

★ Division manager	★ Platform general manager
● Chief engineer	■ Functional manager

Source: Toyota Motor Corporation, "Outline of Technical Center," 1992.

Organizational Problems

Figure 2–1 shows a simplified version of Toyota's product development organization before its reorganization in 1992. There were, at that time, as many as 16 design or functional engineering divisions, and each had a functional manager. There were also about 15 projects proceeding concurrently (the figure depicts only 9 projects). Each project had a chief engineer who belonged to the product planning division and worked under its general manager.

The product development organization was actually a huge matrix that gave roughly similar weights to functional areas and projects. It was not a true project-oriented organization because chief engineers and general managers in the product planning division did not directly oversee the engineering divisions in this structure.

In theory, chief engineers at Toyota had authority over the entire product development process, from concept generation through design and manufacturing. In practice, Toyota's product development organization had become much larger than before, and chief engineers were finding it difficult to control and integrate different functional divisions when developing a new product. In other words, they had difficulty scaling up the matrix approach. As the number of product development projects increased, the number of engineers also increased. At the same time, Toyota's engineers had become more specialized, reflecting the increasing number of different divisions. As of December 1991, there were about 7,000 people in the 16 product development engineering divisions working on the 15 or so concurrent projects. In addition, Toyota had a Research and Advanced Development Group with 2,000 additional people located at the Higashi-Fuji Technical Center.[7]

In 1991, a chief engineer had to coordinate people in 48 departments in 12 divisions to launch a new product effort. This estimate comes from Toyota data on frequent participants in project management meetings.[8] In contrast, when there were only 5,000 people in the entire product development organization in 1976, a chief engineer had to coordinate only 23 departments in 6 divisions. At that time, a chief engineer generally needed to talk with only six division managers to integrate all the design engineering functions. Clearly, over this 15-year period, coordination tasks had become much more complicated for chief engineers.

In addition to this added complexity, another problem made it difficult for some chief engineers to manage new vehicle projects.

Relatively young chief engineers did not always get sufficient cooperation from senior functional managers. Originally, only a limited number of charismatic senior managers rose to the position of chief engineer. Toyota people often considered them gods within their projects, and they were able to negotiate successfully with strong engineering managers. In recent years, however, Toyota started assigning relatively junior people to the position of chief engineer, for two reasons. First, the number of chief engineers required to cover all new vehicle projects had increased, and not enough qualified senior people were available. Second, Toyota recognized that people needed particular talents to be excellent chief engineers, and their seniority was not as important as their ability.

For their part, functional managers also found it difficult to spend sufficient time on managing the details of so many projects. Most of these managers had to oversee work for about 15 different projects at the same time.[9] Not surprisingly, they usually did not have enough time to deal with complicated issues very well, such as interfaces and interdependencies between multiple projects. Due to the large number of functional divisions and vehicle projects, each chief engineer arranged regular meetings with the relevant functional managers only about once every two months.

There was another problem at the engineering level. Because of their narrow specialization, engineers did not have a good "system view" of the entire product. For example, some engineers only knew about a door's inner body structure and did not know much about the outer body because Toyota separated the interior engineering and body engineering divisions. This kind of excessively narrow specialization did not promote the creation of a well-integrated final product. In addition, the narrow specialization caused another problem when Toyota later promoted engineers to become managers in charge of larger engineering tasks, such as developing the entire body. It was difficult to train general engineering managers in the highly specialized organizational structure.

Nor was this organizational structure particularly appropriate for transferring knowledge from one project to another. Because of the narrow specialization and the large number of projects, each engineer frequently had to move among unrelated projects. This practice reduced the sense of commitment to individual products, but managers hoped it would be useful to transfer technical know-how. In reality, however, Toyota found that it could not transfer or utilize "system knowledge" very effectively simply by transferring engineers frequently from one project to another.

Toyota's rapid growth in size partially caused these problems. One way to increase the chief engineer's authority and eliminate narrow specialization is to create a pure product-team organization. Chrysler did this for its LH and Neon projects (see Chapter 3). In product teams, almost all engineers exclusively work for a single project for its entire duration. But Toyota executives did not think that the product team organization would suit their needs. This type of organization can work well for firms with a small number of projects and little technical interdependency between multiple products. Toyota has many projects and a limited number of engineers. Therefore, managers do not want to assign engineers to a specific product for the entire duration of a project. The peak period for design work for engineers in an automobile project lasts only about 1.5 to 2 years out of a 4-year cycle. It follows that, when a project task is nearing completion or "outside the peak," engineers should move to other projects to avoid wasting time. In addition, a change in the competitive environment discussed in the next section made the product team approach especially inappropriate. In the new environment, cost reduction and technology sharing among projects has become much more important.

Even the organization at Toyota prior to 1991 had problems with coordination across projects. One of the policies of Toyota's chief engineer system was to encourage the autonomy of chief engineers and to get them to feel like these are *their* projects. General managers in the product planning division above chief engineers, therefore, did not supervise chief engineers in the details of individual projects. In addition, the number of vehicle projects was too large for managers to deal effectively with multi-project issues such as resource allocation, technology transfer, and component sharing.

Finally, coordination with the Research and Advanced Development (RAD) Group located at the Higashi-Fuji Technical Center proved to be a problem.[10] Toyota kept the center relatively independent of specific vehicle projects so that its engineers could focus on research and advanced engineering. But both those involved in vehicle projects and the RAD group felt dissatisfied with this structure. Engineers working on vehicle projects did not think that the RAD group developed technologies that were useful for their needs. On the other hand, engineers in the RAD group felt frustrated because vehicle projects did not use technologies that they created. Toyota executives concluded that these two groups needed more integration organizationally.

In summary, Toyota's product development organization had five problems. These caused difficulties both in integrating functions within projects and coordinating across projects:

1. There were too many functional engineering divisions and too narrow a specialization of engineers.
2. There were too many vehicle projects for each functional manager to manage the engineering details of each project as well as coordination across projects.
3. It had become much more complicated and difficult for chief engineers to oversee all the engineering functions.
4. The chief engineer organization did not foster coordination across projects.
5. Management did not sufficiently coordinate the RAD group and individual vehicle projects.

Changes in the Competitive Environment

The competitive environment surrounding Japanese automobile firms also started changing around 1991. There were two interrelated issues. First, rapid growth in production levels virtually ended. The aggressive product strategy of Japanese automobile firms in the 1980s, such as frequent new product introductions and replacements, in large part reflected their assumption of continuous rapid growth. The new environment required some changes in this strategy as well as in company organization. Second, the importance of cost reduction became even more critical for international competition than before. In addition to the appreciation of the yen, Japanese advantages in development and manufacturing productivity were diminishing. Both factors had a strong negative impact on the cost advantages the Japanese had once enjoyed.

Because of these changes, Toyota executives decided to revise the existing chief engineer system. This system primarily focused on building the best individual products one at a time and encouraged chief engineers to think first about the success of their own projects. For example, a former chief engineer recalled that, "Each project manager wanted to increase sales of his own product by developing many new proprietary components and by expanding his project's target customer segments into those of other Toyota product lines." He explained that when Toyota's production volume was growing rapidly, these characteristics of Toyota's chief engineer system worked well for the company. Cannibalization of individual product lines was not a major problem. The market in each product segment also expanded, and this growth made it possible for each project to expand its target market.

In addition, in previous years, Toyota often sold more new products than planners had expected. As a result, high development and production costs due to many new proprietary components was not much of a problem. A manager in charge of cost management admitted this: "Prior to 1991, few new products met an original target cost when it was introduced to the market. The sales volume for each new product, however, usually exceeded its original plan. The large sales volume lowered the actual production cost compared to its original plan through scale economies. In the end, a new product usually reached the production cost that had been originally planned when we fully considered the entire production during its life cycle." Because of a faster depreciation of manufacturing equipment than in the original plans, production costs also appeared to be lower than expected. Given this common pattern, it made sense for chief engineers to try to develop hit products rather than to try to meet conservative cost targets.

Starting in 1990, however, Toyota's production volume stopped growing and even declined in some years. Profit from each new product also started decreasing. Under these circumstances, Toyota needed a new strategy and organization, particularly with respect to cost management. Top management considered one aspect of the chief engineer system to be particularly inappropriate in this new environment: The management of individual projects was too independent. Toyota executives concluded that multiple related projects needed more coordination.

In a stagnant market, Toyota executives determined that they needed to position new products more carefully within their portfolio to reduce potential cannibalization. Given a limited total sales volume, one product line could easily take away sales from similar Toyota products. In addition, to reduce production costs, management decided to increase the level of sharing or commonality of components. They could no longer expect sales increases to compensate for high development costs, resulting from the tendency under Toyota's chief engineer system for each project to create too many unique or proprietary components. (This problem is common, as we discuss in the next chapter.)

There remain in 1997 many symptoms of the old product strategy and organization at Toyota. For example, the company still has three distinct platforms for three similar products: the Corona/Carina, the Celica/Carina ED, and the Camry. These exist because the chief engineers for each product wanted to develop their own ideal platforms.

We can understand why Toyota ended up with redundant platforms. At different points in time, no doubt it was important to project managers and engineers to create distinctive new products with new platforms and other innovative technologies. A good engineering organization should be able to do this when necessary for competitive reasons. On the other hand, a good engineering organization should also be able to share technologies and coordinate different projects when efficiency of this sort becomes important. These two objectives—creating well-integrated new products and creating products efficiently by leveraging existing technologies—

are in a sense contradictory. They require a firm to have strong projects as well as a strong functional orientation to promote sharing. Rather than continuing to struggle with how to balance these two extremes, Toyota decided to reorganize.

THE MOVE TO DEVELOPMENT CENTERS

Toyota did not reduce the total number of people working in product development. At the end of 1991, before the reorganization, the company had about 11,500 people in its product engineering organization, and the number even rose to about 12,000 in 1993. Rather, Toyota's two major changes specifically targeted the problems discussed in the previous section.

First, in 1992, Toyota divided all of its new product development projects into three development centers, as shown in Figure 2–2. The center grouping focuses on the similarity in platform design. Center 1 is responsible for rear-wheel-drive platforms and vehicles, Center 2 for front-wheel-drive platforms and vehicles, and Center 3 for utility vehicle/van platforms and vehicles. Each center has between 1,500 and 1,900 people, and works on about 5 new vehicle projects simultaneously. Toyota had considered other grouping schemes, such as by product segment (luxury versus economy versus sporty cars, or small versus medium versus large cars). Toyota management chose platform similarity because this would lead to the highest level of technology sharing among projects within a center. In particular, managers concluded that because new platform development requires such extensive resources, using common platform designs for multiple product lines would save in engineering investments and reduce production costs most effectively.

Second, in 1993, Toyota created Center 4 to develop components and systems for all vehicle projects. It reorganized the Research and Advanced Development Group (the RAD Group) and assigned most people from this group to Center 4. While the RAD Group used to work on research and advanced development independently, Center 4 closely supports vehicle development by providing specific projects with components and subsystems. In addition to engineers

FIGURE 2–2

Toyota's Product Development Organization in 1992

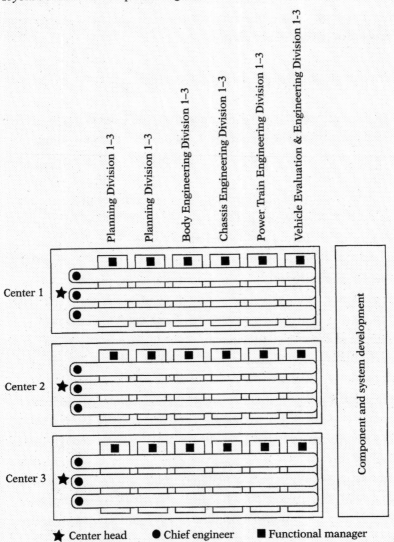

★ Center head   ● Chief engineer   ■ Functional manager

Source: Toyota Motor Corporation, "Outline of Technical Center," 1994.

in the RAD group, Center 4 added engineers working on some components such as electronics and new engines that did not need daily coordination with a vehicle project.

As discussed earlier, Toyota management had hoped that the center organization would improve coordination and sharing across projects as well as functional integration within projects (such as better coordination of different component groups as well as better coordination of design departments and process engineering). The next section focuses on how key aspects of the reorganization led to improvements in these two areas. Important features of this reorganization include:

- Reduction in the number of functional engineering divisions
- Reduction in the number of projects for each functional manager
- Changes in the roles of the center heads for multiple projects
- Establishment of planning divisions in each center
- Adoption of a hierarchical organization for chief engineers in related projects
- The new role of Center 4

1. Reduction of Functional Engineering Divisions

In order to decrease the coordination tasks required to build a well-integrated product, Toyota reduced the number of functional divisions for design engineering. We noted earlier that the complexity raised by the large number of functional divisions had made it difficult for chief engineers to manage individual projects. While the old organization had 16 different functional divisions, each new center has only 6 engineering divisions.

This simplification through the center organization prompted two other changes. First, Toyota lessened the specialization in each functional engineering division. As shown in Figure 2–3, Toyota used to have two separate divisions for designing bodies and interior/exterior equipment: the body engineering division and the interior engineering division. In the new organization, the interior engineering division merged with the body engineering division. Another example is the merger of two different chassis engineering divisions, each of which had been separately responsible for suspension systems and brakes. Each design engineering division now has wider design responsibilities. An important point is that this did

FIGURE 2–3

Old and New Organizations for the Body Engineering Function

Old Organization (1991)

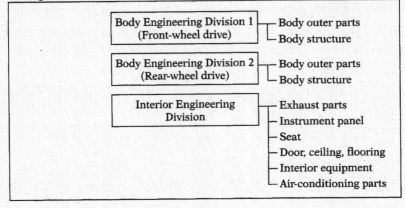

New Center Organization (1992)

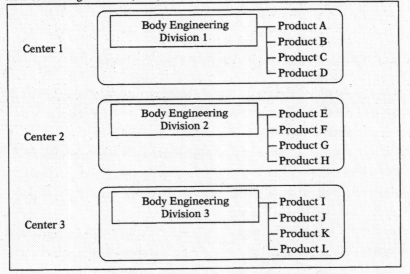

not enlarge the size of each functional division because each functional division is now responsible for only a limited number of projects within the center.

Second, Toyota reduced the number of functional divisions involved in a specific vehicle project (as opposed to a component project) through Center 4, the component and system development center. This simplified the work of the first three centers because

Toyota separated development of some components and subsystems that engineers could manage outside specific vehicle projects.

Toyota considered three factors when determining whether particular engineering functions should be in a vehicle project or in Center 4: (1) Managers decided to keep components that need extensive tailoring for each product within the particular project. (2) They decided to develop within a project components that need careful coordination with other parts of the product design. On the other hand, they concluded that they could develop some components with modular characteristics separately from specific vehicle projects and then insert them into a product design relatively easily. Center 4 should develop these kinds of components and share them with multiple projects. And (3) Toyota managers decided to use Center 4 for components that require a lot of new technical knowledge. Such development efforts usually require a group of technical specialists working together. These types of components also sometimes need a long time to develop and may not fit the time frame of regular vehicle projects.

Following these guidelines, Toyota allocated the development of some components and subsystems to Center 4. For example, the upper-body design directly visible to the customer should be different for each product. Engineers should also carefully coordinate its design with other parts of the product, such as the chassis and interior. Therefore, Toyota decided to manage the upper-body design within a project and to maintain this engineering function within each of the three vehicle centers. On the other hand, components like batteries, audio systems, and air conditioners do not usually need tailoring for each different vehicle project. Therefore, Toyota moved the engineering divisions that developed these electronic components to Center 4.

The example of the electronics engineering divisions is actually more complicated and indicates the extensive thought and analysis put into this reorganization. Toyota carefully examined characteristics and interdependencies of each component so that Centers 1–3 would be relatively simple to manage. At the same time, executives wanted the centers to contain all the engineering capabilities needed to develop all the components that required extensive coordination within each project. For example, among the electronics components, the wire harness usually needs tailoring for each vehicle and has considerable interdependency with the body structure. Therefore, Toyota merged this engineering function into the centers' body engineering divisions and kept wire harness development within the projects.

Another example of eliminating activities from the vehicle development centers is the design of totally new engines, which Center 4 now does. There are many engineering tasks involved in new engine development unrelated to integration tasks within a particular vehicle project. In addition, the time frame of new engine development does not fit that of specific vehicle projects. New engines usually need six to eight years to develop, which is longer than the four-year lead time of the average new vehicle project. But each center still has almost 300 power train engineers who work on project integration because modifying engines for use in particular products requires extensive coordination with each vehicle project. In the old organization, part of Toyota's product development organization took responsibility for both vehicle projects and most component development. This mixture made the former structure complicated and difficult to manage.

In summary, by widening the engineering specialization within each division and by transferring some component development into Center 4, Toyota reduced the number of functional divisions in Centers 1–3. In addition, because Toyota divided each function into three centers, the wider specialization did not require larger functional divisions.

2. Reduction of Projects for Each Functional Manager

Each functional manager is responsible for a smaller number of projects in the new center organization. For example, managers in Center 1 now focus only on vehicle projects with rear-wheel-drive platforms. In some functional areas, there used to be too many projects for functional managers to oversee properly. This is no longer the case.

As shown in Figure 2–3, the functional manager for interior engineering in the old organization was responsible for all vehicle projects—usually about 15 at any given time. In the center organization, functional managers are only responsible for about five product lines, and these all have technological interrelationships. Each functional manager now can spend more time on coordination with each chief engineer. In addition, this reduction of the management scope for each functional manager should result in more effective multi-project management in such areas as resource allocation and technology sharing. Each functional division also can focus on fewer types of vehicle technologies. This focus should lead to more efficient development and accumulation of technical knowledge as a division.

3. Roles of the Center Head for Multiple Vehicle Projects

Each center head officially supervises all product development operations and personnel, including both chief engineers and design engineering functions within the center. Equivalents to the center heads in the old organization were three deputy general managers who supervised chief engineers in the single product planning division. The three deputy general managers used to be in charge of small cars, large cars, and trucks/vans. They reported to the general manager of the product planning division. But they officially managed only chief engineers, not functional managers and engineers, as seen earlier in Figure 2–1. Functional engineering division managers reported to another executive. Toyota did not want general managers above the chief engineers to manage the details of each project. But, in the old structure, it was not clear which general managers—those above chief engineers or those above the functional managers—had more authority.

In the center organization, each of the three center heads now has time to manage more of the technical details for multiple vehicle projects within one center. Therefore, whereas the old organization was officially a matrix both at the chief engineer level and at the general manager level, Toyota has reorganized primarily around projects. Moreover, top management wants the center heads to balance two important roles.

First, management expects a center head to help each chief engineer integrate different engineering functions. One of the key elements of Toyota's former chief engineer system had been the strong leadership of chief engineers. As discussed earlier, however, chief engineers found it difficult to coordinate the growing number of functional managers. In the center organization, chief engineers usually can rely on the center head's support to deal with the different functional divisions. Second, the center heads are responsible for coordinating all the different vehicle projects within the center. Their responsibilities include supervising the functional engineering divisions. Because both projects and functional divisions report to one manager, this structure should reduce conflict. The separate planning division in each center, discussed next, also exists to help the center heads coordinate projects.

4. Planning Divisions in Each Center

Each center has a planning division of 170 to 200 people. These people provide executive support for the center head as well as staff three departments: the administration department, the cost planning department, and the product audit department. The administration department is particularly important. This department takes charge of personnel management, resource allocation, and long-term product portfolio planning for the center. It also conducts advanced concept studies for individual product proposals before these become formal projects with an assigned chief engineer. The management support and portfolio planning that these planning divisions provide are critical to the effective operation of the center organization.

We noted that, previously, Toyota had a single product planning division for its entire product development organization, and chief engineers used to belong to this single division. Most staff members in the product planning division also worked directly for individual chief engineers. For example, Toyota used to divide most cost management staff in the division by vehicle project and had them report to individual chief engineers. In the new organization, cost management staff are more independent of chief engineers and report to the center's planning division manager and the center head, although they continue to work closely with chief engineers. This reflects one of the central concerns at Toyota, which is that each center needs to reduce costs by more efficiently leveraging resources and components across multiple projects.

The management scope used to be so large in the old organization that Toyota found project portfolio planning and resource allocation too complicated to manage well. Now, the center planning divisions can consider technology sharing and resource allocation among multiple projects more carefully because they can focus on a small number of closely related products.

5. Hierarchical Organization of Chief Engineers

Another feature of Toyota's center organization is the hierarchical chief engineer structure for managing product families, as shown in Figure 2–4. This structure also helps strengthen the multi-project perspective of the center organization. For example, there used to be two separate chief engineers for the ES 300 and the Supra projects. Now, there continue to be two chief engineers, but one supervises both the ES 300 and the Supra projects, and primarily

FIGURE 2–4

Hierarchical Chief Engineer Organization for Multi-Project Management

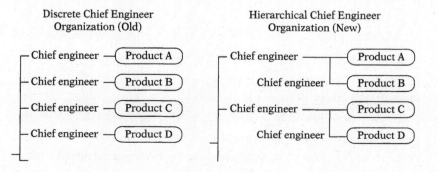

manages the ES 300 project. The other chief engineer manages the Supra project and reports to the chief engineer of the ES 300. Toyota also made the same kind of change for another pair of projects: the Tercel and the Starlet. Although Toyota does not adopt this type of structure for all projects, the company appears to be moving the organization in this direction.

Each pair of projects shares almost identical platform and drive-train designs, even though these two projects target completely different customer segments and have separate product concepts. For example, the ES 300 is a luxury sedan and the Supra is a sports car. Therefore, it is important to manage the two projects separately, so that each project develops a distinctive product that fits with its own target market. A planning division manager at Toyota related that it is difficult for a chief engineer to develop two widely different products and give the same level of commitment to each. At the same time, however, because these two projects share the same platform design, they need extensive coordination. Therefore, the projects have to achieve differentiation in product characteristics and integration in product development simultaneously. The hierarchical chief engineer organization is one way to pursue these two goals in parallel.

6. Role of Center 4

As we explained earlier, Toyota based Center 4 primarily on the RAD group in the old organization. As shown in Figure 2–5, the company has not significantly changed the basic structure of the organization and technical areas. Technical areas of both the old and new organizations include vehicle (body and chassis), engine and drivetrain, electronics, and materials. There was, however, one important change in mission. Center 4 focuses on developing components and subsystems for vehicle projects. In contrast, the RAD Group was more oriented toward research. The relationship between the RAD group and vehicle projects resembled that between upstream and downstream organizations. Now, Center 4 has become a virtual part of the vehicle development organization and is

FIGURE 2–5

Center 4 and Its Original Organization

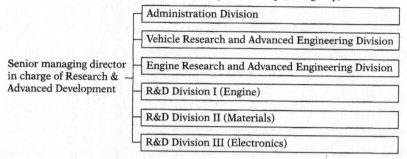

Old Organization: Research & Advanced Development Group (RAD group)

Senior managing director in charge of Research & Advanced Development

- Administration Division
- Vehicle Research and Advanced Engineering Division
- Engine Research and Advanced Engineering Division
- R&D Division I (Engine)
- R&D Division II (Materials)
- R&D Division III (Electronics)

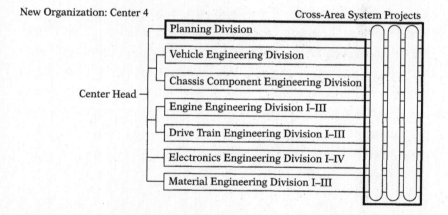

New Organization: Center 4

Cross-Area System Projects

Center Head

- Planning Division
- Vehicle Engineering Division
- Chassis Component Engineering Division
- Engine Engineering Division I–III
- Drive Train Engineering Division I–III
- Electronics Engineering Division I–IV
- Material Engineering Division I–III

responsible for subsystem components that Toyota can better develop outside specific vehicle projects.

The RAD group had about 2,000 people, while there are about 4,000 in Center 4. As discussed earlier, companies can develop some components or subsystems like electronics and new engines outside specific vehicle projects. Centers 1–3 can now focus on creating well-integrated and distinctive products.

One of the most significant improvements regarding Center 4 was the introduction of a new organizational mechanism called the "cross-area system project." Developing some subsystems requires new technical knowledge in multiple areas. To create such new components, Toyota forms project teams containing engineers and researchers from multiple technical areas. Toyota temporarily locates these projects in Center 4's planning division, and the head of Center 4 selects and assigns their leaders. In the old RAD Group, different technical areas usually worked separately, and there was not enough coordination to deal easily with this type of project.

For example, Center 4 recently developed a new low-cost antilock brake system (ABS). In this case, Toyota was able to use similar systems for all its new vehicle projects. It would not be efficient for an individual vehicle project or a product development center to develop new technology that required innovations in the chassis, electronics, and materials. Toyota thus formed a project team including people from these technical areas to develop the new ABS.

The head of Center 4 is also in a good position to integrate the different technical areas. In the old organization, division managers of the different technical areas were relatively independent. The old RAD group also gave top priority to inventing new technologies. As a result, top management gave each division relatively strong autonomy with respect to research agendas and time frames. The introduction of the cross-area system projects represents the new orientation of Center 4 as well as the new important role of this center head.

Toyota did not completely discard its basic research functions. Toyota Central Research & Development Laboratories, Inc., which has about 1,000 researchers, continues to work on basic research as a separate R&D unit. In addition, because Center 4 became less oriented toward research, Toyota established a new internal research division and assigned about 500 researchers to this unit, primarily from the old RAD group.

Summary of Organizational Changes

Figure 2–6 summarizes the changes in Toyota's vehicle development organization. This evolved from the old product development group to Centers 1–3. Meanwhile, the component and subsystem development organization evolved from the RAD group to Center 4.

As we have seen, the new center organization simplified product

FIGURE 2–6

Changes in the Vehicle and Component Development Organizations

Change in Coverage of Product Development Organization

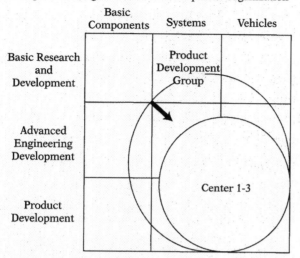

Change in Coverage of Component Development Organization

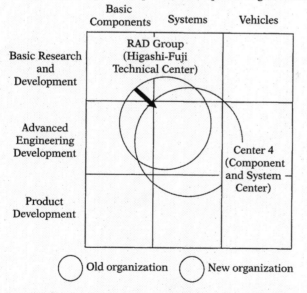

Source: Based on "Outline of Toyota Technical Center," Toyota Motor Corp., 1991 and 1993.

development in two ways. First, it excluded some areas of component development in order to allow projects to focus on the integration of product development activities, rather than component development. This change reduced the number of people in the core development organization from about 7,000 to 5,000. Second, Toyota divided the entire product development organization into three centers. As a result, each center only has about 1,500 to 1,900 people. This is a drastic change with respect to management scope, if compared with the 7,000 people in the earlier product development organization. In component development, Toyota shifted the orientation from research to subsystem development. Because Center 4 is responsible for developing more components and subsystems than the RAD group, the number of people increased from about 2,000 to 4,000.

OUTCOMES OF THE ORGANIZATIONAL CHANGES

After introducing the center organization, Toyota claims to have achieved significant improvements in several areas.

Project Integration through a Streamlined Structure

Figure 2–7 summarizes the impact of the reorganization on reducing coordination tasks for chief engineers as they manage different functional groups. As discussed earlier, before the reorganization,

FIGURE 2–7

Changes in the Number of Divisions Coordinated

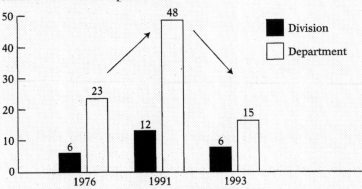

Number of Divisions/Departments

Source: Based on "Activities and Achievements of FP21," Toyota internal document, 1994.

each chief engineer had to coordinate, on average, 48 departments in 12 divisions to develop a new vehicle. Primarily because of the reduction in the number of functional divisions and departments, a chief engineer in the new organization has to manage only 15 departments in 6 divisions. Toyota also compared these numbers with those back in 1976, when there were only about 5,000 people working in product development. At that time, each chief engineer had to communicate with 23 departments in 6 divisions. The change into the new organization reduced the communication complexity down to the level of 1976, when the shusa organization still worked relatively effectively.

Each functional manager and engineer now covers a wider portion of the automobile design. Because of this, cross-functional coordination tasks have decreased among chief engineers as well as engineers, which directly affects the effectiveness and the efficiency of project integration. In addition, it has become relatively easy for functional managers and engineers to see the entire picture of a vehicle project. This change also solved some other problems in the old organization. Engineers can prepare on the job for the time when the company promotes them to managers because they can now learn about a broader scope of component engineering. Engineers also now seem to have more of a sense of achievement and ownership regarding specific products. This should improve their level of commitment and job satisfaction. Because each functional manager is responsible for fewer vehicle projects than before, it also has become easier for a chief engineer to communicate frequently with functional managers. Chief engineers used to meet with all their functional managers only about once every two months. Now, chief engineers and the six functional managers, as well as the center head, have weekly meetings, called the Center Management Meeting.

The appointment of center heads also greatly improved project and product integrity—how well pieces fit together to get a high-quality outcome. Chief engineers, like in the old organization, still have not assumed formal authority over functional managers. On the other hand, center heads oversee all product development projects, including the work of functional managers. The center heads can work directly on integrating different engineering functions. Using their positions, they can support chief engineers if problems arise in coordinating different functions. For example, when chief engineers encounter difficulties in negotiating with a strong functional manager, they can discuss the issue in the Center Management Meeting and seek the support of the center head. This makes it easier for the center management to arrive at decisions and implement them relatively smoothly and quickly. In this sense, with the backing of the center head, chief engineers have regained more of the authority that the original shusas used to enjoy.

Table 2–1 summarizes progress on some important performance measurements.[11] According to Toyota sources, the new organization helped reduce development costs on the average project by 30 percent and the number of testing prototypes by 40 percent. The drop in prototypes was a primary reason for the reduction in development costs. Fewer testing prototypes reflects in part more effective communication and coordination. In order to test many different items in one prototype, projects need intensive coordination among different design divisions and testing divisions. For example, with-

TABLE 2–1

Outcomes of the Center System Reorganization

	Performance Change	Major Factors
Development cost (average project)	–30%	• Reduction of prototypes • Increase in component sharing
Number of prototypes (average project)	–40%	• Intensive coordination between different engineering and testing functions • Increase in CAE usage
Lead time (average project)	Shortened by a few months	• Reduction of prototypes • More extensive simultaneous engineering

Source: Based on "Activities and Achievements of FP21," Toyota internal document, 1994.

out good communication, it would be difficult to combine the testing items for interior equipment and the chassis into a single prototype. Good coordination within a center also enables technically related projects to share some test data like basic platform characteristics regarding handling. In addition, simplified communication and project coordination have enabled Toyota to increase the extent of simultaneous engineering. This has helped cut project lead time by a few months. Stronger project management supported by the center head also may have contributed to quicker decision making and faster progress in development.

Multi-Project Integration Within a Center

The new organization strengthened the multi-project perspective because of the leadership of the center heads and support from the center planning divisions. We noted that, before 1992, the large number of vehicle projects made it difficult to manage Toyota's entire project portfolio and inter-project coordination. Now, participants at the weekly Center Management Meetings discuss the details of multi-project management. In addition, each center has its own building so that all center members can be co-located. Co-location at Toyota emphasizes the geographical integration of the center members rather than just the members of an individual project, which is becoming common in the United States.

In order to achieve better integration within a center, each center also now defines its own vision and theme for product development. Sharing a basic vision that focuses projects within the center helps members effectively coordinate engineering activities. As of the mid-1990s, the development theme or focus of each center was as follows:

Center 1: Development of luxury and high-quality vehicles
Center 2: Development of innovative low-cost vehicles
Center 3: Development of recreational vehicles that create new markets

We can see another example of change in cost management activities. Toyota used to set and monitor targets for development and total product costs at the individual project level, led by individual chief engineers. Most cost management staff members used to work directly for chief engineers and their orientation was the cost performance of individual projects. In the new organization, in addition to cost management at the project level, each center sets and monitors the cost targets for all the projects within the center, led by the center head. Cost management staff members now belong to the planning division in each center and report to the planning division manager as well as the center head. The new cost management activities and center structure thus have increased the concern with multi-project management. Specifically, each center has incentives to increase component sharing among multiple vehicle projects, which is one of the best ways to reduce product costs. Project-centered management and "one-at-a-time" thinking cannot do this.

With respect to component sharing, one critical issue each center is now working on is to reduce the number of basic platforms utilized among different products. For example, Center 2, as of the mid-1990s, offered five distinct platforms:

1. Celica/Carina ED/Caren
2. Camry/Vista
3. Corona/Carina
4. Corolla/Sprinter
5. Tercel/Corsa/Starlet

The planning division manager in Center 2 believes that five platforms for compact-size front-wheel-drive models is too many. The center planned to significantly reduce the number of the platform designs over the next several years. In the past, Toyota managers tended to justify so many distinct designs by economies of scale because they manufactured more than 200,000 units per year of each of the five platforms. It is true that there are scale economies with the different dies needed to make the platform designs. At that level of production, a company does fully utilize each die for its entire useful life cycle. But there are many other areas that could benefit from a reduction of platform designs, such as prototype design, production and testing, and component development and handling.

This manager concluded our interview by admitting that a major challenge for his center was to develop products that use as many common components as possible but still provide customers with differentiated functions and value. The focus of each center's planning division on a limited number of technically related projects appears to have facilitated this objective through more careful project portfolio management.

For parts smaller than the platform, Toyota also has started a sharing program that monitors component and subsystem usage in individual projects. Toyota chose 290 different components or subsystems for this initiative, ranging from instrument panel subassemblies to small parts such as door regulators. A center makes a list of a limited number of variations for each component group. New product development projects then choose components from the list. When engineers from a vehicle project want to invest in a new component, they must come up with a new design that has a better cost-value ratio than existing components on the list. When a new component design meets the requirement, it replaces one of the components on the list, so that the total number of variations will not increase within the firm. Because of the center organization, management of this program has become practical and effective. In the old organization, because of the large management scope, Toyota did not pursue this type of sharing very systematically.

Another sign of better integration among center members is a growing sense of inter-center competition. The three centers now compete with each other to reduce costs, using products developed before the reorganization as benchmarks. Of course, this type of competition could have a negative impact on organizational learning if each center tried to hide its good processes and technical discoveries. At Toyota, however, this does not seem to be occurring. Senior executives and the center heads strongly encourage engineers to learn as much as they can from the other centers and to share innovations with the other centers. For example, each center has its own engineering functional divisions, such as body engineering and chassis engineering. Three engineering divisions for the same type of technologies and components compete with each other. When one body engineering division comes up with an idea for cost reduction, engineers from the other two divisions commonly learn the new technique at least for the next project so they will not fall too far behind best practice.

Other activities have started within each center to strengthen their integration, which directly or indirectly helps multi-project coordination within the center. For example, Center 1 held a design and engineering competition in which groups of young designers and engineers competed with innovative car designs for a public motor show. Center 3 has started an initiative called the Let's Challenge Program to encourage center members to submit interesting and useful ideas for new models. Each center also publishes its own newsletter.

COMMENTS

We review the benefits of Toyota's center structure in Chapter 8, when we make comparisons to other firms. Here, we address some potential problems of the center system, which came up during our interviews.

First, Toyota has found it difficult to balance the autonomy of the chief engineers with the authority of the center head and the objective of improving center integration. Extensive guidelines for chief engineers imposed by center managers would not boost the motivation and commitment of chief engineers or the people who work for them. Nor do Toyota executives want chief engineers to work only on what the center managers want. Therefore, Toyota has encouraged the center managers to provide only basic guidelines and to allow the chief engineers to retain as much authority as possible. Executives also have carefully chosen the center management teams. For example, six people play a critical role in center management: three center heads and three planning division managers. Except for the planning division manager of Center 3, who used to be an engine design manager, five of the six used to be chief engineers. This personnel assignment may help avoid any misunderstandings between the center managers and chief engineers.

Second, Toyota has experienced some problems coordinating

across the centers. The centers' managers group projects based on technology and design relatedness and try to minimize inter-center coordination requirements. Compared to other grouping schemes, such as around market similarities, Toyota's center organization should increase component sharing *and* produce distinct products. But there are still difficulties. For example, when sports-utility vehicles became a hot segment, all three centers wanted to introduce one of these models. Because Toyota did not need to develop three sports-utility vehicles at the same time, executives had to step in and coordinate the plans of the three centers. How to solve this problem was not so clear, however. Either Center 1 or 2, which are responsible for basic sedans, or Center 3, which develops sports-utility vehicles, could have been logical choices to create a sports-utility vehicle based on a sedan platform. Toyota executives eventually decided that only Center 1 or 2 should develop this kind of vehicle to take advantage of the sedan platforms. Improving coordination across the centers could become the subject of another reorganization someday. At the moment, however, the advantages of relatively autonomous development centers seem to outweigh the disadvantages by a large margin.

Chapter 3

Organizing Product Development in the World Auto Industry

The Toyota story illustrates the challenge of creating a product-development organization designed to handle multiple projects. We recognize, however, that firms need to introduce strategies, structures, and management systems that suit their individual circumstances, capabilities, and competitive objectives. Toyota, for example, is large and profitable enough to afford several development centers and tolerate some redundancies in engineering as a trade-off for simplifying project management. Other firms, such as General Motors (GM) and Ford, are also in this category. Many other firms are not, however.

This chapter presents a framework for comparing basic organizational structures used in product development. We also examine nine major auto makers in Japan, the United States, and Europe. Our particular focus is on how these companies coordinate multiple projects and share components in view of their particular strategies and circumstances. We also highlight similarities and differences compared to Toyota. In general, we find that smaller or less profitable companies have tended not to adopt Toyota-style development centers, though they are following common principles as companies grow larger and need to manage more than one project at a time. For example, other companies have introduced multi-project managers and modified conventional matrix approaches, as well as resorted to options such as multi-product projects.

THE RANGE OF PRODUCT-DEVELOPMENT ORGANIZATIONS

In the mid-1990s, we observed four types of product-development organizations in the auto industry.[1] As we saw at Toyota, these organizations vary depending on the size and scope of a company's product portfolio, as well as what functions management centralizes and what functions it locates within projects. Companies also vary on the dimension of whether or not they organize around groups of projects, and what functions they centralize at these group levels. Figure 3–1 summarizes the major variations we have identified.

The first type we refer to as *matrix organizations*, including variations such as platform teams and what we call the differentiated matrix. This latter term refers to the use of a matrix but with different engineering teams working on one or more projects simultaneously, depending on whether the components need to be similar or different for each product. For example, the matrix may include one team that designs a common component such as a brake system for two vehicles, as well as two teams that design different body shells for the two products to ensure different appearances to the customer. (We give more examples of the differentiated matrix later in this chapter as well as in Chapter 7.)

We noted in the previous chapter that Toyota was a matrix before its recent reorganization. Most auto makers seem to have used a traditional matrix structure prior to the mid-1980s. It is still common today in Europe and Korea among medium-size or small producers. Typically, matrix organizations combine projects with permanent functional engineering departments. There is usually a project manager or project coordinator (the actual title for this job varies by firm) who often belongs to a centralized product-planning

FIGURE 3–1

Four Types of Product Development Organizations

1. Traditional Matrix Organization

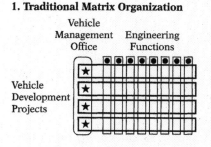

2. Product Team Organization

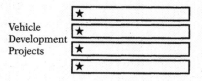

3. Semi-Center Organization   **4. Center Organization**

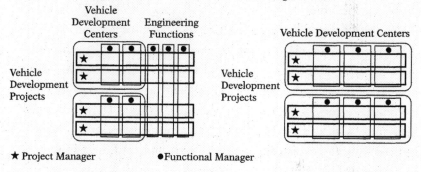

★ Project Manager   ●Functional Manager

department. Companies then impose some form of project organization over relatively strong functional engineering departments. The projects draw members from the functional departments, and engineers usually report both to the project managers and the managers of their functional departments. As we saw at Toyota, companies differ mainly by how much authority they give to managers of projects as opposed to managers of functional departments. In this chapter, we discuss variations of the matrix structure at Renault in France, Mitsubishi in Japan, and Fiat in Europe. We also make some comparisons to other European auto producers.

The second type we refer to as *product team organizations*. Companies that use this structure generally create independent projects that focus on building one product at a time, though they may build multiple variations of the product (such as different body styles) in the same project. There are minimal barriers between the different functional departments because all engineers belong to the project team and usually co-exist physically. This structure means, however, that firms with several projects duplicate many functional activities or component development efforts. In this chapter, we discuss two prominent examples of product organizations in the auto industry: Chrysler in the United States and Honda in Japan. We should also note that many companies use product teams on occasion, but usually for special projects (like the Mazda Miata or the Renault Twingo) rather than as their regular approach to product development. Our descriptions focus on a company's usual structure and process for product development, rather than exceptional cases.

The third and fourth types we refer to as *semi-center* and *center organizations*. As in the case of Toyota, some companies now have many product lines and try to coordinate projects and share components more systematically. To simplify their organizations, they tend to create clusters of similar projects and duplicate some functional departments for these groups of related projects. We can see only two cases of "pure" center organizations that duplicate most functional departments for the different clusters of projects—Toyota and Ford. In this chapter, we discuss the case of Ford and compare it to Toyota.

Rather than full development centers, some companies have utilized structures that we refer to as semi-center organizations. This means that they retain centralized functional departments that provide most of the components or engineering services to all projects. They mix these centralized departments, however, with clusters of projects (semi-centers). The clusters include a matrix structure that breaks up some key functional departments (for example, body design) just for the projects grouped together. In this sense, the semi-center approach resembles the differentiated matrix. In this chapter, we discuss semi-center organizations used at Mazda and Nissan in Japan, and GM in the United States. We also note that Mazda reverted to a matrix organization in 1996 because of its declining sales and increasing integration with Ford.

As the discussions suggest, there does appear to be a strong rela-

TABLE 3–1

Automobile Company Production Levels and Development Organizations

Company	1996 Production (in 000's)	Organization Type
General Motors	8,400	Semi-center
Ford	6,750	Center
Toyota	4,756	Center
Volkswagen-Audi	3,977	Matrix (with multi-project managers)
Chrysler	2,861	Product team (with multi-product projects)
Nissan	2,742	Semi-center
Fiat	2,586	Matrix (with multi-project managers)
Honda	2,084	Product team (with multi-product projects)
Mitsubishi	1,943	Matrix (with multi-project managers)
Renault	1,804	Matrix (with multi-product projects)
Suzuki	1,789	Matrix
Hyundai	1,282	Matrix
Peugeot-Citroen (PSG)	1,147	Matrix
BMW	1,144	Matrix
Mercedes	986	Matrix
Mazda	800	Matrix (semi-center during 1993–96)
Isuzu	673	Matrix
Daihatsu	536	Matrix
Fuji (Subaru)	519	Matrix
Volvo	433	Matrix

Source: Production data is from Automotive News, *1997 Market Data Book.* Our characterization of firms is based primarily on our interviews, as well as some public information. See Appendix 5 for the list of interviews.

Notes: Vehicle output indicates only production in North America, Japan, and Europe, and includes cars and trucks. Production numbers for Mazda include cars produced for Ford. Suzuki numbers include cars produced for GM.

tionship between the type of organization a company uses for product development and the size of the company. Simply ranking companies by vehicle production in 1996 indicates that the largest firms (GM, Ford, and Toyota) all use development centers or semi-centers (Table 3–1). Smaller firms with production levels under 2 million vehicles tend to use matrix organizations. (Before it went back to the matrix, Mazda was clearly an exception with semi-centers because of its small size.)

We see more variety in organizational types at the medium-size firms producing between just under 2 and 4 million vehicles (ranging from Renault to Volkswagen-Audi). Four companies use matrix systems (VW-Audi, Fiat, Mitsubishi, and Renault), two use product teams (Chrysler and Honda), and one uses a semi-center system (Nissan). Of this group, however, all the firms have adaptations for managing multiple projects. They either use matrices or product teams with multi-project managers (VW-Audi, Fiat, Honda, and Mitsubishi), or they use what we might call complex "multi-product projects" (Chrysler and Renault). Multi-product projects consist of large, often multi-stage projects—one team headed by one project manager—that develop multiple body styles or product variations simultaneously or in stages, based on a single platform.

Company strategy and size, and no doubt other factors, such as imitation, all seem to influence the structures that firms adopt. (With regard to imitation, for example, many firms followed Toyota in introducing heavyweight project managers and then product development centers). That various factors influence these decisions seems especially obvious because we can find producers of similar sizes using at least three types of organizational approaches (semi-centers, matrix structures, and product teams), and we can see larger companies adapting to multi-project management in product development in different ways.

But we can also identify some common principles among these variations. As Toyota managers found, if a company produces a lot of different products, then grouping similar models by development centers or even semi-centers is a useful way to simplify project management and promote component sharing. In addition, a simple matrix organization seems to become unwieldy if a firm has too many projects going on at the same time. We can also argue that dedicated product teams, though they promote innovation, are not very economical if a firm has many similar products and wishes to eliminate redundant components or share technologies systematically across projects. Similarly, a small company (like Mazda) should find centers or semi-centers to be very uneconomical because it will have to duplicate so many engineering functions. These common principles become more apparent as we discuss specific examples in more detail.

1. Matrix Organizations and Multi-Project Management

As we noted earlier, prior to the mid-1980s, most auto companies organized product development through a traditional matrix structure. Most companies also faced the same problems that Toyota did. Many moved toward some form of stronger project management organizations but still within a matrix system, and several adopted semi-center or center structures. Renault operates with a relatively conventional matrix, though its projects are large and complex in terms of the numbers of body styles and components that projects build. Mitsubishi and Fiat also have retained the matrix structure, but with more specific adaptations than Renault to handle multiple projects. All three of these companies use project managers that range from middleweight to heavyweight by their own interpretations. Their project managers, however, usually do not have the same scope of authority as true heavyweight project managers at companies such as Toyota, Chrysler, or Honda.

Several other European companies closely resemble Renault, Mitsubishi, and Fiat. BMW, Volkswagen-Audi, Mercedes, and Volvo, for example, all organize projects within similar matrix systems and have histories of strong functional departments. These companies are also moving toward heavier heavyweight project management systems and more dedicated product teams. Mercedes even claims to use centers for product development, though its centers generally produce only one platform and rely primarily on the centralized functional departments for staffing.

Like Renault, multi-project management has not been a primary concern for most of these other European companies. Except for Volkswagen, Fiat, and possibly PSA, they have relatively few product lines and, again like Renault, try to optimize product performance or appearance rather than "cost-performance." These other European companies also compete primarily in luxury or higher-priced niche segments. For high-end customers, producing a highly innovative product may be more important than in mass-market segments, where price and value, or frequent and timely introductions, may be much more important. Volkswagen-Audi, in contrast, is now paying more attention to component sharing and multi-project management because it has similar mass-production product lines, especially since its acquisition of SEAT in Spain and recent plans to share platforms across the Audi and Volkswagen brands.

Renault

Figure 3–2 shows Renault's organization for product development, which contains about 5,000 people. It is a conventional matrix, with permanent functional departments (design, quality, product and process engineering, power trains, purchasing, and manufacturing) as well as projects that draw personnel from the engineering departments. The engineering departments contain smaller sections, such as for vehicle layout and body design within the design depart-

FIGURE 3–2

Renault's Conventional Matrix Organization (1996)

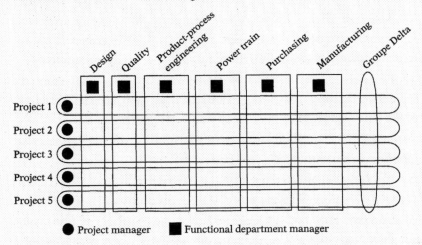

ment. Project managers report to a senior executive, called the Director of Product Planning and Projects (DPPP). Engineers report both to their functional department managers and to the project management staff.

Similar to most other European manufacturers, Renault used to be more functionally organized and continues to have relatively strong functional departments. This is true even though project managers have been increasing their authority in recent years. In the 1960s, Renault's formal product development organization consisted entirely of functional engineering departments, with only informal coordination through engineers that worked on vehicle layout and other integrative tasks. The department managers reported directly to the CEO. In 1970, Renault introduced project committees and formal project coordinators, who were in effect "lightweight" project managers. The coordinators were not highly experienced or respected personnel and held no decision-making authority. Nor did they report to a senior executive. They simply gathered information for the project committees, which consisted of the heads of the functional departments. The functional departments thus remained very powerful and took primary responsibility for product design and manufacturing.[2]

Renault management decided to replace the project coordinator system because this was not particularly good at integrating across functions or controlling costs. The company moved to the current project management system during 1988–1989. At this time, Renault executives appointed more experienced and respected engineers to serve as project directors and designated department supervisors to form a dedicated staff for each project. Under this new system, the project managers also began to report directly to a senior executive (the DPPP) and negotiate contracts with functional managers to determine objectives for product designs, schedules, budgets, and quality. The project management staffs now consist of 12 to 14 people for each project: the project manager, 3 assistants (one each for scheduling, quality, and cost management), and 8 to 10 local project managers for the different engineering functions. Project managers and functional managers also meet monthly in formal meetings to coordinate project work. Unlike at Toyota, Renault's project managers do not have direct authority over marketing, but they can influence this area through a contract negotiation process.

The layout section within the design department handles the earliest stages of concept planning, and then hands over product development to a project manager and project team. The coordinator from the layout group usually moves to the project team as well. The project manager then takes on responsibility for the remainder of the life cycle, from product and process design through the start of mass production. Renault tries to assign engineers to work only on one project, as in a dedicated product team. Renault also opened a new Technical Center in 1996 and this now houses all the product development engineers. Many engineers work on more than one project, however, depending on whether or not the components they are designing need to be different for each product. Renault's structure, therefore, is really a differential matrix.

Renault has continued to use this basic organizational structure since 1989. The diagram in Figure 3–2, however, reflects two changes made in 1994. At this time, Renault decided to combine vehicle product and process engineering as well as to create a separate department for power train design and manufacturing.

Renault first used this project management structure with the Twingo project during 1989–1993. This product required 48 months from initial concept development through the first day of production ("job #1"). Renault used the Twingo project as an opportunity to experiment with more overlapping of project phases and concurrent engineering techniques, as well as to establish closer relationships with parts suppliers. In addition, Renault imposed tighter cost controls by breaking down the project into two dozen sub-projects for various subsystems and activities. The Twingo ended up with a very distinctive design and has been well-received by industry critics and the public. Most observers would consider the project a clear success. Nonetheless, the time to market was still somewhat long. Renault also struggled in sales at least in part because the Twingo competed for customers with another small Renault car, the Clio.[3]

The value of the Twingo project as a model for Renault in project management has been somewhat limited in that this was an unusually simple project, with just one body style and one power train combination. Nonetheless, Renault has tried to reflect on Twingo and other project experiences. In 1990, the company established a small team to encourage learning—the Groupe Delta. The current team consists of seven people. The group began by working with project managers and functional managers as a sort of change agent, helping them introduce better development methods and practices, such as heavyweight project management and more task overlapping. The group has had only mixed success, however, for reasons that reflect the highly competitive nature of the world automobile market as well as specific issues that Renault has faced as a relatively small European auto maker.

First, Renault, like many other auto makers, has been struggling to improve development lead times, costs, and quality while competitors have been improving at the same time. Targets for best practice, therefore, have been moving, and Renault has struggled to keep pace with leading producers in the industry. For example, some older Renault projects from the 1980s were relatively fast, taking around 45 months from concept development to job #1, but quality too often fell short of competitors' products. To improve quality, Renault decided to slow down development times to 58 or 60 months for many projects. The company then produced better products and had some hits, such as the first European minivan. But long lead times on most models (Twingo was an exception) kept costs high and did not help the company respond quickly to changes in the marketplace.

Renault has brought development times back down to around 45 months, but competitors from Japan, the United States, and even Europe are now producing many new products even faster. As a result, Renault is planning to reduce development times further to around 36 months by doing more task overlapping (particularly of prototyping and tooling for assembly and components manufacturing), working more closely with suppliers, introducing more CAD/CAM systems, and increasing the size of some engineering teams (which makes cost reduction difficult).

A second issue for the company is the complexity of most of its projects. By complexity, we mean the number of different product variations or components created as part of a single project. Renault projects tend to resemble Chrysler's in that they usually have multiple stages for developing different body styles and they create a lot of new components. In contrast to Chrysler, however, Renault's average projects seem to build more product variations. Renault also designs several power train combinations for each product, and does this work as part of the individual vehicle projects. Renault in 1994 created a separate power train department to manage more of this work centrally, and projects will share power train technologies and other components when appropriate. Renault also jointly designs and manufactures engines and transmissions with its French competitor, Peugeot-Citroen. Nonetheless, Renault projects still do a lot of integration and design work for power trains that many U.S. and Japanese projects do not.

Renault's recent Megane project is a good example of complexity. This effort produced six body styles, ranging from a hatchback to a minivan, as well as several power train combinations. Renault took 53 months to introduce a hatchback and a coupe. It followed with a minivan, station wagon, and sport model a year later, and then introduced a sixth body type. All this work came from one project manager and one engineering team, making it difficult for managers and engineers to focus on any particular product version. Other companies, such as Toyota and Honda, usually divide this amount of engineering work into smaller separate projects and thus are able to encourage different teams to focus on specific products and streamline development. Toyota, Ford, and GM also reuse more components from other projects because they have more similar products. In contrast, Renault cannot share parts so easily because of its small number of product lines. Renault managers also believed that European customers were part of their problem to the extent that Europeans prefer many different engine and transmission options as well as new technologies.

A third, related issue is Renault's size and competitive strategy. Renault is relatively small and often tries to capture market share by producing a hit product, rather than trying to compete with a full line of products that cover every market niche. This means that project teams are much more interested in creating distinctive products than trying to share platforms or other components. Renault projects do share some components on an ad hoc basis, but projects tend not to share platforms. As a result, the company currently has six different platforms—one for high-end vehicles, three for mid-size vehicles, and two for the low-end (Twingo and Clio). This number is one or two more than Renault really needs, and managers plan to consolidate platforms as they replace models in the future. But, precisely because Renault has relatively few products and replaces them relatively infrequently, managers are concerned that reusing too many platforms and other components will hurt product performance. In addition, the "company memory" as reported by senior managers has not supported much component reuse. Before the 1980s, Renault introduced several products based on modified platforms and reused components, and these vehicles generally did not do well in the marketplace. In the current system, the company would end up reusing mostly old components because of its long lead times and infrequent replacement cycles.

The problem with Renault's strategy is that producing hit products in a fast-moving trend-oriented industry is not so predictable. Missed attempts also can be costly when new products cost billions of dollars to develop and prepare for mass production. This is why many auto makers create portfolio strategies and systematically share platforms and other components. In Renault's case, the use of concurrent technology transfer might help the company introduce new products that are still distinctive but share more platforms and other components. More frequent new product introductions would help the company respond better to changes in auto market demand. Concurrent technology transfers would also be a way for Renault to reduce the complexity of its individual projects.

Mitsubishi

Figure 3–3 is an abbreviated model of Mitsubishi's development organization. There are seven passenger-car groups: luxury cars,

FIGURE 3–3

Mitsubishi's Matrix Organization for Multi-Project Management (1997)

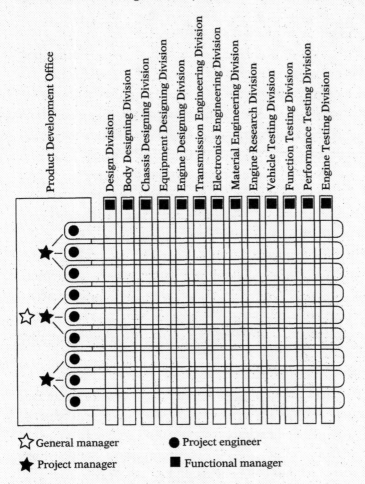

☆ General manager ● Project engineer

★ Project manager ■ Functional manager

sporty cars, mid-size cars, economy cars, recreational vehicles (RVs), light vehicles, and commercial vehicles. A project manager supervises each of the groups and manages several related projects. Project managers also supervise individual project engineers, who head each project. Both project managers and project engineers belong to a centralized product development office that coordinates product engineering and project plans. Each project draws personnel from the permanent functional departments, such as for body design, chassis design, various components, and testing. As in a traditional matrix, engineers working on new products report both to managers of projects and to managers of their home functional departments.

Mitsubishi has not broken up car development into clusters of related projects within separate development centers. Instead, it has retained a matrix system because, compared to larger companies such as Toyota and Nissan, Mitsubishi has relatively few product lines and managers want to spread resources across many projects. We see the same rationale at Renault, which is similar in size (see Table 3–1). Mitsubishi's organization for car development also is not too complex to manage because there are relatively few projects going on at any given time. (Since Mitsubishi has a separate organization for trucks and buses, however, in a sense, the company does manage through centers—one for cars, and one for trucks and buses.)

Of particular relevance to this study is Mitsubishi's approach to platform sharing and portfolio planning. The company adopted a formal system for creating common platforms rather early among Japanese auto makers. In 1984, for example, it established the centralized product development office and the current project manager/project engineer system. As indicated in Figure 3–3, each project manager at Mitsubishi is really a multi-product manager. In addition, since the mid-1970s, the company has been creating long-range product plans (LRPP) that cover product platform strategy over eight-year periods. The product planning division, a separate organization from product development and engineering, drafts this document. Top executives review the plan every six months.

Other firms have similar portfolio planning processes, although Mitsubishi seems to put more direct emphasis on platform sharing and uses its planning process to direct product development activities rather closely. (We also found during our data analyses that Mitsubishi has pursued platform sharing more extensively than most other firms.) As a result, even products that have very different characteristics have shared common platforms since the early 1980s. For example, Mitsubishi's Space Runner (RVR), a sports utility vehicle, borrowed its platform from the Colt (Mirage). The

Eclipse, a sports car, used a platform from the Galant, a mid-size family sedan. The GTO (3000GT), a high-end sports car, shared platform components with the Diamante, a luxury sedan.

Mitsubishi managers also have realized the importance of simultaneously developing multiple products that share a common platform, which we have called concurrent technology transfer. During one of our visits, for example, one engineering manager was creating a master schedule for two projects and was taking into consideration how to optimize interactions and coordination. He was examining issues such as the appropriate time lag between projects as well as when to freeze the common platform design.

Mitsubishi (and other companies) use other mechanisms to coordinate multiple car projects and share component technologies. One is the differentiated matrix, which we also have seen at Renault and most companies with matrix systems. Figure 3–4 illustrates a simplified model of this approach based on Mitsubishi's structure in the early 1990s. This is a matrix in that a project manager and functional managers share authority: The functional engineering departments listed horizontally in the figure each contribute personnel to the projects listed vertically. If we look more closely, however, we can see that there are specific mechanisms in the structure to coordinate some activities across multiple projects.

In this case, the company has analyzed relationships among projects at the component or subsystem level and flexibly formed different groups (making up the "differentiated" matrix) to accommodate these requirements. For example, the chassis used in products A and B is essentially the same, as is the chassis used in products C and D. As a result, one chassis engineering team works for both products A and B, and another for products C and D. In contrast, products C and D share no interior components with any other projects. Therefore, separate engineering groups work on these subsystems.

The body design groups show even more flexibility. To make components such as the outer body shell completely different for each product, separate engineering teams work on the body shells. The different teams ensure that the finished products have some distinc-

FIGURE 3–4

Simplified Example of a Differentiated Matrix

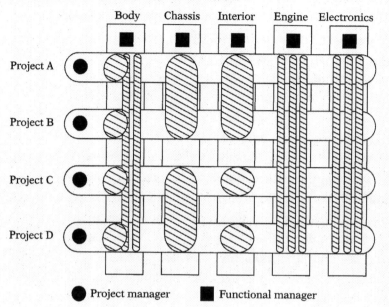

tive characteristics apparent to customers. On the other hand, the company can standardize some body components, such as inner structural parts or door handles, because they are not visible to the customer or are not necessary to differentiate. In this case, single teams work on such body components for four products simultaneously. The company standardizes other components, such as engines and electronics, across the four products and builds them with single-component groups.

In addition, Mitsubishi employs what we call the "dual responsibility system" for engineers. In this system, managers charge specific engineers with sharing information and coordinating with other engineers working on similar components in other projects. We have seen other companies (such as Chrysler and Mazda) that do something similar to this at least informally. Mitsubishi's approach, which we discuss in more detail in Chapter 7 as part of a broader discussion of matrix management, seems particularly formalized.

Finally, we should note that Mitsubishi presents examples of joint platform and vehicle development with other firms. This type of partnering also allows a firm to gain some additional scale or scope benefits in product development as well as manufacturing and procurement without establishing another brand or product line within the company. In past years, Chrysler owned part of Mitsubishi and used the Japanese company as a source of components (such as engines) as well as whole vehicles. This relationship gave Mitsubishi extensive experience with multi-firm product development and manufacturing. More recently, Mitsubishi and a new partner, Volvo, developed a platform together and, in 1995, introduced the mid-size Mitsubishi Charisma and the Volvo S40/V40 models. The two companies and the Dutch government formed a joint venture in the Netherlands, called NedCar (Netherlands Car), to participate in the engineering work and manufacture vehicles based on this platform.[4]

Mitsubishi did most of the work on the common platform, with some requirements from Volvo and feedback from Volvo engineers. The two companies then developed separate products based on the common platform. Their efforts were similar to concurrent technology transfer except that the two overlapped projects took place in two different firms. The two companies also designed most other components separately to achieve maximum differentiation between their products, although they shared some minor components such as the air-conditioning system, power window and door regulator mechanisms, and sun roofs, as well as various nuts and bolts. (Because of the success of this first joint development effort, Mitsubishi and Volvo appear to have designed a recreational vehicle using the same platform, called the MPV, and to have scheduled this for production in 1998.)

Fiat

One of the auto industry's most active companies in product development during the 1990s has been Fiat. Like many of its competitors, in the 1980s Fiat suffered from high-cost manufacturing and engineering as well as products that were becoming old and noncompetitive. In 1990–1991, the Italian company announced plans to introduce or replace dozens of models within a 10-year period, representing an investment of billions of dollars.[5] At the same time, Fiat began changing its product development organization in order to reduce development costs by approximately 10 percent and lead times by 12 months. In 1991, it adopted a 48-month project schedule from concept generation to production, and then reduced this target schedule to 36 months in 1996. In the 1990–1991 reorganization, Fiat also adopted specific goals to share more platforms and components across the Fiat, Lancia, and Alfa Romeo brands.

Figure 3–5 depicts Fiat's development organization. Like Renault and Mitsubishi, we classify Fiat as a matrix organization, although it has made some important modifications to this structure. Since 1990, Fiat has utilized what it calls platform teams that build families of similar products from the three brands using the same platform. It also has given platform directors (Fiat's multi-project managers) as well as project managers (which Fiat calls "product managers") more authority than in a traditional matrix. As a result, Fiat is a hybrid, combining a differentiated matrix with elements of a semi-center structure and a product team organization.

Fiat's five main platform teams correspond to different market segments, as indicated in Table 3–2. This table also provides examples of Fiat, Lancia, and Alfa Romeo models built on common platforms. A sixth platform team (segment H) also exists and recently built a minivan from a platform developed jointly with Peugeot-Citroen. Each platform team consists of a management group (the platform director, product managers, engineering managers, platform manufacturing manager, plant general manager, purchasing manager, and controller) that meets weekly for managing projects and monthly for budget evaluation and control. There are usually between two and five project teams ongoing for each platform, covering the three different brands. A different product manager heads each project and acts as a member of the platform management group. The different brands usually have different major components that help distinguish the products, such as different engines and transmissions, suspensions, interiors, and, of course, body shell designs. Fiat usually manufactures all the products from one plat-

FIGURE 3–5

Fiat's Platform Team Organization (1997)

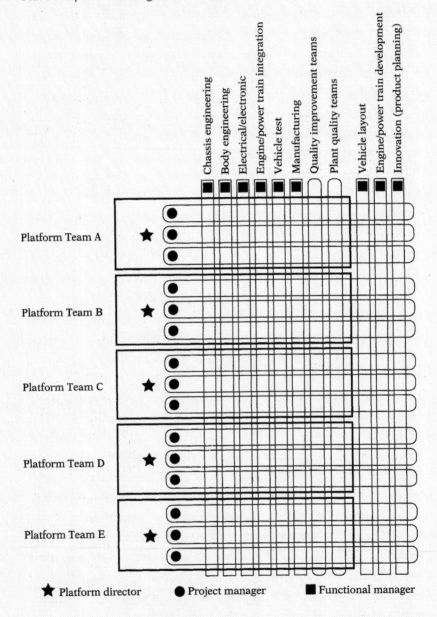

★ Platform director   ● Project manager   ■ Functional manager

form on the same manufacturing lines. Because factories usually handle more than one platform, however, plant general managers belong to more than one platform management team.

TABLE 3–2

Fiat Platforms, Brands and Representative Models

Platform	Brands			Segment Description
	Fiat	*Alfa*	*Lancia*	
A/B	500			Subcompact/small vehicles
	Panda		Ypsilon	
B	Uno			Small vehicles
	Punto			
	Palio			
C	Tipo	33	Delta	Medium vehicles
	Tempra	145		
	Bravo	146		
	Brava			
D		75	Dedra	Medium/large vehicles
		155		
E	Croma	164	Thema	Large vehicles
			Kappa	
F	Ulysse		Zeta	Large vehicles/minivan, from common platform with PSA

Source: Fourin, no. 140 (April 1997), pp. 8–13, 39.

As in a typical matrix, Fiat retains several key functions outside the platform teams: vehicle layout, engine development, innovation, and component or subsystem development. Vehicle layout does product architectural design, such as to determine which subsystems will be in the product and how these subsystems will interact. This work occurs prior to the more detailed subsystem and component engineering design done by the platform teams. (Because vehicle layout is critical for properly integrating thousands of components, we were a bit surprised that this group is not directly part of the platform or project team, which is generally the case in

Japanese firms as well as at Chrysler.) Engine development creates new engine technologies and families for use by the different platform teams. The innovation group has two main responsibilities. One is long-term product planning, with a focus on encouraging the introduction of new product concepts and designs. The second is development of concept vehicles, which might or might not become production vehicles built by the platform teams.

The functional engineering departments staff the platform teams with engineers that work on the chassis, body, electrical and electronic components, as well as engine and power train integration. There is also a group in the platform team for vehicle testing. Fiat calls the component groups "simultaneous engineering" or "SE" teams to emphasize their goal of doing as much work as possible in parallel to reduce calendar time and speed up problem solving. Most projects use at least 19 separate SE teams—16 for specific components or subsystems (such as side panels, suspensions, power train, and fuel supply) and three for "virtual parts" (layout, bodywork, and final inspection). Since Fiat does not break apart and repeat these departments by platforms or product teams, we characterize Fiat as a matrix structure, rather than a product-team, semi-center, or center organization.

The component engineers that are part of the platform teams do not develop new technologies. These innovations come from engineers who remain in the functional departments. The platform team engineers mainly work on integrating components or tailoring components for specific products. Fiat also designates specific application engineers for each component or subsystem within the platform teams (called "RPAs") to make sure that each project uses the best available technology and engineering practices.

Again typical of a matrix organization, both project managers and functional department managers evaluate engineers working on the platform teams. Fiat uses a conventional management by objectives (MBO) system to do this. On a daily basis, however, engineers assigned to the project teams report mainly to the project managers, unless they are working on standardized components that cut across different projects and occasionally different platforms—again, the differentiated matrix approach. Fiat also tries to co-locate the platform team engineers as much as possible to facilitate cross-functional communication and integration. In this sense, Fiat tries to create more of a product team atmosphere. Co-location is sometimes difficult, however, because some component engineers work on multiple projects and sometimes belong to more than one platform team.

Because it has different brands and many models with distinctive images but similar size and performance characteristics, portfolio planning is a particularly important exercise for Fiat. For several years, the company has been creating ten-year plans for new models. Marketing generates these plans and revises them annually, although the company president and the board of directors have to approve them. In addition, platform directors now make most of the decisions regarding what models Fiat decides to build. Manufacturing, which recently became part of the platform teams, also has considerable input into the plans so that new model plans fit into existing manufacturing systems or planned investments.

Figure 3–5 also shows quality improvement and plant quality improvement teams. These used to be independent but have been part of the platform teams since 1996. They implement minor changes to existing models in between the major model changes, which usually incorporate new platform designs. The quality teams also contain staff experts who assist the platform teams in transferring know-how from one project to the next and from one platform group to another.

Between 1990 and 1995, Fiat had used a menu-type system for component sharing. The component engineering departments developed long-term plans for approximately 60 subsystems and components. Project managers had less actual power than functional managers in that management wanted them to choose most of their components from these lists. As it turned out, too many products from the three different brands ended up being too similar in appearance and performance. Fiat managers still place considerable emphasis on sharing platforms and other components. The functional departments, for example, maintain "component family managers" who work on standardizing components across different platform teams. Fiat even stated objectives in 1996 to reduce the number of distinct components 30 percent by the year 2000. But senior managers realized in the mid-1990s that the company had pushed this objective too far, and standardization now takes second place to product plans. In line with this thinking, the changes in 1996 gave the authority to platform directors to determine, first, what products they wanted to design, and second, what components they needed to build these products.

Overall, Fiat has made significant progress in reducing lead times and development costs. The platform team structure, as well as the maintenance of permanent component departments, ensures that new products will combine new and reused platforms and technologies. Fiat also has introduced several successful designs with this organization, including the Palio "world car" for developing countries. Fiat customers have had problems distinguishing products that rely on common platforms and components from the different brands. Managers hoped that the 1996 changes would result in more independent platform teams that still shared key components across brands but produced more distinctive products.

2. Product Team Organizations and Multi-Project Management

In a product team organization, a company assigns the engineers working on a product to a specific project more-or-less full time, at least until they complete their main tasks. Many companies also like to bring together—co-locate—all the engineers on a team. Product teams are probably the *best* way to coordinate and integrate functional departments for a particular product.[6] To the extent that companies create separate project teams, this approach would seem opposed to multi-project management. This is not really the case, however. As we discussed earlier, and especially with the example of Toyota's development centers, the objective of multi-project management is to coordinate *both* across functional departments and across projects. Therefore, as a first step, it is important for firms to be able to manage effectively the functional groups that make up individual projects. Second, they might try to tackle the more complex process of coordinating functional groups across multiple projects.

We think that Chrysler and Honda are good examples of product team organizations as well as lean practices for managing individual projects. Both companies also have recently become more concerned with sharing and coordinating across different projects, and we discuss some of the mechanisms they use. We must note as well that Honda does not use pure product teams as a formal organizational structure, but it is the closest to this among the Japanese auto makers.

Chrysler

In February 1989, Chrysler abandoned its traditional matrix organization in favor of product teams, which (like Fiat) the company refers to as platform teams. These teams have not been so lean in the sense that Chrysler continued to use several hundred more engineers per project than comparable Japanese projects. Nonetheless, this was a revolutionary reorganization because it involved major changes in product strategy, organizational structure, and work processes.

In its old matrix system, as in other companies, Chrysler had powerful functional engineering departments as well as rather weak project managers who served as little more than project coordinators. Typical of other companies using a matrix system, including Toyota, Chrysler's project coordinators had great difficulty overseeing the work of so many powerful functional departments. In the 1989 reorganization, Chrysler split its single chassis and body design organization into two departments, and then divided these as well as other functional departments among five new platform teams—one each for small cars, large cars, minivans, jeeps, and trucks (see Figure 3–6). Chrysler also eliminated a central R&D department and decided to rely on the product teams to develop new technologies.

With the introduction of platform teams, Chrysler abandoned its strategy of sequential technology transfer, which it had relied on throughout the 1980s. Management charged the platform teams with quickly building new designs as well as producing multiple models based on these platforms. Each platform team is essentially one large project (or product) team working on multiple body styles. According to our definitions of strategy types, therefore, Chrysler in the 1990s has relied primarily on the new design strategy. Nonetheless, its relatively large multi-stage projects, which are similar to Renault's, resemble concurrent technology transfer because Chrysler projects try to build multiple products relatively quickly based on the same platform.

For example, following the 1989 reorganization, Chrysler's first product team built the new LH platform and then introduced three new products in 1992: the Chrysler Concord, Dodge Intrepid, and

FIGURE 3–6

Chrysler's Platform Team Organization (1994)

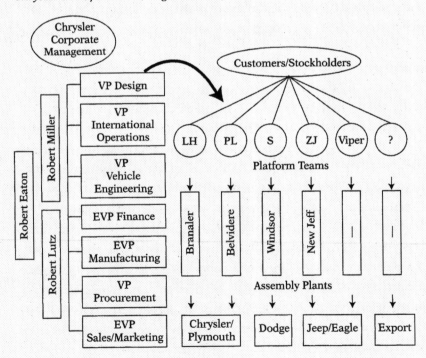

Source: Scott 1994a, p. 13, provided from Chrysler.

Eagle Vision. In 1993, Chrysler followed with another product line based on the same platform, the Chrysler New Yorker and LHS. It took the company about 39 months to bring each of the LH family products to market after choosing the design—about two years faster than its usual product development pace.

In November 1991, to speed up development even more, the company opened the Chrysler Technology Center (CTC). This co-located most platform team members on individual floors in one huge building. The CTC also provides common facilities for the different teams, such as for prototype construction, pilot manufacturing, and vehicle or system testing. More than 300 engineers from component suppliers also work together with Chrysler engineers to improve and speed up design activities. The first product to come out of the CTC, the Neon, took only 31 months to develop.

Also similar to Renault and some other auto makers, Chrysler had relatively few models in the early 1990s and little need for formal multi-project management. Still, executives recognized the value of sharing technologies, coordinating work, and spreading good practices or knowledge across more than one project. To promote more sharing, company executives encouraged engineers to establish an informal organization of Tech Clubs. These consist of small groups of engineers from different platform teams working on similar components or problems, such as audio technology and wire harnesses, or vibration reduction and safety improvement. These resemble Mitsubishi's dual responsibility system for engineers, though they are less formal. The size and frequency of Tech Club meetings varies among the different clubs, but most have between 5 and 10 members, and meet monthly or every other month. Occasionally, Chrysler has also organized task forces from Tech Club members to promote technology transfer and cross-project problem solving, or to launch R&D efforts such as for new engine technology development.

Perhaps because Chrysler is still relatively small, the platform teams and the informal network of Tech Clubs are still working relatively well. But the company has been gradually increasing its model lines, and the product team approach may not continue to work as effectively in the future. Already, we have observed that co-ordination tasks among multiple platform teams and project assignments for different platform team members have become complicated to manage. Nonetheless, Chrysler's new strategy and structure of the 1990s—independent product teams, new platform designs, and the rapid introduction of multiple models based on common platforms—clearly have been a successful departure from the sequential design transfer strategy and the old matrix organization of the 1980s.

Honda

Among Japanese auto makers, Honda has a reputation for innovative product designs and advanced engine technology. This reputation has required an effective mix of project management skills and functional skills in engine R&D. With regard to project management, Honda tends to assign most engineers full time to specific product teams. In contrast, at other Japanese firms and at most other auto makers in Europe and the United States, component engineers usually take responsibility for two or three vehicle projects at the same time. Spreading technical expertise across multiple projects is one of the major characteristics of a matrix organization, as opposed to independent product or project teams, such as at Chrysler. Nonetheless, Honda's product teams are not as formalized as Chrysler's. When it starts work on a new product, Honda forms a temporary project team that resembles a task force of engineers from different functional areas. The team members disperse after they deliver the final product (unlike Chrysler's "permanent" platform team organizations). Honda also does not co-locate all the engineers on one project (though they work relatively close together in Japan).

Honda does have strong project managers, which it calls Large Project Leaders (LPLs). Although top management has slightly reduced their authority in recent years, the LPLs are still more powerful than project managers in traditional matrix organizations such as Renault and Mitsubishi. Therefore, they really have been close to the ideal heavyweight project manager. In addition, the exclusive assignment of engineers to particular projects has strengthened the authority of project managers. This factor, as well as the company's tradition of changing project team members after the launch of a new product, seem to have helped Honda create distinctive products that reflect the different personalities of the project managers and dedicated engineering teams.[7]

As with other Japanese companies, however, the heightened competitive environment of recent years has had a major effect on Honda. During the 1980s and early 1990s, the company rapidly increased the number of product lines it offered. As sales increases slowed down in the 1990s, reducing design, engineering, and related manufacturing costs became much more important. For example, Honda was by far the most active company in introducing new engines during the 1980s and early 1990s—at least a billion-dollar investment decision for each engine.[8] Often, project managers made these investments simply because they did not want to reuse engines from other Honda products. Of course, Honda also had major successes with highly innovative engine technologies, such as the high-performance low-pollution CVCC. Nevertheless, by the early 1990s, Honda management had recognized the need to coordinate its engineering groups and projects better in order to promote more technology sharing and cost reduction.

As a first step in this direction, in March 1991, Honda established a planning office for four-wheel vehicles that reports directly to the president. (Honda is also the world's largest producer of motorcycles and motor scooters, which it manages separately.) The explicit intention was to bring together managers from engineering, manufacturing, and marketing in order to coordinate these functions better across multiple projects.[9] The four-wheel vehicle planning office also established a new position, Representative of Automotive Development (RAD). Honda initially appointed five senior engineering managers to these positions and made them responsible for multiple product lines. Managing strong-willed project managers accustomed to high levels of autonomy was no simple task, however. To do this, for the RAD positions, Honda chose respected senior engineers and managers, most of whom had experience as LPLs. (This approach is similar to Toyota, which chose mostly experienced and well-respected chief engineers as its center managers.)

The idea of sharing components was hardly new to Honda. As we saw in Chapter 1, in the 1980s, Honda frequently transferred platforms across multiple projects. We gave the example of the Civic platform, which had the innovative double wishbone suspension system. Honda quickly transferred this technology to the separate Honda Concerto and Acura Integra projects. But even when multiple product lines used the same basic platform, each project team often modified many smaller components related to the platform, such as brakes or components that linked the power train to the platform. This practice resulted in many different underbody component specifications, even with common platforms. In addition, for other components as well as for engines, Honda was much less strategic. It had far too many redundant components in similar products because project members tried to maximize *their product's* distinctive appearance or performance. For example, the Accord and its close cousin, the Inspire, shared similar platform technologies but few other components. (Some Honda engineers even admitted that, in the past, they had felt "ashamed" if they used exactly the same components that were in other products.)

Under the RAD system, during 1991–1992, Honda made considerable progress in standardizing not only the platform but also approximately 50 percent of the components across three product lines—the Civic, Integra, and Domani (successor model to the Concerto).[10] In addition, Honda's 1994 hit product, the Odyssey RV recreational vehicle, used a large number of the same components as the Accord as well as the same assembly line. Honda then developed two completely new sports utility product lines in 1996, the S-MX and the Stepwagon, partially based on the Odyssey platform. This platform-leveraging strategy quickly produced multiple distinctive products that targeted the most popular market segment in the auto industry. These new products contributed significantly to Honda's unprecedented profit performance in 1996.

The RAD system also led to some constraints in new engine development, Honda's special area of expertise since the beginning of the company.[11] Since the early 1990s, project managers have not had the freedom to build new engines whenever they want. Unless they have top management approval and special budgets, engineers must create new engine designs that reuse existing manufacturing equipment.

Because of the RAD system's success in promoting sharing and standardization of both product technology and process equipment, in 1994, Honda executives elevated the four-wheel vehicle planning office to the status of a division. The RADs have continued in their roles, though senior executives have appointed some managers to this job with backgrounds in manufacturing and marketing, in addition to engineering. The hope is that RADs from different backgrounds will help the company balance issues that cut across these different functions.

In general, like other companies that try to share more components and reuse existing manufacturing equipment, Honda faces a dilemma and potential trade-off. Companies may save on development and production costs, but they risk placing too many restrictions on the creativity of engineers. In Honda's case, placing constraints on project engineers and engine developers would seem to be particularly risky because the company is known for design creativity and innovation in engine technology. On the other hand, more strategic use of engineers and equipment investments, and elimination of redundant components, also can free up resources that a company could put to better use. This seems to be Honda's strategy. Indeed, one manager insisted that the RAD system and the strategy of reusing components have not reduced the creativity of Honda engineers. Rather, he believed that through the more effective use of resources, Honda is now able to develop attractive and distinctive products even more quickly and efficiently than before— when speed is important. The evidence we have suggests that this seems true, although Toyota and other competitors also are introducing attractive products very quickly. In addition, Toyota has been cutting prices, such as on its best-selling family sedan, the Toyota Camry. This competes head-on every year with the Ford Taurus and the Honda Accord as the best-selling sedan in the United States.

3. Semi-Center Organizations for Multi-Project Management

After Toyota established development centers in 1992, several other Japanese companies followed its lead, as did Ford. Our discussions with managers indicated that Toyota's example had influenced these firms, although at least one manager (from Nissan, Toyota's historical rival) argued that it is natural for companies to adopt similar organizations when facing similar problems. Whatever the specific motivation, Mazda, Nissan, and GM decided to group multiple projects around shared platforms. Meanwhile, Ford adopted a structure that, like Toyota, disperses most design and component engineering departments across several development centers. Mazda, Nissan, and GM have not broken up their entire engineering organizations, however, and keep a lot of key development work centralized. This is why we refer to them as "semi-center organizations." In practice, they fit somewhere in between matrix and center organizations. Because the Mazda and Nissan organizations are easier to understand than the structure at GM—which is the world's largest auto maker—we begin with a discussion of the two Japanese companies, and then discuss GM and Ford.

Mazda

In August 1993, Mazda abandoned its traditional matrix organization in favor of product development centers. Like Toyota, it established three centers, as indicated in Figure 3–7. At the end of the 1970s, Mazda also adopted Toyota's old term *shusa* for its project managers, and it has continued to use this term even after moving to a semi-center system. As we noted earlier, however, declining sales and increasing integration with Ford have led Mazda management to revert to a matrix system for product development. To illustrate the organization of a semi-center system and its potential difficulties, we describe the structure that Mazda used through 1995 and briefly note the changes it has made since then.

Mazda's semi-center structure differed from Toyota's in two key respects. One was the grouping of vehicles. As we discussed in

Chapter 2, Toyota groups its products by common platforms and has one center each for front-wheel drive, rear-wheel drive, and recreational vehicles. Mazda also separated its recreational vehicles

FIGURE 3–7

Mazda's Semi-Center Organization (1995)

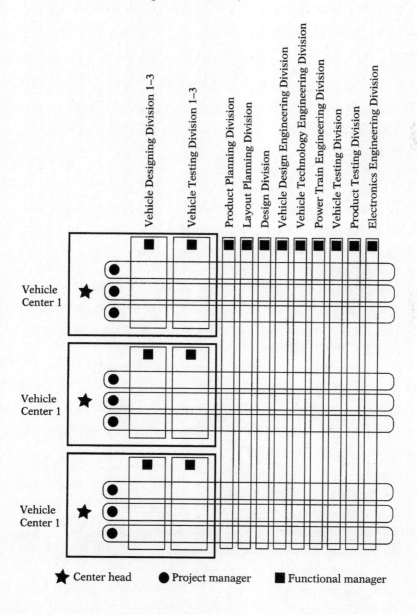

from other passenger cars, but it divided products for its two other centers largely by size and price. Mazda's Product Center 1 focused on higher-priced cars (the 626/Kronos/Capella and above) and Center 2 on lower-priced cars.

The result was not so logical from a technical point of view. Product Center 1 developed products with completely different platforms—both front-wheel and rear-wheel drive. This made it difficult for Mazda to achieve the kind of integration and standardization of components that Toyota achieves with its centers. Mazda also developed the rear-wheel drive RX–7 sports car in Product Center 3, which otherwise worked on recreational vehicles.

Another difference from Toyota was the scope of Mazda's centers. Toyota has a fourth center to develop a limited number of common components (such as electronic parts and new engines) that do not need close coordination with individual projects. It then provides these components to the three vehicle development centers. Otherwise, Toyota has dispersed engineering functions to the different centers, where the center managers and functional managers work together to share components and manufacturing investments for projects within each center. Toyota also established large planning groups in each of its vehicle development centers. In contrast, Mazda kept exterior and interior design (styling) as a centralized department. It also retained a centralized product planning department.

Also different from Toyota is the way Mazda limited design and development work in its centers. As seen in Figure 3–7, each of Mazda's centers had vehicle design and prototype testing departments that incorporated work from most of the other engineering functions. But Mazda kept a relatively large organization outside the centers. This took the form of centralized departments for vehicle design, vehicle engineering, power train development, vehicle testing, product testing, and electronic components.

Of course, compared to Toyota, Mazda has fewer product lines, much less volume, and far fewer financial and human resources. Management had planned to expand product offerings as well as sales, and thereby make better use of the semi-center organization. As it turned out, however, the company has had difficulties making profit and sales targets, and has encountered major financial losses in recent years. Mazda thus failed to implement its original expansion strategy. Accordingly, top executives decided that moving back to a matrix structure would help them keep engineering departments centralized and small, with no redundant groups or component development. Related to this decision was pressure from Ford to use more common platforms and components. Clustering products by market segments rather than by platforms may have helped Mazda segment markets more carefully and avoid products that cannibalized each other. In any case, without a major expansion of sales, Mazda could not afford to maintain three semi-center organizations for very long, and could not seriously contemplate creating three separate development centers on the Toyota model.

Mazda reverted to a matrix structure in stages. First, in July 1995, it reduced the number of development centers to two, one for sedans and sports cars, and another for recreational vehicles. Then, in September 1996, Mazda went back to a pure matrix organization. Managers and engineers welcomed this change because, in practice, the semi-center structure had never worked very well. Our interviews pointed to three reasons why.

First, because Mazda was unable to increase the number of its product lines, managers found it difficult to separate technically related products into three separate groups. There was always a lot of overlap in components. Second, given this technical overlapping as well as a shortage of money and people, it did not make economic sense to try to divide limited engineering resources into three groups. As a result, management always allowed each center to borrow engineers from other centers whenever projects needed more resources. This borrowing, which occurred often, clearly went against the concept of the center organization, which aimed at creating specialized groups of engineers, with closer coordination and integration of projects within a center. (In contrast, to maintain the separate identities of its centers, Toyota executives resisted moving engineers across centers even when project managers requested this and resources seemed to be available in other centers.) Third, since a Ford manager became president of Mazda in 1996, sharing platforms between Ford and Mazda has become more important as an objective than sharing components across Mazda projects. The matrix system makes it easier to manage projects centrally and co-ordinate development work with Ford.

Nissan

Compared to Toyota and other Japanese auto makers, Nissan's engineering organization has been more functionally oriented for many years. For example, in Chapter 2 we noted that Toyota established a product planning division to coordinate and support the shusas (project managers) in 1965. Nissan did not create a product planning office to coordinate and support its project managers until 1979. Prior to this time, Nissan only had "representative engineers" in a vehicle engineering department that coordinated multiple engineering functions. One reason why Nissan delayed moving to a project-oriented system was the company's strategy: Nissan executives generally have emphasized innovation in specific areas such as engine technology or body design styling as their primary method for competing against Toyota, and they gave primary authority over budgets and people to managers of the functional engineering divisions.[12]

Even after the reorganization in 1979, project managers at Nissan still did not obtain similar authority compared to their counterparts at Toyota. In particular, Nissan managers were not fully responsible for concept creation for new products. As a result, marketing staff and project managers often disagreed over product concepts and marketing plans. In addition, the heads of the functional engineering departments retained most of their authority, at least partially because Nissan's culture and traditions were difficult to change quickly.

In 1985, however, Yutaka Kume became Nissan's new president. He decided to strengthen the project management organization by giving more authority to project managers and instituting more of a matrix system. First, in January 1987, he expanded the responsibilities of the product planning office and reorganized this into three product-market strategy divisions. In addition, general managers who headed the three new divisions took on the role of multi-project managers, coordinating the work of several projects. Shortly thereafter, project managers formally took on full responsibilities for new product development, from concept creation to manufacturing and sales.

At this time, Nissan's new matrix of multi-project general managers, project managers, and functional department managers resembled Toyota's structure before its 1992 reorganization. There was, however, an important difference. Nissan grouped products into three divisions based on market characteristics rather than platform similarity. For example, Nissan developed the Sentra (sold in Japan and the United States) and the Pulsar (sold in Japan and Europe) in separate divisions, even though these products shared a common platform. This structure thus required managers to coordinate platform development and usage across different divisions. Because this was not a particularly efficient structure, in 1992 Nissan changed its product grouping scheme from market characteristics to platform similarities.

Nissan produced several new products under the new structure that greatly improved its reputation for creativity in product development. These products included new versions of the Bluebird, Maxima, 240SX, 300ZX, and other specialty cars sold in Japan.[13] Like several other competitors, however, high engineering and manufacturing costs, and declining sales, led to low profitability or losses for Nissan from the mid-1980s through the early 1990s. Despite the improvements, top management decided that the matrix organization was still inadequate to respond to this situation. In March 1993, Nissan made another fundamental change. It established three product development centers as a way to reduce costs in engineering. (Nissan does not use the English term *center* for these organizations, as Toyota and Mazda have done, but uses a Japanese equivalent, *kaihatsu honbu.*)

Nissan's semi-center system continues to evolve, so we discuss the structure that existed through 1996. As seen in Figure 3–8,

FIGURE 3–8

Nissan's Semi-Center Organization (1996)

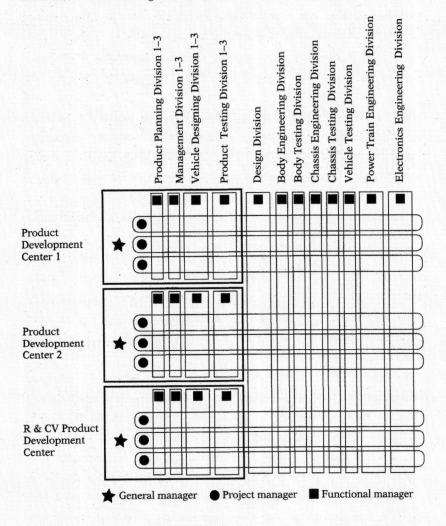

General manager ● Project manager ■ Functional manager

similar to Toyota, Nissan's three centers group vehicles by platform commonality: front-wheel drive (Center 1), rear-wheel drive
(Center 2), and recreational and commercial vehicles (Center 3).
Similar to Mazda in 1996, however, Nissan limits the scope of the
engineering work done in each center, as opposed to centralized
functional departments. Because of their limited scope, Nissan's

product development centers have fewer than one-third the number of engineers as Toyota's centers, even though Nissan is about two-thirds the size of Toyota in terms of production volume and develops a full line of vehicles. Each of Nissan's centers has between 400 and 600 engineers, compared to 1,500 to 2,000 at Toyota. The total number of product engineering employees at Nissan is quite large, however, numbering about 10,000, compared to about 12,500 at Toyota.

Nissan continues to use project managers (which it calls *tanto shukan*) to manage projects, but these managers now work within one of the product development centers. Since the reorganization, project managers also have slightly more direct control over critical engineering functions, such as vehicle design and prototyping. They do not have the same level of authority as project managers in Toyota or Honda, however. This is because they directly oversee fewer functions, and senior management subjects their products to centralized control, as in Mazda.

Again like in Mazda's semi-center system, Nissan keeps exterior and interior design (styling) and power train (engine and transmission) development completely centralized. Toyota also does this with its fourth center, although Toyota's vehicle centers each have a large number of engineers dedicated to adapting components from Center 4 to the individual products in their centers. Mazda did not have such groups in its centers, and neither does Nissan. In addition, like Mazda before its reorganization, Nissan uses centralized functional departments to promote scale economies and technology sharing across different projects. Nissan even does most new chassis design in a centralized chassis development department. Although its centers have chassis design sections within their vehicle design departments, these primarily adapt existing designs to the individual products. It is the same with body designs. Nissan has one centralized design department, and this does most of the development work at the beginning of a project. In short, Nissan's centers mainly take charge of product integration work. Engineers continue to do most technology and component development outside the centers in centralized functional departments.

Nissan management is still trying to improve efficiency in engineering. In mid-1997, the company announced a new initiative to reduce the number of platforms it develops. Nissan currently makes 15 different platforms or platform variations—a huge number for a mid-size auto producer, especially because each product development center could theoretically produce vehicles based on only one or perhaps two platforms. Nissan announced that it hoped to reduce the number of platforms it makes to five by the year 2000. The company plans to do this, for example, by standardizing the platform used in the popular Sunny/Sentra compact car with the mid-size Bluebird/Altima. It also wants to utilize just one platform for new mini-car, station wagon, and sport-utility models being produced in Europe. Nissan expects to save approximately $2.6 billion a year in engineering and manufacturing expenses by eliminating so many platforms.[14] To implement this strategy successfully, however, Nissan still has to overcome the functional orientation of many of its engineers. The company also has to streamline and integrate projects more within each center, and move more decisively to multi-project development based on shared platforms and common components.

General Motors (GM)

Though it is the world's largest auto maker, GM has also suffered from relatively low profitability, especially in North America and compared to Chrysler and Ford. This has been due in part to manufacturing inefficiencies but also to costly and slow product development and components organizations. On the other hand, GM has actually been sharing platforms across its different brands for decades, and has about the same number of platforms as the world's number two producer, Ford (approximately 24 worldwide). GM has not been so effective, though, at sharing lower-level components or making products from its historic car brands (Chevrolet, Buick, Oldsmobile, Pontiac, and Cadillac) look very distinct from each other. The following statistics are typical of GM's problems: Despite having too many products that looked very similar, its 1993 models had more than 200 different steering columns, 89 steering gears, and 44 power-steering pumps. GM executives hoped to reduce these numbers to 50, 14, and 5, respectively, by the year 2000. In the future, GM also hoped to reduce the 19 platforms made in North America to as few as 5.[15]

Like most other auto makers in the 1990s, GM has launched a number of major initiatives to revamp how it does product development. It has emphasized process improvement in managing individual projects, moving toward faster lean techniques, with overlapping phases and heavyweight project managers. It has tried to reduce platforms and non-standard components while simultaneously building more new models. In addition, GM has consolidated different development and marketing groups, physically co-located development teams in their early phases, and coordinated more product development work between its North America and European engineering operations (Opel and Saab) as well as within Europe. The new Saab 9[5], for example, which competes with the BMW 5-series, shares its platform with the Opel Vectra.[16] In the United States, GM introduced a system of centers to share key technologies and knowledge across projects, especially in the details of how to launch new products.

GM's reorganizations and refinements are ongoing, and the company's structure for product development is complex and difficult to follow. Nonetheless, we have created a simplified organization chart (Figure 3–9). We also summarize several key changes introduced in the mid-1990s that seem to be effective for improving multi-project management.

The most recent round of reorganizations began in 1992, when GM started to bring together its various design, marketing, components, and manufacturing groups. In particular, management imposed centralized control over all design, engineering, and technical staff by combining these under the umbrella of a Vehicle Development and Technical Operations (VDTO) Group, also known as the GM Technical Center organization. At various times it has included the Vehicle Launch Center (VLC), the Design and Engineering Center, the Quality Center, and the Metal Fabrication Division, as well as the R&D Center, Manufacturing Center, Marketing Center, and GM's Electric Vehicle Program.

FIGURE 3–9

GM's Semi-Center Organization (1997)

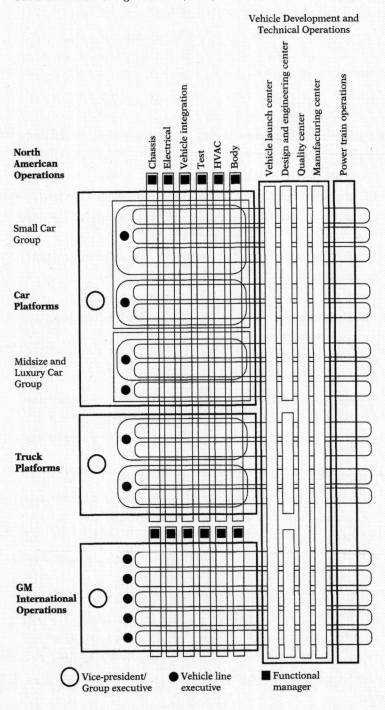

Another key date is October 1994. At this time, GM merged its four separate passenger car development groups in North America into two groups—one for small cars (including the formerly separate Saturn division) and one for mid-size and luxury cars. It retained a third group for truck platforms. These groups do design and some component engineering work for multiple products that GM sells under different brand names. In essence, they operate as three semi-independent centers, although most engineers work through the Technical Center and the Vehicle Launch Center. We also consider the GM International Organization (consisting primarily of Opel's engineering operations in Germany) to comprise a fourth center. In addition, GM now appoints "Vehicle Line Executives" (VLEs) that take charge of product development based on common platforms. They function like heavyweight multi-project managers, somewhat like Toyota's center managers, with extensive technical and marketing responsibilities for multiple products.

Figure 3–9 shows the organization that GM expects to have in place by the end of 1997 or 1998. This shows Power Train Operations and the VDTO Group as worldwide organizations. In reality, GM's Europe operations currently duplicate some of these engineering functions located in North America. This is an improvement over the past, however. Europe used to duplicate everything in North America and once operated as an almost separate company. This has changed, and GM is actively eliminating redundancies and centralizing more engineering work. Because GM centralizes so much product and process engineering, we characterize the four development groups in North America and Europe as semi-centers, similar to Nissan, and not as full development centers, as in the case of Toyota or Ford.

For example, GM keeps concept design, prototyping, engine and transmission development, manufacturing preparations, and some other components development and testing in centralized organizations. In North America (and increasingly worldwide), GM's Design and Engineering Center handles the development of product concepts, exterior and interior styling, and prototyping. The engineers typically stay in the center but work with staff in the Vehicle Launch

Center to develop product specifications. Some engineers then physically move to the VLC. Other engineers stay in the engineering centers and operate more like a traditional matrix organization, mixing functional areas with projects, and negotiating contracts with their "customers" in the product divisions. The VDTO contains separate centers for electrical, information, and control systems; exterior body; interior body; noise and vibration; safety and restraints; systems engineering; and vehicle dynamics and chassis.

The Vehicle Launch Center is a particularly important organization for multi-project management. It acts as an incubator for new products, allowing projects to share process knowledge as well as components more easily. Engineers working on a new product come to this center for the first two years of a project. As in the Chrysler Technical Center, GM co-locates product teams on one floor in the same building to foster face-to-face communication. The VLC also has a permanent staff of approximately 40 new product development experts. They work on development process standardization, cost reduction, and components sharing across projects, as well as group dynamics, problem solving, and quality management. After two years, the product team members return to their functional departments to complete development work, although the VLC staff remain. Their accumulation of experience, as well as documentation and other information they collect, help GM replicate their product launching process with different groups.

Another key practice at GM is the coordination of components development, selection, and procurement through a new "bill of materials" process. This is similar to the component sharing process we described at Toyota. In fact, most auto companies that strategically attempt to share components—including Ford, Mazda, Nissan, and Fiat, as well as Toyota—do something similar to this. They divide the product into a relatively small number of subsystems (ranging from 25 in the case of Ford to 50 or so at Mazda and 290 at Toyota). Then they try to standardize products around these modules by asking product engineers and project managers to design new products from this menu of components.

GM appears to be effectively using the Vehicle Launch Center staff to promote this type of menu-based components standardization. The challenge it still faces, however, is to share more components but still create products that have distinctive images. Because GM centralizes so much development for its different brands, product teams have had trouble creating products with unique designs and performance characteristics. We described a similar problem at Fiat. The best solution, as we see it, is the differentiated matrix. This requires strong individual product teams at least for those components that differentiate a particular product and are visible to the customer, as well as an effective system for designing common components. GM, as well as Fiat and other companies, appear to be moving in this direction.

4. A Global Center Organization

Figure 3–10 shows a simplified picture of Ford's vehicle center organization. Similar to Toyota, each center includes most engineering functions, except for concept design. Ford created this structure between 1993 and 1995. First, in 1993, management announced a corporatewide innovation program called Ford 2000 and began restructuring its product development organization as part of this program. Then, in January 1995, Ford divided its product development organization into five vehicle centers, one each for small/medium, large front-wheel-drive (FWD), rear-wheel-drive (RWD), light-truck, and commercial-truck vehicles. One of the vehicle centers, which develops small- and medium-size vehicles, is spread over two locations in Europe (England and Germany). Ford located the other four vehicle centers in Michigan (USA). Mazda will also contribute more to the work of the centers in the future, although Ford managers are still working with their Japanese partner to define its role.

The structure and strategy of Ford's center organization resemble Toyota's, even though Toyota locates nearly all its engineering organization in Toyoda City. The centers specialize in particular types of vehicles and design products for world markets. Company executives also want engineers to develop new products more fre-

FIGURE 3–10

Ford's Vehicle Center Organization (1996)

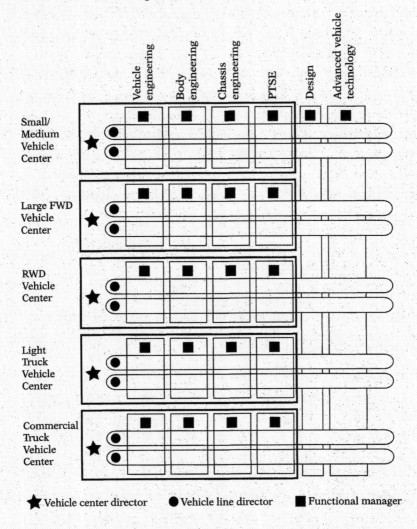

★ Vehicle center director   ● Vehicle line director   ■ Functional manager

quently and quickly while lowering development costs. Ford's goal is to shorten lead time (from the concept decision to the start of mass production—job #1) from the current 36 months to 24 months. Another goal is to design more vehicles in parallel from common platforms. The company objective is to reduce platform variations from 24 (a huge number) to 16 by the year 2004 while increasing product offerings per platform by 45 percent. This means that Ford would increase the average number of variations per platform from less than six in 1996 to eight in 2004.[17] We noted earlier that Ford also encourages projects to reuse its 25 standardized modules in different product lines. This is an important practice for effective multi-project sharing.

Before the move to centers, Ford had already started reducing platform variations. For example, Ford introduced the Mondeo in 1993 to replace the Sierra in Europe. It then used the same platform in the Ford Contour and the Mercury Mystique, both of which Ford introduced in 1994 in the United States to replace the Ford Tempo and the Mercury Topaz. These older U.S. models and the Sierra once had completely separate platforms despite being similar in size and other characteristics. Ford also will use the Mondeo/Contour/Mystique platform, as well as the same engine and transmission, in the replacement model for the Mercury Cougar. (The Cougar previously shared a platform with the Ford Thunderbird that Ford has temporarily discontinued.)[18]

This last example reflects Ford's efforts at what managers call "global platform integration," although designing one product to fit all markets has proved to be expensive and difficult—for Ford and other auto makers. The Mondeo (with some local variations), for example, was supposed to be a true world car—virtually the same in every market. But it cost $6 billion to develop (at least twice the cost of comparable cars at many other auto makers), and has not sold equally well in all markets.[19] Nonetheless, the vehicle center organization should improve Ford's ability to standardize more technologies as well as manage multiple projects concurrently that share the same platforms.

Like GM, Nissan, Mazda, and other auto makers we have talked about, Ford continues to restructure its development organization. In August 1996, the company announced a refinement of its new development process. Then, in 1997, Ford merged the large front-wheel-drive and rear-wheel-drive vehicle centers into one center, and the light-truck and commercial-truck vehicle centers into another center. Ford now has three centers, the same number as Toyota. This restructuring reflects Ford's attempt to reduce the amount of redundant engineering work in the different centers and share more components in different product lines. Through these changes, Ford expects to reduce engineering costs per vehicle, material costs, servicing costs, and manufacturing equipment investment.

COMMENTS

We can see considerable evidence of lean thinking in how auto makers in the 1990s are managing individual development projects. Most firms that we visited are speeding up projects by overlapping phases and giving more authority to project managers and product teams, as well as suppliers.[20] The examples we cited in this and the previous chapter, however, indicate that most auto makers, even if they introduce product teams, still try to manage across projects by sharing platforms and other components. We see the most variations occurring around decisions on how to do this most effectively.

Among firms that have moved beyond simple matrices or product teams to coordinate multiple projects, the most popular organizational innovation seems to be *multi-project managers*. These exist by definition in companies that have centers or semi-center organizations and managers for these organizations (Toyota, Ford, GM, Nissan). But we can also see multi-project managers at a wide range of other companies (see Table 3–1). Relatively few firms (and no large producers) manage projects one at a time in complete isolation of other projects. Even Chrysler and Honda, which utilize the most independent product teams, have various mechanisms to share technology or coordinate development efforts across different projects. Chrysler uses the Tech Clubs and task forces. Honda has RAD executives supervising project managers.

Even firms that have a tradition of strong functional departments and only weak project managers, such as Renault and Fiat, have changed their matrix systems. They have adopted more powerful project managers, product team or platform team concepts, and engineering teams that develop components for multiple projects as part of a differentiated matrix. We also saw how Mitsubishi adapted its matrix to multi-project management by introducing different component groups (the differential matrix) as well as a dual responsibility system that requires engineers to share information with counterparts in other projects working on similar components.

We do not see many semi-center structures, and this is probably because of their inherent disadvantages. Semi-centers do not simplify functional management as much as pure centers. They put some functions within centers, but keep most component development and functional departments outside the center structure. As a result, this structure can improve scale economies in some areas of engineering. But it also creates very complex matrices and debates over authority between functional department managers and project managers as well as among project managers, especially if a company has a lot of products. We can certainly see this high degree of complexity and potential confusion at GM as well as Nissan.

On the other hand, the reorganizations at Mazda and Ford reflect a potential problem of development centers: how to minimize redundancy in engineering work. Some redundancy is desirable, as Toyota determined, to simplify the span of control for project managers and multi-project executives. But companies generally want to maximize scale or scope economies in engineering through centralized departments, an objective that runs counter to the product teams. Scale or scope economies can be difficult to achieve also for center or semi-center organizations, unless firms adopt appropriate product grouping schemes, as well as effective management techniques within the centers. Furthermore, at times, most companies want to create independent projects with strong project managers to maximize their chances for innovation and hit products. Even multi-project organizations need to be flexible enough to handle these exceptional projects.

Chapter 4

Strategies for Product
Development and Multiple Projects

I t is clear from the previous chapter that there are different ways to think about and organize product development. This is true even for firms of similar sizes in the same industry. In this chapter, we examine some of the thinking behind these differences. First, we discuss common ways of categorizing product strategies and then relate these to the concept of radical versus incremental innovation. We next discuss the relationship between a multi-project strategy and the utilization of common product platforms. Finally, we link these ideas to our particular framework for distinguishing multi-project strategies—new design, concurrent technology transfer, sequential technology transfer, and design modification.

We believe that our framework is new and useful for managers and researchers of product development. Relatively few studies have analyzed product development by measuring both the newness of the technology being moved from project to project as well as the timing or speed of the transfer.[1] Understanding these two factors better should help any firm manage product development and technology transfer more efficiently.

TWO BASIC CATEGORIES

Most studies of product strategy fall into two basic types. One set of studies tends to categorize a company's product strategy based on how it relates to the strategies of competitors. For example, Ansoff and Stewart distinguished three strategic types: leaders, rapid followers, and followers (the low-cost approach).[2] Products that were leaders generally targeted particular customers and brought extraordinary profits to the first-mover.[3] In the case of the follower strategy, companies succeeded only if they realized a low-cost position through superior development and production processes. Porter's discussion of differentiation as well as low-cost strategies is another illustration of this type of categorization.[4]

But classifying a strategy based on a contrast with competitors is not always useful for managers. It is a reactive, rather than a proactive, way of thinking about strategy. In many cases, whether a company is a leader or a follower is obvious only after the fact. Nor does this type of analysis help managers put a particular strategy into practice. For example, several companies often try to be leaders in a particular market, but one usually ends up leading because of superior organizational capabilities. In this case, the key issue seems to be implementation—*how* to be first to market. This is more important than selecting a strategic category that becomes clear only after the market selects a winner.

Another approach to classifying product strategies looks at the relationship between strategy and how a particular firm has accumulated capabilities in technology or organization from past activities or investments. Probably the first study to use this approach was by Johnson and Jones, who focused on "technological newness" and "market newness."[5] They defined newness according to whether a product was new to a particular company, rather than making a comparison to a competitor's offerings. This definition enabled researchers to distinguish products by how similar or innovative they were compared to a company's previous offerings. Many subsequent writers have adopted a similar type of analysis.[6]

Our concept of multi-project management adheres more closely to this second way of thinking about product strategy. To us, the primary strategic issue is to what extent managers want to utilize the technology as well as other knowledge or capabilities their firm has already accumulated in past projects. This other knowledge can take the form of how to organize and manage projects as well as engineering work more rather than less effectively. The concept of multi-project strategy and management, therefore, requires a linkage between technology and organization. It emphasizes the *leveraging* of accumulated firm-level resources or capabilities. This theme also has become common in recent strategy and organizational literature.[7]

RADICAL VERSUS INCREMENTAL PRODUCT INNOVATION

The product strategy literature makes another basic distinction: whether a firm pursues "radical innovation" in product development or "incremental innovation."[8] Our concept of multi-project strategy and management also builds on this distinction. Again, however, we base our analyses not on whether a product is radical or incremental in terms of what is available in a competitive marketplace. We want to know how new or old it is compared to a firm's previous products—and thus existing capabilities.

One of the problems we see in existing research on this topic is that the findings and the implications for managers are ambiguous. For example, some studies indicate that if a firm can introduce an innovative product, then it should have a greater chance of leading the market and earning higher profits than less innovative competitors. Other research indicates that in competitive markets, leading firms—to remain leaders—need to make special efforts to be more innovative.[9] At the same time, we know that successful firms have relatively little incentive to introduce radical innovations precisely *because* they are successful in what they are doing. It is also difficult for firms to overcome the tendency toward organizational inertia, which is usually necessary to do in order to become more innovative.[10] In the watch industry, for example, which moved from mechanical to quartz technology, only firms that followed a radical innovation strategy were able to make the transition.[11]

More recent research has argued that incremental technology development is critical to a firm's ability to compete effectively.[12] In many industries, product life cycles have shortened while product variety has increased. These factors make it relatively more difficult for firms to sustain a competitive advantage for a long period of time based purely on technological superiority. This is especially true because technological capabilities may not differ as much among firms due to increasing flows of information and people from one company to another.[13]

Other research emphasizes the importance of producing incremental innovations in continuous streams of new products, particularly in relatively stable industries.[14] There are also numerous cases of firms that created radical innovations and then lost out to technological followers who led in commercializing a series of incremental innovations. Xerox's invention of the technologies that went into graphical personal computers and then its failure to commercialize these for the mass market is one famous example.[15] Another is Microsoft's success with the Windows operating system, patterned after Xerox and Apple Macintosh products. Microsoft followed the same strategy with a range of applications, including Word (initially patterned after WordStar and WordPerfect) and Excel (patterned after Lotus 1-2-3).[16] Japanese firms also are renowned for this strategy of continuous incremental innovation based on technologies invented in the United States or Europe. Consumer electronics products ranging from the television to the videocassette recorder are prominent examples.[17]

Still other studies indicate that companies have a better chance of succeeding if they develop products related in technology or markets to their previous product offerings. This seems better than trying to introduce totally unrelated products to totally new sets of customers. Data to support this conclusion comes from studies of diversification both at the firm level and the product level.[18]

We also know that radical and incremental innovation strategies imply different organizational capabilities. To develop truly innovative products, a firm often must change its existing organizational processes or at least create a separate organization.[19] In contrast, to create incremental innovations, a firm often needs to do no more than make key organizational processes routine in order to maximize organizational effectiveness.[20]

Of course, a firm is unlikely to remain competitive simply by following a strategy of incremental product innovation, especially in competitive markets. Yet it is not always easy or necessarily useful for companies to make a clear distinction between radical and incremental product innovations. Perhaps the best strategy is to develop highly innovative products very frequently, as long as these innovations are not so radical that they alienate customers or take too long to find a market. Realistically, however, few companies can produce useful radical innovations on a frequent or continual basis. As a result, companies need a way to think about product development that does not simply try to distinguish between radical and incremental innovations.[21] A better strategic framework would allow a firm to take advantage of its existing organizational capabilities as well as acknowledge that both radical and incremental innovations have advantages and disadvantages.

Indeed, other researchers have proposed concepts that combine aspects of radical and incremental innovation. In particular, the notion of core competence can refer not only to developing highly innovative technologies but also to utilizing these core technologies later on in multiple products.[22] Another popular concept, "architectural innovation," refers to how companies innovate in putting components together, rather than in designing the components themselves.[23] Other researchers have viewed products as subsystems that can combine both new and old technologies.[24]

In this book, we take a broader approach than most other researchers in that we do not treat individual product development projects as single events. Rather, we treat product development as an investment in technology at the level of the firm and over time. The objective of the firm should be to optimize the attractiveness to customers and the profitability of its entire product portfolio. This involves a set of related decisions, including what kind of and how much new technology to develop, how much technology to share and across which projects, what timing to follow in project planning and new product introductions, and how to create an organization to carry out this type of an integrated portfolio strategy for products and projects.

MULTI-PROJECT STRATEGY MAPS AND THE PLATFORM CONCEPT

One way to illustrate the concepts we have talked about is to create a multi-project strategy map.[25] This is a tool to visualize a company's product strategy by mapping out patterns among several generations of products. These patterns can produce a picture of long-term product-development strategy.[26] But multi-project strategy maps are useful not merely to illustrate a company's product lines and their life cycles. The maps also can show the technological relationship among products. This is important because central issues in a multi-project strategy should be which technologies are new to particular development projects, what other projects have utilized these core technologies, and when did the firm transfer them. This mapping also resembles Prahalad and Hamel's concept of a "strategic architecture" for a company's products and underlying technologies.[27]

Figure 1–3 in Chapter 1 is actually an example of a multi-project strategic map of the new products for three auto makers during the 1979–1991 period. The analysis in this figure and in the next two chapters focuses on what industry experts often consider a core technology of the automobile, its platform or underbody structure. The platform consists of the floor panels, suspension system, fire wall, and rocker panels. It is essentially the "architecture" of the product, even though modern automobiles contain some 30,000 parts. The platform provides a structure for major components by determining the body size as well as the size and type of engine and transmission. It also significantly affects the style and performance characteristics of the product (such as front-wheel or rear-wheel drive, or sporty versus luxury-style handling).

The platform is usually the most expensive subsystem for a new motor vehicle in terms of design and manufacturing preparation costs, with the possible exception of the engine. In addition, it incorporates critical aspects of design and manufacturing know-how. This is why automobile makers around the world are paying increasing attention to reusing platforms in as many distinct products as possible. They have to modularize platforms and related components, though, to transfer platforms easily across projects. For these reasons, platform standardization and reuse are key elements of any multi-project strategy and rely heavily on the organizational capabilities needed to coordinate across multiple projects and different component engineering groups.

In recent years, through effective multi-project strategies, various automobile companies around the world have been able to standardize platforms across a number of products that previously had unique platforms. Use of common platforms also has made it possible for firms to introduce a variety of new products relatively cheaply and quickly, and respond speedily to new market trends. This trend is by no means limited to the automobile industry. A recent book, in fact, titled *The Power of Product Platforms*, contains illustrations ranging from laser printers and household appliances to computer software programs.[28] Other researchers have explored product families in industries such as consumer electronics.[29] The examples we have selected below illustrate the rising importance of common platforms in the auto industry.[30]

1. Rapid Expansion of the Market for Recreational Vehicles

The rapid expansion of demand for recreational or sport-utility vehicles has had a major impact on the automobile market of the 1990s. This product has become a huge and highly profitable new segment around the world. Chrysler pioneered the market in the United States by building a minivan on top of an existing car platform. GM and Ford quickly followed with a variety of products, though some resembled trucks and had less-than-adequate performance. The Japanese were late into this market as demand took several years to grow in Japan. Most automobile companies today are still scrambling to introduce new products or replacement products into this segment.

Some companies have developed new platforms as the basis for their recreational vehicle products. For economic reasons, however, most companies have reused existing passenger car platforms that provide better handling characteristics than commercial vans or trucks. For example, to catch up in this market, between 1994 and 1996 Japanese auto makers quickly built a series of recreational vehicles based at least partially on car platforms. As indicated below, the name in parentheses is the car model that provided the platform:

Toyota Ipsum (Corona)
Toyota Raum (Tercel)
Nissan Rasheen (Sentra/Pulsar)
Nissan Stagea (Laurel/Skyline)
Honda Odyssey (Accord)
Honda CR-V (Civic)
Honda Orthea (Civic)
Suzuki Wagon R (Alto/Cervo)
Daihatsu Move (Mira)
Daihatsu Pizer (Charade)
Mazda Demio (Revue)

2. Intra-Company Platform Standardization Across Brands

Various auto makers sell products under different brand names. In Europe, the Fiat Group contains the Fiat, Lancia, and Alfa Romeo brands; the Volkswagen Group has the Volkswagen, Audi, SEAT, and Skoda brands; the PSA Group has the Peugeot and Citroen brands. In the United States, General Motors markets products under the Buick, Cadillac, Chevrolet, GMC Truck, Oldsmobile, Pontiac, and Saturn brands, as well as Opel, Saab, and Vauxhall in Europe. Ford has the Ford, Lincoln, and Mercury brands. Chrysler has the Chrysler, Dodge, Plymouth, Eagle, and Jeep brands. Reducing the number of platforms needed to support these different brands has become a major strategic issue, especially in Europe, where companies generally have relied on distinct platforms for their different product lines.

For example, Fiat and PSA have already made considerable progress toward common platforms, although they are still in the process of finding an effective way to do this. In 1988, Fiat introduced the Fiat Tipo and then transferred this platform to the Lancia Dedra (introduced in 1989), the Alfa Romeo 155 (1992), and the Lancia Delta (1993). PSA standardized platforms for the Citroen ZX (introduced in 1991) and the Peugeot 306 (1993), as well as for the Peugeot 605 (1989) and the Citroen XM (1989).

But both companies have experienced difficulties. Fiat has had problems differentiating its products. Alfa Romeo and Lancia customers do not like paying more money for cars that are too similar in style and performance to Fiat models sharing the same platforms. The Fiat brand is supposed to be cheaper and less sporty and luxurious. PSA, on the other hand, has kept its brands more distinctive. It has done this by maintaining large numbers of unique components for each model, even though it has standardized some elements of the platforms used in the Citroen and Peugeot brands. But the large number of non-shared components has limited the amount of cost savings. Both companies need more effective multi-project strategies in order to achieve a better balance between cost reduction through platform standardization and brand differentiation.

Volkswagen presents yet another case. The German company used to make it a priority to keep the Volkswagen and Audi product lines separate. Even for products in the same size category, such as the Volkswagen Passat and the Audi 80 (A4), the company deliberately developed different platforms to ensure that these brands remained distinctive. Recently, however, Volkswagen has vigorously pursued a strategy of moving to common platforms. The new versions of the Volkswagen Passat and the Audi A4 share the same platform, as do the new Volkswagen Golf and the Audi A3.

We can see similar movements in the United States. General Motors, in particular, has launched a major effort in recent years to reduce the number of distinct platforms and components used across its numerous brands and models. As we discussed in Chapter 3, along with this initiative, GM has made numerous changes in executive management, product design, engineering, marketing, organizational structure and processes, and components sourcing. One plan discussed in 1995 aimed to reduce the 19 or so distinct platforms made in the United States to as few as 5. GM had at least another 5 platforms for its European brands, which it was also planning to consolidate.[31]

Japanese companies have fewer brands under one corporate structure. But they are increasingly facing similar issues of platform as well as component standardization, such as between Honda and Acura products (made by Honda), Toyota and Lexus products (made by Toyota), and Nissan and Infiniti products (made by Nissan). Japanese and other auto makers also face the issue of sharing more platforms and other components across similar product lines. As we saw in Chapter 2, this is particularly an issue for the largest Japanese producer, Toyota. This company offers many similar niche products in Japan, such as the Corona, Carina, Camry, Celica, and Avalon passenger cars. It has many opportunities to use common parts, design concepts, and technologies, even though it has only one mass-production brand (Toyota) and one luxury brand (Lexus).

3. International Platform Sharing

Sharing platforms across development groups in different parts of the world has been a particular problem at Ford and GM.[32] Both companies have had separate international divisions for many years and deliberately developed different platforms even for models that were practically identical in terms of market segments, size, and performance objectives.

For example, in the mid-size segment, Ford used to offer the Sierra in Europe and the Tempo/Topaz in the United States—each with completely different platforms. In 1992, however, as a successor to the Sierra, Ford introduced the Mondeo in Europe with a new platform, and then used this same platform for the successor to the Tempo/Topaz models, the Contour/Mystique. As we discussed in Chapter 3, Ford also reorganized into development centers to manage this global platform standardization effort more effectively. These centers span several locations around the world (with Mazda as a partner). Ford's plans for the future include a 33 percent reduction in platforms (24 to 16) along with a 50 percent increase in the number of different models offered.[33]

GM has had similar problems integrating its European Opel unit with its American engineering operations. Previously, Opel operated almost as a separate company. Recently, GM has been using or modifying some Opel-built platforms for new models introduced in the U.S. market.

4. Platform Sharing Through Alliances
(Multi-Firm Multi-Project Strategy)

We also can see the importance of common platforms in the attempts of some firms to share platforms—in essence, a multi-firm multi-project strategy, as we proposed in Chapter 1. In the past, it has been common for companies with equity relationships to share some platforms. For example, since the 1980s, Ford has done this with its Japanese partner, Mazda, in which it is the largest shareholder. The Mazda 323 (Familia) and Ford Escort, and the Mazda 626 (Capella) and Ford Probe, are well-known examples.

In recent years, however, even firms without equity relationships have pursued the strategy of sharing platforms. For example, from the latter 1980s through the present, covering two product generations, the Mazda Carrol and the Suzuki Alto have used the same platform. We also noted that Mitsubishi and Volvo developed a new platform in a joint project and in 1995 introduced the mid-size Mitsubishi Charisma and the Volvo S40/V40 models. PSA and Fiat developed a common platform for minivans and in 1994 introduced the Peugeot 806 and the Fiat Ulysse.

OUR MULTI-PROJECT STRATEGY TYPOLOGY

Managers need a relatively sophisticated methodology to create a good multi-project strategic map. This map should capture the technical relationship among projects. It also should allow managers to measure the impact of their strategy on market performance as well as on development costs for related products. Our typology—new design, concurrent technology transfer, sequential technology transfer, and design modification—enables us to make these measurements. We present our findings in the next two chapters. Here, we would like to point out that we do not focus simply on the distinction between incremental or radical innovations, or the technical relationship between projects. In addition, we have identified two other issues that are critical for strategic product development: the specific *application* and the specific *timing* of technology leveraging across multiple projects.

With regard to applications, firms can leverage key technologies from existing products in two different ways.[34] They can use existing technologies in a product redesign or replacement project. In other cases, firms can transfer the technologies to another product line that targets a different market segment from the original product. In the first case, firms try to enhance the competitiveness of their original product. In the second case, they try to extend their investment to move into a new market segment and achieve economies of scope in development. Both applications involve incremental changes, but they have vastly different implications on market competition at the corporate level. We can best analyze the impact of these incremental changes by separating the effects of the simple product enhancement strategy (i.e., technology leveraging within the same product line) from the economies of scope strategy (i.e., technology leveraging to create or enhance another product line).

With regard to timing, the speed with which a firm can exploit existing technologies should be another critical factor that affects its competitiveness. The technology that a firm modifies and exploits may be nearly obsolete or still relatively new. It is reasonable to assume that even competitive technologies eventually become outdated as time passes. Therefore, if a firm is going to utilize the same technologies in different products, how fast it can accomplish this transfer should affect how products do in the marketplace. There have been numerous studies focusing on the scope strategy.[35] Researchers have all but ignored, however, the timing of reuse activities or technology transfers among multiple projects.

The timing of technology leveraging also has significant organizational implications, both at the level of project management and at the level of corporate-wide structures and processes for managing engineering work. For example, a project might try to borrow new components from another ongoing project that started before it did. In this case, engineers from the base project developing the new component technology can interact with engineers from the follow-on project. They can make unilateral or mutual adjustments in their designs if needed because the two projects overlap chronologically. When there is no chronological overlapping between projects, engineers cannot coordinate their work or make mutual adjustments in their designs. These adjustments might be necessary to avoid lowering the performance of the product that relied on technology borrowed from the base project.

COMMENTS

We wish to reemphasize two points that follow from the discussion in this chapter. First, we believe that the *speed* with which a firm can transfer component technologies from one project to another may have a significant impact on the market performance of a firm's product lines. The case of Chrysler in the early 1980s illustrates that technology transfers, even if they are slow and sequential, can be highly economical and better than not reusing technologies at all. But the Chrysler case also indicates that too many transfers of old technology may provide a firm with little or no competitive advantage. Reusing old technology may even be a disadvantage if products do poorly in the marketplace and create no scale or scope economies in development or manufacturing.[36]

Second, we believe that *strategic portfolio planning* is important to transfer component technologies and effectively utilize them in more than one product. This planning involves technical issues such as product family architectures and component modularity, as well as more subtle design issues, such as the character of particular brands or models. (We say more about these issues in Chapter 7.) There are also organizational issues such as the allocation of engineering resources and the structuring of design work.[37] For example, we noted that it should be particularly useful for firms to schedule projects sharing components so that they overlap chronologically. Overlaps make it possible for engineers to combine tasks and design components for more than one product but still adapt their designs as the products evolve.[38] Other studies have reported that the ability of engineers to make mutual adjustments when necessary can lead to greater efficiency and effectiveness in transferring technology from upstream functions to downstream functions.[39] The same benefits should apply to leveraging technology among multiple projects.

Chapter 5

Multi-Project Strategies and Project Performance

In this chapter, we examine the impact of the four multi-project strategy types (new design, concurrent technology transfer, sequential technology transfer, and design modification) on lead time and engineering hours in new product development. The data we examine comes from a survey we conducted of 103 projects at 10 automobile firms in Japan and the United States. We also discuss some organizational issues that appear in Toyota and other companies and seem to affect project performance.[1]

Our findings indicate that projects using the concurrent technology transfer strategy are by far the most efficient in terms of engineering hours. The reason for this seems clear: Only through concurrent technology transfer can a company reuse technology from a base project in another project and effectively share tasks among projects as well as make mutual adjustments and conduct joint design work. As we discuss in this chapter and other parts of the book, there are several reasons why isolated product teams and functional organizations are not as effective as multiple projects that are technologically linked as well as ongoing simultaneously.

LEAD TIME AND ENGINEERING HOURS

When we began this study, we believed two things with regard to project performance: First, we thought that new car projects using platform designs completely new to the firm should require the longest lead time and the largest number of engineering hours.[2] Developing a new platform requires time and engineering resources in all areas, including drawing, prototype testing, and process engineering. In addition, because it is a core subsystem of the automobile, a new platform often requires new parts or extensive modifications for the other primary components.[3] These include the body structure and drivetrain, as well as technologies that link these components. Second, we believed that, of the four multi-project strategies, concurrent technology transfer should require the fewest engineering hours. We assumed that this strategy should best facilitate task sharing, joint design, and mutual adjustments among engineers.

Numerous studies have provided ideas and empirical evidence suggesting that mutual adjustments lead to greater efficiency and effectiveness in transferring technology from upstream functions to downstream functions.[4] These studies also have argued that projects can most effectively and efficiently implement mutual adjustments when there exist overlapping and intensive communications among the functional groups. We can apply the same concept to interfaces among multiple projects, as shown in Figure 5–1. Even when a new car project uses an existing platform as a base, it develops new proprietary components for other parts of the product design, such as the exterior body. Engineers also must devise complicated linking technologies between the platform design and other components, such as the body shell and the engine. Not surprisingly, engineers identify many potential problems only after a new project starts. Without any overlaps among the base project and the new project, it is impossible for engineers to adjust the base platform design so that the new project can avoid these problems.

Transferring and reusing an old design may not be efficient if engineers apply the old design or reuse old components in ways that do not properly meet new customer needs or match competitors'

FIGURE 5-1

Concurrent Engineering and Technology Transfer Across Projects

Concurrent Engineering

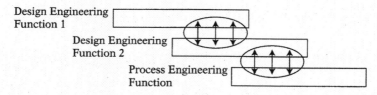

Concurrent Technology Transfer Across Projects

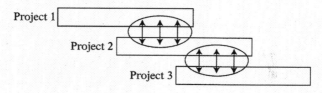

products. This is a problem not only in automobiles but also in many other relatively fast-paced industries, where technologies and customer requirements are continuously evolving. In another study, for example, we found that reusing existing designs and components in computer software without appropriate planning for different user needs may have a *negative* impact on development productivity and quality because of the time required to rework components.[5] In particular, we believe that when there is a long time lag between a base project and a follow-on project, it is less likely that engineers created specific plans for technology transfer while managing the base project.

Using the survey data we collected, we decided to explore three propositions: (1) Projects using the new design strategy should require the longest lead time and the most engineering hours because these projects build most components from scratch and probably try to maximize innovation. (2) Concurrent technology transfer projects should require the fewest engineering hours and perhaps the shortest lead time because of potential task sharing and the ease of making adjustments in the designs. And (3) the lead time and engineering hours for sequential technology transfer and design modification projects should fall somewhere in between new design and concurrent transfer projects.

THE DATA

To explore these questions, we surveyed 103 project managers of new car and truck development projects: 78 at seven Japanese firms and 25 at three U.S. firms. We conducted this questionnaire survey in the spring of 1992; most projects dated from between 1986 and 1992. One central contact person at each company distributed the questionnaires to project managers. These contact persons decided the actual number of questionnaires to distribute and the selection of projects. The only guideline we gave them for consistency was to distribute the questionnaires to at most 15 project managers in each firm who had recently worked on relatively large projects building new products. The sample included some variations in project contents that we discuss later.

In the questionnaire, we defined product variations such as different body types and trim levels developed within a distinct project as part of a single product. We pretested questionnaires with three project managers. We also discussed with several project managers and engineers the definitions and measurements of lead time and engineering hours described in Appendix 2. Overall, between September 1991 and May 1993, we interviewed approximately 130 engineers and 30 project managers at five Japanese, three U.S., and four European firms.

Project Strategy Type

One survey question asked whether the platform design each project developed was new to the firm or based on a preceding design. We categorized new projects that developed their platform design without any base design as following the new design strategy. We categorized as design modifications all of the new projects based on the platform design of their direct predecessors that companies planned to replace with these new projects. Those projects based on the platform design of other product lines we categorized as either concurrent technology transfer or sequential technology transfer. We determined the category depending on the answer to our question about overlaps and interactions between the new project and the base project with respect to platform development. Additionally, a project meets the definition of a transfer only if the managers of the base project and the new project are different. If there is only one project manager, we consider these development efforts to be one project.

The average time lag between a new project and the base project with respect to market introduction was, as shown in Figure 5–2, 15.0 months for concurrent technology transfer and 66.6 months for sequential technology transfer. This difference convinced us that the question adequately distinguished between these two strategies.[6] At 81.2 months, the average time lag for projects using the design of one of their direct predecessors, the design modification strategy is even longer than that of sequential technology transfer projects. For exam-

FIGURE 5–2

Multi-Project Strategies and Average Lead Times

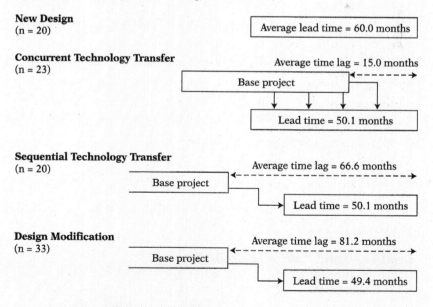

Source: Nobeoka and Cusumano, 1995, p. 400.

ple, some U.S. projects utilizing this strategy replaced predecessor platforms that were more than 10 years (120 months) old.

Project Content and Control Variables

It is always important to control for differences in project or product complexity in order to compare lead time and productivity across different projects accurately. First, we measured design complexity and newness by the ratio of new components versus carried-over components in two separate areas, body/interior and engine/transmission. The automobile design consists of three primary component groups: body/interior, engine/transmission, and platform. Therefore, these new component ratio variables cover the rest of the automobile design not contained within the platform.

Second, many components in new products are completely new but do not add any new technical features or functions. We should distinguish them from components that incorporate technology new to the firm. Therefore, in addition to the new component ratio, we added a rough measure of innovation in each project. We asked whether the technology used in each component area brought new technical features to the firm (yes = 1, no = 0). We then calculated the average of the answers in these two areas to create an innovation index that ranges from 0 to 1.

Third, we measured price in the market and the number of body types for each new product because these factors may also significantly affect project complexity. Finally, a vehicle type variable denotes whether a project is for a car or a truck. The other design complexity variables we used did not capture the different design and market characteristics for these two kinds of vehicles. We felt that such differences might potentially affect project performance.

ANALYSIS AND KEY FINDINGS

Lead Time and Engineering Hours

Table 5–1 summarizes the raw data on project content, lead time, and engineering hours for each multi-project strategy type. The set

TABLE 5-1

Sample Raw Data on Project Content and Performance

		Platform Design			
	New Design	Concurrent Technology Transfer	Sequential Technology Transfer	Design Modification	Total
Projects	27	23	20	33	103
Japan	19	20	13	26	78
United States	8	3	7	7	25
Price ($)**	21,200 (8,860)	15,540 (7,610)	16,380(7,720)	15,290 (7,220)	17,090 (8,100)
Body types**	1.7 (0.6)	1.6 (0.5)	1.7 (0.8)	2.1 (0.9)	1.8 (0.7)
Truck/van	7	5	3	8	23
New Design Ratio (%)					
Engine/transmission	72 (32)	57 (40)	61 (35)	58 (36)	61 (36)
Body/Interior	92 (20)	91 (20)	95 (12)	82 (31)	89 (23)
Innovativeness index (0–1)***	0.35 (0.33)	0.30 (0.36)	0.23 (0.30)	0.07 (0.18)	0.23 (0.31)
Lead time (months)**	60.0 (15.6)	50.1 (11.9)	50.1 (12.4)	49.4 (14.9)	52.5(14.5)
Engineering hours (millions)	1.89 (1.60)	0.72 (0.48)	2.02 (2.55)	1.95 (2.03)	1.66 (1.87)

Source: Nobeoka and Cusumano, 1995, p. 401.

Notes: Difference statistically significant at: ***1% Level, **5% Level, *10% Level (One-way ANOVA). Standard deviations are in parentheses.

121

of projects we studied are relatively major projects as opposed to minor face-lifts. We can tell this from the high average percentage (89) of new body and interior components, indicated by the new design ratio.

With respect to multi-project strategy applied to the platform, 27 of 103 projects (26 percent of all projects) developed completely new platform designs. The other projects used existing designs or transfers from on-going projects. Among the remaining 76 projects, 23 (22 percent of all projects) followed the concurrent technology transfer strategy that borrowed a platform design from other projects in progress. Twenty of the 23 concurrent technology transfer strategy projects were Japanese, a much higher proportion of projects than for the other multi-project strategy types. Twenty of the 103 projects or 19 percent followed the sequential technology transfer strategy, and 33 projects or 32 percent were design modification projects. Figure 5–2 presents the average project time lag for each multi-project strategy.

There are some differences in project content among the different multi-project strategies that we controlled to compare the impact of each strategy type on project performance. For example, except for some specialty luxury cars, auto makers tend to develop new platform designs more often for more expensive products than for less expensive products. We suspect that this is why the average price for a new design project ($21,200) is much higher than the average price for other types. Less expensive products may be more cost-constrained and may use more existing components. Because of the "system" nature of automobile design, a new platform, which is a core subsystem, also may necessitate more new component designs in the rest of the product. For example, a new platform tends to come with more new components in the engine and transmission. In addition, projects utilizing a new platform tend to focus on technical innovation and design quality as opposed to product costs. This difference in objectives may be another reason why new design projects develop more new engine and transmission components.

New projects categorized under the design modification strategy, on average, developed more body variations and offered less technical innovation than the other types of projects. This did not surprise us. Established bread-and-butter product lines such as the Nissan Sentra and the Toyota Corolla often have a large number of body variations and frequently use the design modification strategy. On the other hand, the number of body types for concurrent technology transfer projects tends to be small. This may be because concurrent technology transfer projects tend to produce derivative products.

Table 5–2 lists the results of our analyses of lead time and engineering hours.[7] The first analysis uses only basic control variables, including firm nationality, vehicle price, and vehicle type. The second two analyses contain all important variables, including those for project complexity and multi-project strategy types. The first analysis shows that more expensive products and trucks tend to require more time, and that Japanese projects tend to be shorter than the U.S. projects. The second analysis, which introduces the multi-project strategy variables, shows that the new design strategy requires by far the longest lead time. Nationality and price factors disappear when we include the multi-project strategy variables.

With respect to engineering hours, in the first analysis with only basic variables, Japanese projects require far fewer hours, but product price or vehicle type are insignificant. In the second analysis, engineering hours for the new design strategy are again larger than the other three multi-project strategies. There is, however, a marked contrast with the results regarding lead time. Only concurrent technology transfer projects required significantly fewer engineering hours than the new design strategy. (As seen in the third analysis, this result does not change when we adjust engineering hours for supplier contribution in design to include engineering hours for both internal and external tasks. See Appendix 2 for the adjustment method.) In order to visually compare lead time and engineering hours among the four multi-project strategies, Figure 5–3 illustrates adjusted results from the regression analyses in Table 5–2. (This adjustment scheme used the average numbers for all independent variables listed in the table for Appendix 4.)[8]

The adjustments allow us to compare the different strategies, assuming that all factors are similar for the different projects. But the

TABLE 5–2

Regression Analysis of Lead Time and Engineering Hours

Independent Variables	Lead Time (months)		Engineering Hours (millions)		
	Model 1	*Model 2*	*Model 1*	*Model 2*	*(Supplier Adjusted) Model 3*
Constant	43.38	37.74	13.30	11.27	11.56
Nation (United States = 1, Japan = 0)	5.60*	3.67	1.35***	1.13***	1.16***
Product's price ($ in ten thousands)	3.20*	1.81	0.01	0.00	0.02
Vehicle type (Car = 0, Truck = 1)	10.26***	10.01***	0.13	0.25	0.20
Project task complexity					
Number of body types		3.76**		0.57***	0.59***
New design ratio % (engine/transmission)		–1.40		0.10	0.00
New design ratio % (body/interior)		6.30		1.20***	1.30***
Innovativeness index (0–1)		10.10**		0.65**	0.68**
Inter-project strategy type of platform design					
1. New design		—		—	—
2. Concurrent technology transfer		–6.99*		–0.55**	–0.60**
3. Sequential technology transfer		–7.22*		–0.18	–0.18
4. Design modification		–7.36**		–0.06	–0.18
Adjusted squared multiple R	0.16	0.25	0.32	0.58	0.57
Sample size	103	103	76	76	76

Source: Nobeoka and Cusumano, 1995, p. 402.

Notes: Statistically significant at: *10% Level, **5% Level, ***1% Level.

FIGURE 5–3

Lead Time and Engineering Hours for the Four Strategy Types (Adjusted)

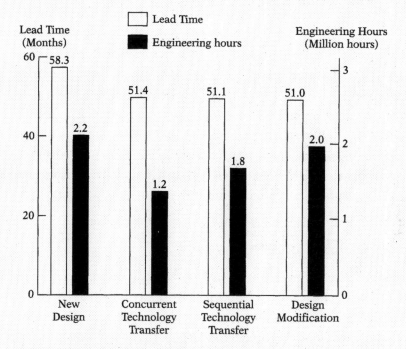

Source: Nobeoka and Cusumano, 1995, p. 402.

adjusted numbers do not realistically capture what occurred in the actual projects. For example, the adjusted engineering hours for design modification projects are close to those for new design projects. As shown in Table 5–1, however, a new design strategy for the platform tends to come with newer designs and technologies in the engine/transmission and the body/interior components. On the other hand, design modification projects do not usually introduce many new technologies or designs. Therefore, we also calculated adjusted numbers that use the average values of the new component ratios and the innovation index for each strategy. We still used the average of the total sample for other independent variables.[9] In this adjustment scheme, new design projects require far more engineering hours than the other strategies.

We collected engineering-hour data only for concurrent technology transfer projects and not the combination of a given concurrent technology transfer project and its preceding base project. Consequently, there may be questions regarding negative effects on the base project. If the impact is severe enough, concurrent technology transfer might not be so useful. In order to test for this possibility, we asked in the survey whether there was a subsequent concurrent project with which the respondent's project shared the platform design and had significant overlap and interaction. The results showed that other concurrent technology transfer projects did not significantly add engineering hours to the respondent's projects.[10] This leads us to believe that a concurrent technology transfer project does not significantly constrain a preceding base project.

Influence of Project Task Complexity

Other significant findings exhibited in the analyses in Table 5–2 include the influences of project task complexity upon lead time and engineering hours. First, the number of body types and the new design ratio of body/interior components only have a strong influence on the required number of engineering hours, not on lead time. The innovation index, though, greatly affects both lead time and engineering hours. Projects may design additional body types or additional new components in parallel and may require little extra time. Therefore, these additional tasks necessitate more engineering hours, but not additional lead time as long as engineers design variations in parallel. Developing technologies new to the firm requires extra time for concept generation, producing prototypes, and testing that companies cannot do completely in parallel. New technologies tend to require new manufacturing equipment that they cannot prepare completely in parallel either. Therefore, developing more new components that incorporate technological features new to the firm requires both a longer lead time and more engineering hours.

Second, trucks have a longer lead time than cars in this sample, although there is no significant difference in engineering hours. For example, product life cycles for cars at Japanese firms are, on average, about four or five years, while those of trucks are generally eight years or more. This difference primarily reflects variations in the competition and the nature of each market. A truck project manager at a Japanese firm explained to us that it is not necessary to shorten the lead time of trucks as much as that of cars. That is one of the reasons why the lead time for truck projects tends to be longer. This data supports the idea that not only can organizational capabilities affect lead time, but so can the nature of the market and strategic objectives.

In addition, our data suggests that, after controlling for project characteristics, the U.S. firms are not significantly behind Japanese firms with respect to lead time, although there are still great differences in engineering hours. This is similar to the findings in the recent update to the Clark-Fujimoto survey (see Table 1–2) and reflects improvements in U.S. projects in the early 1990s. Our interviews with U.S. companies suggested that in the 1990s they generally set targets of shorter lead times at the beginning of new projects and used cross-functional product teams and relatively heavyweight project managers to move as quickly as possible. The result is faster lead times but more independent projects than are common in Japan. A question in our survey revealed that, on average, 66 percent of engineers in the U.S. projects fully dedicated their time to a single project, while only 41 percent of the Japanese engineers did.[11]

But the dedicated product team approach, while fast because team members have few distractions, does not seem to be so efficient in engineering hours. In particular, dedicated product teams make sharing tasks between multiple projects difficult to implement. In our field studies, we also found that at two of the three U.S. firms, managers were still debating the advantages and disadvantages of the product team approach and co-location of engineers.

Differences in Priorities Among the Four Strategic Types

Our survey also asked questions that allowed us to examine the strategic intentions or priorities of managers involved in each of the four different types of projects. We expected there to be a spectrum between two extremes. One extreme would be projects that emphasized new technology or improved product performance and functionality more than resource efficiency, such as short lead times or low development costs. The other extreme would be projects that emphasized resource efficiency more than new technology or product functionality and performance.

The results, reported in Table 5–3, do reflect these different priorities. Most managers reporting from new design projects placed more emphasis on new technology (63 percent) than on efficiency and more emphasis on new technology than lead times (74 percent). Far more managers valued functionality and performance than cost (74 percent) or lead time (78 percent). In contrast, few managers from sequential technology transfer projects emphasized new technology more than efficiency (28 percent). Cost appeared to be an especially critical objective in these projects because only 20

TABLE 5–3

Project Priorities for Each Strategy Type

	New Design (n = 27)	Concurrent Technology Transfer (n = 23)	Sequential Technology Transfer (n = 20)	Design Modification (n = 33)
Efficiency is more important than new technology[1]	63%	53%	28%	40%
New technology > Cost	52	44	20	30
New technology > Lead time	74	61	35	49
Functionality and performance are more important than efficiency[2]	76	55	43	54
Functionality/performance > Cost	74	44	35	46
Functionality/performance > Lead time	78	65	50	61

Notes: [1]Differences are statistically significant: at the 1 percent level between New Design and Sequential Technology Transfer, and at 5 percent between New Design and Design Modification.
[2]Differences are statistically significant: at the 1 percent level between New Design and Sequential Technology Transfer, and at 10 percent between New Design and Design Modification.

percent of managers attached more importance to new technology over costs. A larger number, but still relatively few managers from design modification projects, emphasized new technology more than efficiency (40 percent).

The data also suggests that concurrent technology transfer projects tried to achieve a balance between new technology and product performance as well as the efficient use of resources. Lead time was not a major issue with more than 60 percent of the respondents from these projects. More than half the respondents (53 percent and 55 percent, respectively) valued new technology and functionality and performance more than efficiency. A large but somewhat smaller number (44 percent) believed that new technology or functionality and performance were more important than costs.

ORGANIZATIONAL IMPLICATIONS OF CONCURRENT TRANSFERS

We have already suggested several reasons why companies might require fewer engineering hours for concurrent technology transfer compared to other project strategies.[12] In concurrent technology transfer, engineers can transfer a design from a preceding base project to a new project more efficiently than in sequential technology transfer or design modification. There are two basic factors that may contribute to this difference. First, the time lag between completing a base project and a new project is much shorter in a concurrent technology transfer project than in the other two types of transfer strategies. Second, there is overlap between a preceding base project and the new project only in the concurrent technology transfer strategy. These two factors create specific advantages and disadvantages in productivity for each multi-project strategy.

The first factor, the time lag between completion of a base project and a new project, may affect the difficulty of advance planning and of incorporating old designs into a new design architecture. The second factor, overlap between a preceding base project and a new project, may influence the feasibility and efficiency of communication across different projects. We can break down these factors into five areas: (1) advance planning; (2) mutual adjustments, task sharing, and joint design; (3) transfer of fresh versus dated designs; (4) problems of anonymous designs; and (5) the role of a general manager for multi-project management.

1. Advance Planning for Technology Transfer

When a new project transfers a platform from a preceding project, the new project usually needs to adjust the base platform design to fit the new product's individual architecture or specifications. Many factors may prompt changes in the platform design, such as different target markets, different performance requirements, and changes in fashion. For example, a company might redesign a platform from a mid-size family sedan to make a sportier car or a minivan, or widen a platform originally designed for the Japanese market for reuse in the United States. In addition, linking technologies between the platform and other components, such as the exterior body, engine, and suspension system, often differ between a base product and the new product. Because body designs usually differ between two products, this change alone usually requires some adjustments to the base platform.

We think it is more efficient for companies to make advance plans during the base project for future reuse of a platform. For example, Figure 5–2 shows that the time lag between a base project and a concurrent technology transfer project is much shorter than between a base project and other transfer strategies. Sequential technology transfer and design modification projects have long time lags between the base project and the new project—66.6 months and 81.2 months, respectively. These long time lags may indicate that a company designed a base platform without any plans to transfer it to future projects. To probe this question, in the survey we asked the project managers about the timing of decisions to make use of the base platform designs in new projects. In only 33 percent of the sequential technology transfer and design modification projects had companies made a decision to reuse the platform before completing the base project.

More important, even with an advance plan during the base project describing how a future project would reuse the platform design, there were often unexpected adjustments required during the new project. It is almost impossible to make accurate plans to modify the base platform for reuse in the new project when there is a long time lag between two projects. It is difficult for engineers in the base project to predict problems a future project may have in reusing the old platform design. In particular, many problems in the linking technologies surface only after the new project starts and engineers design other components and begin testing prototypes. In many cases, platform engineers cannot complete the necessary adjustments or changes in linking technologies without consulting the component engineers.

2. Mutual Adjustments, Task Sharing, and Joint Design

Adjustment processes are often so complicated that engineers can do these more efficiently through multiple iterations of feedback between two projects. This is true whether or not there are advance plans, partly because of complex interdependencies between component sub-systems. Because only concurrent technology transfer projects have significant overlap with a base project, only in concurrent technology transfer can engineers designing components make mutual adjustments with the base projects.

In addition to mutual adjustments, because of the overlapping and interactions, two linked projects also can share engineering tasks and project resources (we call this "task sharing"). For example, in our interviews, some engineers explained that multiple interrelated projects can share the same testing prototype when engineers in both projects cooperate closely. Moreover, in other cases, engineers from two projects can jointly work on certain engineering tasks as a group, such as creating one braking system to go into two different products (we call this "joint design"). Mutual adjustments, task sharing, and joint design with a base project, which only concurrent technology transfer projects can implement fully, may have contributed to the reduction in engineering hours required.

Figure 5–4 shows a simple model of how we think mutual adjustments, task sharing, and joint design occur. We also can cite a typical example from our interviews of concurrent technology transfer between two projects sharing the same platform. In this case, companies tend to develop the platform (the chassis, suspension system, and other under-body components) in a joint team that includes engineers from a base project and the follow-on project. At the same time, the two projects create two separate groups to develop upper-body components. Engineers from the two projects also coordinate their work and make mutual adjustments to create common linkage components between the two different upper bodies and the platform. Companies often use this type of task structure because, as we have noted elsewhere, the upper body should be different for each product, while the platform and linkages with the upper body can be the same or very similar between two products sharing the same platform.

3. Transfer of Fresh Designs Versus Dated Designs

There are also fundamental problems with use of a dated platform design as a base in a new project following sequential technology transfer or design modification. In our data, even projects using an existing design as a base developed mostly new components, includ-

FIGURE 5–4

Mutual Adjustments, Task Sharing, and Joint Design in Multiple Projects

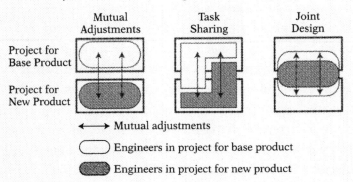

ing body and interior components. This mixture may create some difficulties in linking the old platform with new components in other parts of the product.

For example, usage of computer-aided design (CAD) is becoming more extensive each year. Engineers from 10 years ago probably drew designs on paper instead of using a CAD tool. Another example is the increasing use of plastic or aluminum materials for the body panels that may not fit properly with older platform designs. Some engineers also commented that design requirements often change after they complete the original design for non-technical reasons. These reasons include changes in perceived customer needs, market competition, or governmental regulations, especially when the time lag between the completion of the base design and the transfer to a new project is long. Design changes tend to increase engineering hours in the sequential technology transfer projects because the modifications touch many different components.

4. Problems of Anonymous Designs

In sequential technology transfer or design modification projects, companies usually transfer the design from base projects through drawings and written specifications. This is because engineers may have completed the base projects already and started working on other products. Some engineers even may have already left the firm. Therefore, engineers on the new project can have a hard time finding and communicating with engineers who worked on the old base platform. Even if they are still around, it may not be convenient for engineers who designed the base platform to help engineers on the new project. Engineers from the old project may be working on totally different products and they may not have much time or motivation to cooperate with engineers from the new transfer project.

These issues are important because face-to-face technology transfer can be much more efficient than transfer through specifications and drawings. This seems particularly true for complex knowledge transfers, such as for vehicle layouts or subsystem integration.[13] Our data suggests that an old base platform usually needs modification when other products use it, and this reuse requires information that is hard to codify. For example, several engineers in our interviews mentioned that, in order to modify a base design, they often need to know more details than they can find in standard drawings or CAD data. Drawings do not show the relationship between design modifications and consequent changes in functionality.

One engineer explained this issue to us with a particularly good illustration. Suppose a new project tries to transfer and reuse a brake design (which is closely related to the platform components) from a preceding project. Engineers from the new project believe it is possible to reuse the brakes because they are suitable in terms of size and shape. But they still cannot determine whether or not they can actually reuse the brake design as is. This is because engineers in the previous project designed the brakes after extensive analyses and tests assuming the performance and weight characteristics of the preceding product. In order to apply the old brakes to a new product with different performance and weight characteristics, engineers in the new project need to know some of the details behind the development process and design decisions for the existing brakes. Otherwise, the new project needs to redo all the analytical and proof-of-concept work to ensure that the brakes work correctly with the new product. Only engineers who actually worked on the base design are likely to have that kind of information—but in their minds or notebooks. In general, as other researchers have found, it is difficult to transfer intangible or tacit understanding of design details without chronological overlap and direct interaction with engineers familiar with the original technology.[14]

5. Role of a General Manager for Multi-Project Management

Finally, there is another organizational factor that may differentiate the productivity of concurrent technology transfer from other multi-project strategies. Companies with lots of technology transfers usually have general managers or vice-presidents responsible for product development above the project managers. These higher-level general managers supervise multiple products and projects.

(As we discussed in Chapters 2 and 3, companies give them various titles, ranging from "center managers" at Toyota to "platform managers" at Fiat and "vehicle line executives" at GM.) These executives also are likely to oversee both a base project and a concurrent technology transfer project because the time lag between these projects is short. With a long time lag, it is less likely that the same general manager is responsible for both a base project and a sequential technology transfer project, or for both a base project and a design modification project.

Changes in executive leadership can clearly affect the efficiency of technology transfer between two projects. For example, a general manager is likely to consider the total productivity of the base project and the concurrent technology transfer project together. The manager might authorize extra time or staff to develop components suitable for more than one project. Such concerns are less likely if managers and engineers expect to move on before a related follow-on project starts. Independent product teams and heavyweight project managers also generally work with tight budget and schedule targets for their individual projects, and they may not have the extra time or money to spend to benefit future unrelated projects. (This is a common problem in designing software components for reuse, leading some firms to create organizations that manage multiple projects simultaneously from libraries of reusable designs and components.)[15] In other words, the shorter the time lag between multiple interrelated projects, the greater the potential benefit of a strong general manager who can lead and manage multiple projects.[16]

COMMENTS

We have pointed out that the efficiency of managing projects through concurrent technology transfer is somewhat analogous to the efficiency of managing overlaps among different functions within a single project. Multiple functions, at least to some extent, often require sequential tasks. For example, manufacturing preparations for a new product cannot begin until engineers have completed a significant amount of work on the details of a product's design. As a result, an attempt to overlap functions too much, such as in aggressive concurrent or simultaneous engineering approaches, could lead to wasted effort and other problems. In particular, component engineering groups or manufacturing engineering may have to do considerable rework if design engineers continue to make changes in the product specifications late in a project.[17] As in software development, engineers can avoid some of this rework through frequent exchanges of information and continual integration of design changes, although managing in this way requires special concepts or techniques for project organization and management, component integration, and product testing.[18]

Overlaps among multiple projects through concurrent technology transfer also enable a firm to avoid wasted or redundant work. Managers can coordinate project objectives and engineers can adjust designs as they go along—rather than rework designs later. We believe that the ability to overcome problems of concurrent engineering and task overlapping at least partially explains why concurrent technology transfer projects demonstrated such high levels of productivity. Simply overlapping projects, however, does not automatically provide a firm with all the efficiency benefits of concurrent transfers. Overlapping projects that share components creates significant interdependencies between these projects and makes it difficult to coordinate across projects as well as across interdependent functions (which can cut across overlapped projects), like body or component design and process engineering.[19] Companies need to figure out which components to share. Then they need to introduce specific organizational structures and processes that facilitate coordination across projects and functions as well as the process of mutual adjustments, task sharing, and joint design.

Chapter 6

Multi-Project Strategies and Company Performance

F rom the viewpoint of product development, companies are, in essence, collections of projects. Therefore, efficient performance in individual projects, as well as effective strategies for linking projects and creating a product portfolio, should result in superior performance at the firm level. Accordingly, in this chapter we examine the impact of different multi-project strategies on market share and sales growth, which we believe are important indicators of a company's competitiveness.[1] For the analysis, we again rely on our four strategy types—new design, concurrent technology transfer, sequential technology transfer, and design modification. Our data come from 210 new products introduced by 17 automobile manufacturers.

Of particular significance is the finding that our second strategy type—concurrent technology transfer—has by far the largest impact on market share and sales growth. In other words, when companies develop a new platform and quickly transfer this technology to another project to create a second product, they grow much faster than their competitors. Companies have used this technique for technology transfer to add and replace similar products as well as to move quickly into new market segments. For example, in the past few years, recreational or sport-utility vehicles have suddenly become very fashionable. These vehicles stole large numbers of sales from traditional sedans and station wagons. Only firms that introduced recreational vehicles built on car platforms or using significant levels of existing components were able to quickly adapt to this market transition.

SALES GROWTH AND NEW PRODUCT INTRODUCTIONS

When we started this research, one question we had was whether firms that introduce more new products than competitors actually increase sales more over time. This thinking resembles other studies suggesting that frequent product introductions have a positive influence on sales growth. The reason is that a higher rate of new product introductions should enable a firm to replace existing products or extend product offerings faster than competitors.[2] And broader product lines should enable a firm to grow and meet consumer needs more effectively by covering a wider range of market segments as well as targeting specific market niches.[3]

Therefore, in addition to measuring linkages across projects such as whether a platform is new or transferred, and looking at the speed of the transfer, we created a company-level output metric directly related to multi-project strategy. This is the *new product introduction rate*, which measures the frequency of new products within each firm. We define this as the ratio of the number of new product introductions adjusted by the number of product offerings in a base year.

The impact of the new product introduction rate on market performance may be particularly important in industries, such as automobiles, where two general conditions hold. First, the technology improves steadily in small increments, instead of through radical improvements only once in a while. This makes marginal superiority the basis for product competition in the marketplace. Second, customer expectations appear fragmented and change at a rapid pace, predicated by current fashion trends and social values. Therefore, "freshness" in styling, in addition to product functionality, has a significant influence on sales.[4]

Another question we had is which type of multi-project strategy is the most appropriate to develop a large number of new products. One of the primary corporate goals for new product development may be to introduce new component technologies and designs into a single product line. But companies also may want to introduce new products as quickly as possible into a family of product lines targeting different market segments. Firms may achieve this by developing unique designs for each new product, using the new design strategy. Projects that develop more new components, however, generally require more lead time and engineering resources as well as larger investments in new manufacturing equipment.[5] Otherwise, frequent introductions of new designs may reflect incomplete development efforts and result in products that suffer from problems in design quality and perform poorly in the marketplace.[6] An exclusive use of the new design strategy, therefore, may result in either too few new products or weak new products. This strategy may be effective preserving the market competitiveness of an individual product line, and may result in one or more new hit products. On the other hand, it does little to help a firm systematically improve or expand its *portfolio* of products.

Extensive usage of concurrent technology transfer or sequential technology transfer may provide firms with a greater advantage in leveraging their competencies and engineering investments than the other two multi-project strategy types. But a new product based on sequential technology transfer by definition incorporates relatively older technologies than products based on concurrent technology transfer. Repeated use of old components may then have a negative impact on market competitiveness. For example, one reason to introduce new products frequently is to meet changes in customer tastes and needs with new technologies and designs. Reusing an old design may conflict with this objective. It may also impose constraints on introducing new designs for other components. In contrast, the rapid reuse or transfer of new technologies among multiple ongoing projects may improve the average level of newness and technological sophistication of a firm's overall product offerings.

Automobile firms often try to develop more new products or better products than their competitors without relying on old technology. For example, Clark and Fujimoto implied that some Japanese manufacturers depended heavily on the engineering and development capabilities of outside suppliers in order to avoid a trade-off between new designs and reused designs.[7] Our study explores the idea that successful manufacturers also may have multi-project strategies that differ from those of low-performing manufacturers in order to mitigate this trade-off.

If firms want to utilize their investments effectively and still maintain a high new-product introduction rate, then they may try to decrease the number of new components in each project and carry over substantial portions of existing designs. That is, they may reuse existing core technologies as often as possible.[8] This is similar to how "flexible" factories in software and other industries assemble different products from standardized parts or modules.[9] Particularly when specific technologies reflect a firm's core competencies, managers may want to utilize these technologies quickly in a wide range of end-products.[10] Other researchers also have found firms that stick to core technologies and leverage these in new products gained more market share than companies developing new technologies for each new product.[11]

In recent years, many authors also have written about the importance of "time to market" for individual products. As mentioned above, however, we believe that another critical issue is *speed in technology leveraging.* This refers to the time a firm requires to develop and then transfer key technologies among multiple projects in order to deliver new products or replace existing products. In short, firms may best utilize new technologies across multiple projects by quickly transferring them while these technologies are still relatively new in the market as well as in the company.

There is also an organizational advantage to concurrent rather than sequential technology transfer, which we discussed in Chapter 5. Only when projects overlap in time can engineers working on the different projects transfer a technology from one project to the other and communicate directly, share tasks, and adjust designs as necessary. Overlapping projects is similar to overlapping functions like product planning and process engineering within a single project through simultaneous or concurrent engineering. In single projects, simultaneous or concurrent engineering that overlaps functional groups and activities can enhance both the speed of a project and the quality of the final product.[12] In multiple projects, concurrent management should enhance both the speed and the effectiveness of technology transfer between the interdependent projects.[13] Effective transfers should then enhance engineering productivity and enable a firm to develop more or better products with the same investments, thus leading to improved performance in sales growth and market share.

Finally, focusing on design modifications may not be advantageous to a firm either in terms of leveraging designs or creating new core technologies. Under this strategy, a firm enhances an existing design relatively slowly over multiple generations of the same product. It does not take advantage of new technology developed in other product lines. Only when we consider an individual project as a one-time event does the design modification strategy seem to be effective. In our framework of multi-project strategies, however, design modification should be the least effective in contributing to a firm's growth.

Using the database we constructed, we decided to explore three propositions: (1) Firms that develop more products than their competitors over the same time periods should have greater increases in market share and sales. (2) Firms that frequently follow the concurrent technology transfer strategy should increase market share or sales more than firms that do not follow this strategy so frequently. And (3) firms that rely on design modifications primarily for new products should not increase their market share or sales as much as firms following the other three strategies.

THE DATA

For this part of the study, we collected data on the 17 largest passenger car manufacturers in the world. They consist of five Japanese

(Toyota, Nissan, Honda, Mazda, Mitsubishi), three U.S. (General Motors, Ford, Chrysler), and nine European producers (Volkswagen-Audi Group, Mercedes-Benz, BMW, Opel, Ford of Europe, PSA, Renault, Fiat Group, Volvo).[14] These firms introduced 210 new car products into the U.S., European, and Japanese markets between 1980 and 1991, the period we choose for our analysis when we created this database. To make sure we examined comparable products, we excluded low-volume specialty products, minivans (which were few during our sample period but included some truck platforms), and products that had platforms jointly developed or shared across more than one firm.[15]

We collected data on new products primarily from *Automobil Revue*, an industry journal published annually in Switzerland. This covers introduction dates and design feature details for all new car products worldwide. We also referred to such automobile magazines as *Motor Trend, Car and Driver, Car Graphic, NAVI,* and *Car Styling,* as well a weekly industry journal, *Automobile News,* for detailed product information. We had to develop a methodology to categorize the 210 projects that produced the new cars into different strategies and then validate this. As a result, we conducted interviews with approximately 130 engineers and 30 project managers primarily from Toyota, Nissan, Honda, Mitsubishi, Mazda, General Motors, Ford, Chrysler, Fiat, Volkswagen, Renault, and Mercedes.

We divided the data into four three-year time periods: 1980–1982, 1983–1985, 1986–1988, and 1989–1991. The 17 firms and 4 time periods make 68 combinations or data points. Among the 68 combinations, we did not use 3 periods when firms introduced no new products. As a result, our final sample consists of 65 data points describing company-level strategies and sales growth over a series of three-year periods.[16]

Sales Growth and Market Share Change

We calculated sales growth and market share change using estimates of revenues for each product in North America, Japan, and Europe. We determined revenues by multiplying the total unit production for each product by an average sales price.[17] We collected the production data from a single source, *Motor Vehicle Statistics in Major Countries* (published by the Japan Automobile Manufacturers Association), to maintain consistency. Sales growth tracks the percentage change in a company's car sales revenues from the beginning to the end of one three-year period.

New Product Introduction Rate and New Product Definition

We calculated the new product introduction rate for each manufacturer during each of the three-year periods by determining the number of new product introductions and then dividing this by the number of product offerings in the base year. We defined a new product as a car newly introduced with mostly new interior and exterior styling, as opposed to a product with a minor face-lift or a variation that consists of minor cosmetic modifications.[18] This analysis focuses on the management of multi-project strategies and organizational interactions across projects, rather than on the development of minor product variations such as multiple body types. Therefore, we counted as only one new product any variations designed within a single project led by a single project manager. For example, one project and one project manager produced the Ford Taurus and Mercury Sable, so we counted these two variations as one product. One project and one project manager also produced all of the multi-brand variations that came from the General Motors GM10 project. Therefore, we counted the different models sold under the Pontiac Grand Prix, Oldsmobile Supreme, Buick Regal, and Chevrolet Lumina brand names as only one product.

Usage of Multi-Project Strategy Types

We measured the use of different multi-project strategies by a particular company by categorizing the products that a firm introduced during each three-year period. For example, a firm might introduce 10 new products during a three-year period. If three of these new products are concurrent technology transfers, then we would calculate the usage of concurrent technology transfer during this period as 30 percent. We also had to determine whether a firm newly developed or transferred the platform of a new product from a preceding product. To do this, we developed a point scheme after consulting with industry engineers (see Appendix 1).[19] Through this methodology, we were able to categorize product strategies using publicly available data on product specifications.[20]

We categorized projects that created new platforms from scratch as following a *new design* strategy. All other projects derived platforms from an existing design. Products that simply carried over the platform of the predecessor model we categorized as *design modifications*. Products that shared platform designs with previously existing products that were part of other product lines we categorized as either *concurrent technology transfers* or *sequential technology transfers*. We determined the distinction between concurrent and sequential transfers by the transfer time lag.

We defined concurrent technology transfers as projects where the transfer of the platform design from a base project occurred within two years of the introduction of the base design. Our interviews with company engineers indicated that when the time lag is shorter than this, there are almost always interactions or coordination efforts between a base project and a new project. In our definition, a key factor that conceptually differentiates concurrent from sequential technology transfer is whether an overlap in platform design activities exists between the new project and the base project. Two years is also close to midway for the average new car project in the early 1990s (about 54 months, or 4.5 years—see Table 1–2). We also sent a questionnaire survey to project managers in Japan and the United States. This data supports the two-year cutoff point as well (see Chapter 5).[21]

EXAMPLES OF DIFFERENT MULTI-PROJECT STRATEGIES

The way we categorize product strategies plays a key role in this study. The following examples illustrate how we defined each of the four multi-project strategies.

1. New Design

In most cases, it was easy to identify new designs because firms often adopted new technologies for their platforms during our 12-year sample period. Some products changed from rear-wheel drive to front-wheel drive, and others introduced new suspension technologies such as multi-link or compact double-wishbone systems. To incorporate such major changes requires completely new platform designs.

For example, the new 1987 Civic project developed wide product variations including the basic Civic, the CRX (three-door coupe), and the Shuttle (five-door hatchback). We counted these variations as one product because a single project or product team developed all of them.[22] *Automobil Revue* in 1984 and 1989 described the suspension system and the chassis of the previous product, the 1983 Civic, and the 1987 Civic, as follows:

> "1983 Civic: Integral body; front independent suspension with McPherson struts, front lower A-arm and torsion bar spring, some models with antiroll bars; rear trailing arm, torsion beam axle and Panhard rod with strut, semi-rigid. Some models with antiroll bars."[23]
> "1987 Civic: Integral body; all-round independent suspension with coil springs and air adjustable shock absorbers, front upper A-arm, lower control arm and coaxial tension struts; rear trailing arms, swinging arm, with upper and lower control arms. Some models with front and/or rear antiroll bars."[24]

The suspension system in the new Civic is a variation of the four-wheel double-wishbone type. The older Civic uses a variation of McPherson strut types in the front and a variation of semi-independent torsion bar types in the rear. The new Civic has a completely different system compared to either the 1983 Civic or any other existing designs at that time in Honda. This platform was technically innovative because no other products of this size had a double-wishbone suspension. The wheelbase/track for the new Civic four-door sedan and the old Civic four-door sedan are 2,450/1,400 mm and 2,500/1,450 mm, respectively. The difference in both the wheelbase and track of the new and the old Civic indicates that the floor panels for the new Civic are also new. Therefore, we categorized the 1987 Civic as a new product under the new design strategy.

2. Concurrent Technology Transfer

In May 1988, 13 months after introducing the 1987 Civic with a completely new platform, Honda introduced a new product line, the Concerto. The Concerto project and the Civic project were organizationally separate and managed by different project managers. The Concerto project developed two different body variations as well as exterior and interior stylings completely different from any variations of the 1987 Civic. However, the Concerto's suspension system is identical to the 1987 Civic.[25] The Concerto sedan's wheelbase is 2,550 mm, 50 mm longer than that of the Civic sedan, while the Concerto's front track is identical to the Civic sedan. Therefore, we concluded that the Concerto project shared the same platform as the Civic but stretched the wheelbase by 50 millimeters. Because Honda introduced the Concerto only 13 months after the Civic project, we categorized the Concerto project as following the concurrent technology transfer strategy.

3. Sequential Technology Transfer

We noted earlier that Chrysler primarily relied on sequential technology transfers to introduce new products during the 1980s. It began in September 1980 with the K-car project. This introduced a completely new platform for the front-wheel drive Dodge Aries and the Plymouth Reliant. *Automobil Revue* in 1982 described the chassis of this platform as follows: "Integral body. Front McPherson strut and A-arm; rear rigid axle with trailing arm and Panhard rod, front and rear coil springs, telescopic damper and antiroll bar."[26]

Chrysler then used this platform as a base for several other distinctive products. These included the 1985 H-car project (the

Dodge Lancer and the Chrysler LeBaron GTS), the 1987 P-car project (the Dodge Shadow and the Plymouth Sundance), and the 1988 C-car project (the Dodge Dynasty and the Chrysler New Yorker). For example, the P-cars, introduced in March 1986, employed exactly the same chassis specifications and the same front track, 1,460 mm, as the original K-cars.[27] Because the wheelbase of the P-cars (2,465 mm) is 75 mm shorter than the K-cars, we concluded that the platform of the P-car is a shortened version of the K-car platform. The platform design of the P-cars at the introduction date was already 5.5 years old (the time difference between September 1980 and March 1986). Because it is longer than 2.0 years, we categorized the P-car project as following the sequential technology transfer strategy.

4. Design Modification

In 1987, Toyota introduced a new Corolla. We categorized this project as following the design modification strategy. Product body variations of this Corolla included the basic Corolla, the FX, the Levin, the Sprinter, the Cielo, and the Trueno. Again, we counted these variations as one product because Toyota developed all of them within one project. *Automobil Revue* in 1989 described the platform design of the new Corolla as follows: "Integral body, front and rear independent suspension with McPherson struts, front lower A-arm, rear parallel control arm and trailing arm, front antiroll bars, some models also rear antiroll bars."[28]

Automobil Revue (1987) also described the suspension system in the previous model, the 1983 Corolla; this is identical to the description for the 1987 Corolla. With respect to the change in floor panels, we compared the wheelbase and track dimensions of the 1983 Corolla and the new Corolla. We found them to be the same (2,430 mm and 1,430 mm, respectively). The new Corolla and the old Corolla shared the same suspension system and the same wheelbase/track. Therefore, it seems that the new Corolla used the old Corolla platform at least as a base. Accordingly, we consider the new Corolla a design-

TABLE 6–1

The Number of Projects Introduced by Sample Firms

Strategy Type	Periods				Total
	1	**2**	**3**	**4**	**Total**
New design	27 (57%)	26 (50%)	24 (48%)	29 (48%)	106
Concurrent technology transfer	4 (9%)	3 (6%)	10 (20%)	11 (20%)	28
Sequential technology transfer	8 (17%)	14 (27%)	9 (18%)	11 (18%)	42
Design modification	8 (17%)	9 (17%)	7 (14%)	10 (14%)	34
Total	47 (100%)	52 (100%)	50 (100%)	61 (100%)	210

Source: Nobeoka and Cusumano, 1997, p. 180.

modification project. The platform design of the 1987 Corolla was already four years old when Toyota introduced it in May 1987.

Trend of Project Characteristics in the Sample

Table 6–1 shows the total number of new product introductions and the number and the percentage of each multi-project strategy type during each period. The total number of new product introductions increased rapidly after 1989, from 50 in 1986–1988 to 61 in 1989–1991. Use of the concurrent technology transfer strategy also increased sharply in the middle of the 1980s, from 6 percent in 1983–1985 to approximately 20 percent in 1986–1988 and 18 percent in 1989–1991. The increase in the concurrent technology transfer strategy reflects the accelerating speed with which firms have been leveraging new platform designs to other product lines. The adoption of concurrent technology transfer also implies that managing multiple overlapping projects, as opposed to managing one project at a time, has become more important to automobile manufacturers. In fact, the percentage of concurrent technology transfer, about 20 percent during 1986–1991, means that firms probably had to coordinate twice this number (about 40 percent) of all projects. We reached this conclusion because each concurrent transfer requires, by definition, overlapping (and, according to our interviews, coordination) with at least one other project from which the platform design originates.

ANALYSIS AND KEY FINDINGS

To examine the impact of different multi-project strategies on market performance, we first conducted a simple cluster analysis of the different strategic groups.[29] As we explained before, the sample consisted of 17 firms over four three-year periods, and excluded three periods when firms introduced no new products, for a total of 65 data points. This analysis measures the utilization rate for the four different multi-project strategies as well as the new product introduction rate, for a total of five variables.

As seen in Table 6–2, there were 26 three-year periods when firms were primarily following the new design strategy, 15 for concurrent technology transfer, 11 for sequential technology transfer, and 13 for design modification. Looking at the first strategic group, for example, we see that 92 percent of the products they introduced during these three-year periods consisted of new platform designs. Therefore, we can say that this group had a "primary orientation" toward the new design strategy. Within the second group, 41 percent of the products they introduced during these periods consisted of concurrent technology transfers, while 46 percent were new designs (which provided the new platforms to transfer). In the third group, 72.1 percent of the products introduced represented sequential technology transfers, compared to 22.6 percent of new designs. In the fourth group, 54.7 percent of the products were design modifications, 25.2 percent new designs, and 19.1 percent sequential design transfers.

If we look at these data by region, we see that at different points in time, firms from all regions used nearly all the strategies. (The Japanese are exceptions in that they did not utilize sequential

TABLE 6–2

Cluster Analysis of Strategy Types

	Group 1 New Design	Group 2 Concurrent Technology Transfer	Group 3 Sequential Technology Transfer	Group 4 Design Modification
Total sample	26	15	11	13
By region				
Japan	6	9	0	5
United States	4	1	3	4
Europe	16	5	8	4
Multi-project strategy usage				
New design	**92.0%**	46.0%	22.6%	25.2%
Concurrent	0.6	**41.0**	0.0	1.0
Sequential	4.4	5.8	**72.1**	19.1
Modification	3.0	7.3	5.3	**54.7**
New product introduction rate	0.45	0.69	0.51	0.47
Average platform age (years)***	0.37	0.91	3.75	5.54
Market share change (%)***	3.4	23.4	9.1	–15.6

Notes: *** Differences among the strategy types are significant at the 1% level (ANOVA). Market share change measures a ratio and therefore does not total zero.

technology transfers during the period we studied.) Firms from the different regions, however, tended to have different strategic orientations. For example, Japanese firms accounted for by far the largest number of periods (9) dominated by the concurrent technology transfer strategy. European firms had by far the largest number of new design periods (16); they also had the most sequential transfer periods (8). U.S. firms were less clear in their strategic orientation and combined rather evenly the new design (4), sequential technology transfer (3), and design modification (4) strategies.

A high new-product introduction rate should result in relatively new products in the marketplace. To examine this, we tracked the average platform age (measured since its first usage in a product) for each product introduced during the period under study. On this measure as well, there is a clear distinction at least partially due to the definition of strategic types among the strategic groups. As seen in Table 6–2, the new design group, not surprisingly, had the lowest average platform age for their products during these periods (0.37 years). The concurrent technology transfer group also had relatively new platforms—on average, only 0.91 years old. This reflected the high number of new products that this group introduced as well as the practice of rapidly reusing platforms in concurrently ongoing projects. In contrast, the sequential technology transfer group (3.75 years) and the design modification group (5.54 years) had rather old platforms in their products.

Lastly, Table 6–2 presents data on market performance. We defined this as the change in a firm's share of the total world car market (measured in estimated dollar values) over each of the three-year periods under study. A particularly striking finding is that companies focused on concurrent technology transfers increased their market share an average of 23.4 percent over these three-year periods. For example, a firm that started out with a 10 percent market share would have grown to 12.3 percent in share by the end of the three-year period—a huge increase for the relatively stable auto industry. This growth seems to reflect the ability of firms to introduce a popular product and then quickly transfer the platform technology to other products. In contrast, equally striking is the observation that firms following the design modification strategy lost an average of 15.6 percent in market share over their three-year periods. For example, a firm with a 10 percent share would have dropped to 8.44 percent over three years if it only introduced design modifications. This seems to reflect that customers do not respond well to old technologies (seen in the 5.54-year average platform age for design modification products). This seems true even if products undergo complete exterior and interior styling changes.

It is also notable that companies which concentrated on new designs did not do very well in the marketplace either. They increased in share only 3.4 percent, badly trailing companies that followed not only concurrent technology transfer but also sequential technology transfer, which we can associate with an increase in market share of 9.1 percent. For example, firms with 10 percent market shares would have increased to only 10.34 percent following the new design strategy versus 10.92 percent following sequential technology transfer. This difference seems to reflect the large resources required to develop new products and the limits a new design strategy placed on the number of new products companies were able to introduce during these three-year periods. Thus sequential technology transfer and, in particular, concurrent technology transfer seem to result in better market performance than the other two strategies.

The cluster analysis supports our three propositions. We had suggested that firms should grow faster when they introduce more products, and that concurrent technology transfer should result in the highest growth levels and design modification in the lowest growth. But cluster analysis does not allow us to separate the effects of other factors on sales performance, or examine the interrelationship among different factors. To test our propositions more formally, we relied on more sophisticated statistical techniques.[30]

Table 6–3 shows descriptive data and a correlation matrix for major variables. The average sales growth across all manufacturers is 5.2 percent. The new product introduction rate, on average, is 51.8 percent. This number means that, for example, if a firm focused only on replacing existing products with new products, it would have replaced about half of all its products during any of the three-year periods we considered. The new product introduction rate has a strong correlation with sales growth. In addition, an analysis of sales growth and the different multi-project strategies indicates that only an extensive use of concurrent technology transfer has a strong positive correlation with sales growth. Conversely, an extensive use of design modification has a negative correlation. These findings confirm what we saw in Table 6–2.

TABLE 6-3

Descriptive Data and Correlation Matrix (N = 65)

	Ave.	S.D.	1	2	3	4	5	6	7
1. Sales growth change	.052	.249	—						
2. New product introduction rate	.518	.308	.45***	—					
Multi-project strategy type									
3. New design	.563	.354	.03	−.08	—				
4. Concurrent technology transfer	.099	.180	.29**	.23*	−.18	—			
5. Sequential technology transfer	.191	.294	.05	−.01	−.65***	−.25**	—		
6. Design modification	.147	.246	−.32**	−.05	−.54***	−.17	−.09	—	
7. Market coverage	6.62	2.73	−.14	−.24*	−.28**	.04	.13	.23*	—
8. Sales growth change (t−1)	.105	.235	−.20	−.14	−.03	.33***	−.08	.11	−.13

Source: Nobeoka and Cusumano, 1997, p. 181.

*p < .10; **p < .05; *** p < .01.

Table 6-4 presents results from our analyses of the influence of different multi-project strategies on sales growth. We used a regression model that controls for different variables. This enables us to simulate statistically the sales growth performance of firms that utilize different product strategies. The first analysis (model 1) contains the control variables without any multi-project strategy variables. The second analysis (model 2) adds the new product introduction rate. The third (model 3) has both the new product introduction rate and the multi-project strategy variables.

As our first proposition suggests, the new product introduction rate significantly predicts differences in sales growth even after controlling for other relevant factors. The results also support our second

TABLE 6–4

Regression Results for Sales Growth

Independent Variables	Model 1	Model 2	Model 3
New product introduction rate		0.435***	0.456***
		(0.160)	(0.145)
Multi-project strategy (%)			
New design			—
Concurrent technology transfer			0.510 ***
			(0.185)
Sequential technology transfer			0.125
			(0.091)
Design modification			−0.321**
			(0.128)
Market coverage at beginning	−0.038*	0.002	0.032
	(0.021)	(0.019)	(0.024)
Sales growth change (t–1)	−0.415***	−0.352***	−0.330***
	(0.148)	(0.130)	(0.105)
Period (Dummy)			
80–82	0.016	0.064	0.080
	(0.077)	(0.066)	(0.061)
83–85	−0.106	−0.069	0.271**
	(0.080)	(0.074)	(0.075)
86–88	0.008	0.036	0.148*
	(0.078)	(0.072)	(0.062)
89–91	—	—	—
Adjusted R Square	0.186	0.312	0.510

Source: Nobeoka and Cusumano, 1997, p. 182.

Notes: Heteroskedasticity-consistent standard errors are in parentheses (White, 1980). All results are for a fixed-effects model and therefore include 16 firm dummy variables.

*p<.10; **p<.05; ***p<.01; two tailed tests.

and third propositions. Extensive use of concurrent technology transfer has a strong positive influence on sales growth. On the other hand, design modification has a significant negative influence on sales growth.[31] The third analysis also indicates that the full set of variables explains about 51 percent of a company's sales growth.[32]

TABLE 6–5

Relative Increases in Sales Growth over Three Years

Strategy	Sales Growth over Base Year (%)
New design	–7
Concurrent technology transfer	+35
Sequential technology transfer	–2
Design modification	–33

Note: This data is calculated from a simplified regression model based on Table 6-4.

We also can estimate the relative sales performance of the different product strategies from these numbers (although we had to simplify the regression analysis to do this). According to Table 6–3, the average firm had 6.62 product lines in the base year (the market coverage variable) and then introduced approximately 3.5 new products during the three-year period (the new product introduction rate is 51.8 percent). Suppose a hypothetical firm created three new products and then used concurrent technology transfer to create three additional products—one derived from each of its new products. Then, the analysis in Table 6–4, which is based on the historical data from our sample, indicates that sales for this firm would increase by about 35 percent over the three-year period. On the other hand, if the firm introduces no other products based on the three new designs, then sales would fall by about 7 percent over the next three years. If the firm used sequential technology transfer to introduce at least some additional products, sales would decrease only by 2 percent. A firm following the design modification strategy would fare the worst, with sales dropping about 33 percent over the three years (Table 6–5).[33]

Finally, we must point out the variable for sales growth change in the previous period (t-1) in Table 6–4. In all three analyses, the negative sign indicates that firms had difficulty sustaining high growth rates from one three-year period to the next. This variable is also significant in the correlation matrix (see Table 6–3). We think these results reflect the importance of maintaining a consistent strategy that emphasizes the introduction of many new products in each time period. We also conclude that following the concurrent technology transfer strategy for multiple periods leads to very high growth rates.

COMMENTS

Concurrent technology transfer helps firms perform better in the marketplace. This strategy promotes the effective use of investments in product development by quickly diffusing new technologies across a portfolio of products. In particular, by overlapping and coordinating the work of multiple projects, concurrent transfers make it possible both to share key components and differentiate end products.

We realize that the variables we used to analyze market performance have limitations, although our primary purpose in this part of the study was not to develop a comprehensive model to predict sales growth. Selling products is a complex phenomenon and ultimately results from the ability of a firm to do a better job than competitors in designing, building, and marketing products that customers want to buy. This ability relates to product styling, quality, prices, functional performance, advertising, product availability, service, and numerous other factors. Nonetheless, we have highlighted an important strategy for the management of product development—concurrent technology transfer. Our findings demonstrate that even a few variables describing multi-project strategy can explain about half of a company's growth rate. This is a powerful result that few managers can afford to ignore.

Chapter 7

Organizational Requirements for Multi-Project Management

I n Chapters 2 and 3, we discussed how Toyota and other companies have introduced different strategies and structures for
multi-project management. In Chapters 5 and 6, we demonstrated the impact on project performance and then sales performance of concurrent technology transfer—rapidly reusing key
technologies and architectural elements, such as in an automobile
platform, in multiple projects that are simultaneously ongoing. We
also noted that overlapping projects that share technology make it
possible for engineers to combine project tasks—for example, to design one platform or brake system that fits two products. In addition,
overlapping allows engineers to make adjustments in specifications
for final products or shared components to avoid rework later on and
to ensure the distinctiveness or integrity of the individual products.

In this chapter, we return to the issue of organizational requirements for effective multi-project management and technology transfer.
To manage multiple projects well, companies need specific organizational capabilities that promote coordination and communication
across functions as well as across projects. Fortunately, during the

1980s, many firms in a variety of industries improved their ability to integrate the work of different functional departments. We noted in Chapter 1 that a popular concept also found in companies practicing lean principles is "cross-functional" management. This approach brings together engineers and staff from different functional areas to form multi-disciplinary teams. It has clearly helped firms move toward more project-centered rather than functional product-development organizations. It also has helped component groups and functional departments communicate better, share knowledge more easily, and establish common goals. In addition, many companies have tried to overlap phases within projects, such as beginning manufacturing preparations while creating detailed designs, as advocates of concurrent engineering and lean product development encourage. This overlapping has helped engineers speed up development and solve various problems simultaneously.

These two trends—cross-functional teams and concurrent engineering—have led to more effective management of individual projects.[1] We have argued in this book that while firms need to manage single projects well, they can go beyond this. Managers need to coordinate *multiple* projects in order to achieve *optimal* efficiency and effectiveness from the perspective of the corporation as a whole. To manage in a multi-project mode, however, they need to understand the relatively complex organizational capabilities and processes that this new way of thinking requires.

FUNCTIONAL VERSUS PROJECT-CENTERED ORGANIZATIONS

Prior to the 1990s, most writings on organizing product development emphasized the management of different functional groups through separate departments or the integration of functional activities through cross-functional projects or product teams.[2] Shortening lead times and improving product concepts have become key competitive issues in recent years, prompting many companies to adopt cross-functional teams as well as other practices that we place together under the heading of lean.

We saw in the case of Toyota and other auto makers that companies tend to introduce matrix structures rather than eliminating functional departments completely. These matrix structures combine functional departments and cross-functional product teams in the form of projects. Projects within a matrix structure usually succeed in integrating across functions while maintaining some functional expertise within the organization. As a result, relatively few companies have adopted pure product-team organizations with no matrix of functional or component departments. The debate that companies have continued to face with the matrix system, however, is how much should they make their development organizations project-centered versus functionally oriented. In concrete terms, the distinction usually comes down to issues such as how much authority should project managers have relative to functional department managers over product concepts, detailed component designs, component reuse, schedules, budgets, and personnel.

Project-centered organizations have certain advantages. They help break down walls between functional departments and bring different departments together toward a common product concept (such as a sporty sedan or a high-quality, luxurious economy car) and common project goals (such as a shorter lead time or lower costs). This consensus occurs because project engineers generally do not think only about their individual components. They usually have numerous opportunities, through cross-group meetings and interactions with other engineers, to influence the whole product concept or the broader project effort. For example, engineers from different departments might work together to design parts for easier manufacturing, or to modify manufacturing systems to make unique product components. Engineers from different specialties might combine to make product development more innovative. (A famous case is Sony's CD Walkman, where electronic, mechanical, and laser engineers all cooperated in a joint project to design this unusual miniaturized product in a very short period of time.[3])

On the other hand, functional organizations have certain advantages of their own. Engineers in these organizations are more likely to be aware of the latest technologies and accumulate special technical expertise because they tend to specialize more and stay together, rather than forming and disbanding project groups every time they complete a product. Functional departments may thus be in a better position to produce radical innovations in particular technologies or be state-of-the-art in selected areas.[4] They may, for example, produce the best component designs and performance, possibly at the expense of total product integrity. Some customers will want this type of excellence—cars with the fastest engines or the most unusual body designs, or CD players with the longest battery life.

A matrix that combines projects with functional departments may obtain some of the advantages of both approaches, but it also creates particular problems. Two common areas stand out: One relates to the level of authority held by the project manager as opposed to the functional department managers that he or she has to work with. This issue can become cumbersome when difficulties arise that cut across areas and there is disagreement on how to solve the problem. Should functional department managers have the final say based on their technical expertise? Should the project manager have the final say based on his or her responsibility for the whole product? Or should more senior managers resolve disagreements between functional managers and the project manager?

The second common debate relates to the responsibilities and physical location of engineers. Should an engineer be responsible for a particular technology or component and remain with a functional group in order to be among other engineers working on the same component for other products? Or should management view engineers as members of a project team and co-locate them with other engineers working on the same product? The issue, again, is strategic, not simply organizational: Do managers want to optimize a particular technology or component, and maximize the chances of innovation in specific domains? Or do they want to optimize integration of components and balance the cost, quality, and performance of the whole product?

A number of researchers have studied this dilemma. Allen, who provides a good summary of the literature, concluded that three conditions determine whether a project-centered or a functional organization is more appropriate: (1) the rate of technological change, (2) the length of the development project, and (3) the degree of interdependency among the functional components being developed for the product.

In the case of rapid technological change, there is a higher chance that engineers located within a project will become detached from information on the latest advances in their field. If the project takes a long time, even if the pace of change is not that rapid, engineers located in the project are also more likely to fall behind the state of the art in their fields. According to this line of argument, functional organizations help a firm's long-term competitiveness because they do not simply pursue the short-term goals of a particular project. And if there are few interdependencies among the functional components in a product, then there is little need for a project-centered organization. The opposite case also holds: If engineers cannot design good components without interacting extensively with engineers making other components because there are significant technical interdependencies, then a project-centered organization is best.

These arguments are fairly easy to understand. Whether or not a company should be more functional or project-oriented in product development depends on management's long-term strategic goals, short-term competitive objectives, the technology, and the competitive environment. It is also clear that these alternatives involve different organizational structures and processes. In the next section, we consider another set of issues that previous writers on product development have largely avoided: What type of organizational structures and processes are necessary for firms to coordinate *multiple* functional groups in *multiple* projects, rather than simply coordinate multiple functional groups for one project?

ORGANIZATIONAL REQUIREMENTS FOR MULTIPLE PROJECTS

To manage multiple projects effectively, a functional organization would seem to be better than a project-centered organization because functional managers generally have considerable authority that cuts across various products. For example, if lowering costs is a major objective, then functional departments are useful since they have the ability to standardize components across multiple products. It follows that functional departments should be better than project organizations at transferring technology as well as reducing task duplication (including both design and manufacturing preparations) in different product development efforts.

Our case studies, interviews, and data suggest, however, that functional organizations are not very good at the kind of multi-project management that we argue for in this book. A key benefit of project-centered organizations is the ability to create differentiated products with an integrated or cross-functional management style. Companies should want to combine this ability with an important advantage of functional organizations—a direct mechanism to share technologies and knowledge across multiple product lines and projects. We also believe that simply promoting technical excellence through a functional organization is inadequate in today's competitive markets. Customers around the world now expect high-quality, reasonably priced products that reflect a skillful integration of different components or subsystems as well as different functions, such as design and manufacturing. For complex products, it is not possible to create individual components and sub-systems independently; companies have to integrate functional departments in some way.

This integration across departments is especially important because of the potential impact it has on the speed of a project, which has become key in recent competition in many industries. For example, at one auto firm, 70 percent of design changes during a project (which are the primary causes of schedule delays) come from interference problems between sub-system components. In order to reduce these problems, cross-functional coordination and project-centered management are both essential, even when a project transfers common components from other projects.

Coordinating multiple projects does not reduce the need to integrate the functional areas of individual projects—it probably makes this coordination even more important, as well as more difficult. We have noted that there are differences between a single-project organization and multi-project management. In contrast to functional organizations, however, the common theme between project-centered organizations and multi-project management is the importance attached to *projects* in both approaches.

In other words, multi-project management is a way to manage multiple product lines without resorting to the disadvantages of a purely functional structure. The objective is to share as many components among different product lines as makes sense, without overly reducing the integrity or the distinctiveness of each individual product. Functional organizations cannot easily do this. Integrating the various components or subsystems of a product is a task better suited to project teams, and integration work has to be a separate task in itself.[5] Thus, to manage multiple projects effectively, companies need more integration across product lines than even strong functional departments can provide.

The framework illustrated in Figure 7–1 summarizes our arguments by comparing a multi-project organization with both functional and single-project approaches. The horizontal axis indicates the degree of integration across functional areas, which is stronger in a project-centered organization. The vertical axis indicates the level of integration across projects, which is higher in a functional organization compared to a project-oriented structure. The multi-project orientation that we recommend, in contrast, provides a balance between these two extremes: It has a relatively strong project orientation in that it emphasizes integration across functional areas; but it also presupposes a strategy and organizational mechanisms to coordinate these functions across various projects.

Figure 7–1 is more than simply a hypothetical drawing: It reflects findings from the survey we described in Chapter 5 that involved 256 design engineers at 10 automobile companies in the United States and Japan during 1992. The data indicated that, for effective multi-project management, both cross-functional integration and cross-project integration are necessary. Integration across different functional groups as well as across projects had a significant effect on project lead time and cost when engineers worked on components being used in more than one project.[6]

FIGURE 7–1

Positioning of a Multi-Project Organization

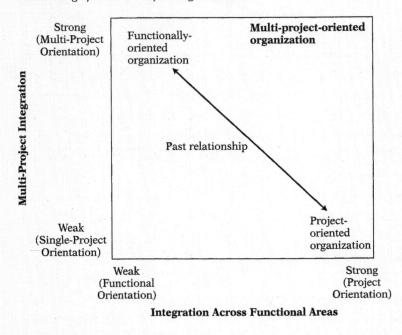

Figure 7–2 provides another perspective on how a multi-project organization differs from a functional organization. To integrate across one or more projects, multi-project management requires a level of control above the project manager that coordinates different projects as well as individual functional departments and individual engineers. As indicated here, though a functional structure can handle multiple projects, it cannot effectively integrate across these different levels.

COMMUNICATION AND COORDINATION MECHANISMS

In order to utilize concurrent technology transfer, project managers and engineers in related or overlapping projects have to communicate well and coordinate their work properly. Engineers or functional department managers cannot operate in isolation, such as in a platform design department or a process engineering department

FIGURE 7–2

Multiple Levels of Product Development Management

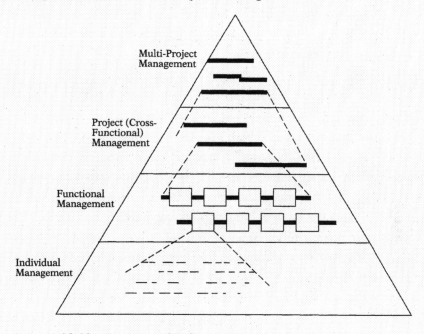

Source: Modified from Kamimoto and Hashimoto, 1995.

that has minimal contact with other departments or projects. If they have insufficient communication, then functional managers and engineers are not able to adjust their activities or designs to the requirements of multiple projects.

Communication and coordination are so important because an automobile is a system of mostly interdependent components or sub-systems. Engineers cannot transfer a component without considering its particular interdependencies with other components of each specific product. As Clark and Fujimoto discussed, only strong project managers can effectively manage cross-functional interactions caused by such interdependencies. Therefore, coordination between multiple project managers may be particularly important in the transfer of a platform design across multiple projects. This is in addition to coordination through functional managers who are responsible for specific components in multiple projects and coordination between engineers for different projects. In other words, even the component-level interactions between multiple projects may require project-level or system-level coordination when the components are parts of sub-systems and interdependent with other components within the project.[7]

It follows that in concurrent technology transfer, project managers in follow-on projects probably have to communicate extensively with project managers in base projects. In order to examine this question, we asked the 103 project managers in our questionnaire survey (see Chapter 5) how frequently they met with managers from other projects as well as with functional managers. Although we understood that the frequency of meetings may have varied during the course of the project, the questionnaire asked the project managers to estimate an average over the project's duration. The meetings as defined in the questionnaire include both formal and informal interactions. Table 7–1 displays the results.

Managers of concurrent technology transfer projects had meetings with other project managers more frequently (4.3 times a month) than managers for other kinds of projects (2.9 times). Managers for concurrent technology transfer projects also met with

TABLE 7–1

Communication of Project Managers with Functional Managers and Project Managers for Other Projects

	Concurrent Technology Transfer Projects	Projects in Other Multi-Project Strategies
Frequency of meetings each month		
Functional managers	2.2	3.2
Project managers for other projects	4.3	2.9
% of project managers who had meetings more frequently with other project managers than with functional managers**	48%	24%

Source: Nobeoka and Cusumano, 1995, p. 405.

**Difference significant at the 5 percent level.

functional managers less frequently than with managers of other projects. As a result, almost half of the managers (48 percent) of concurrent technology transfer projects had meetings with managers of other projects more frequently than with functional managers. This number is significantly larger than the equivalent number for managers of other kinds of projects (24 percent).

These data suggest that project managers for concurrent technology transfer needed to spend more time on coordination with other projects through meetings with other project managers. In addition, managers on concurrent technology transfer projects seemed to shift the focus of their activities from cross-functional integration alone to both cross-functional integration and coordination with other projects.

In addition, our interviews indicated that auto companies used four different organizational mechanisms to coordinate multiple projects. First, is mutual coordination among the project managers, such as through meetings. Second, is coordination by executives who supervise the project managers. For example, all project managers in Toyota prior to 1992 reported to one project planning division, headed by a general manager and an assistant general manager. Third, is coordination of multiple projects by functional department managers. Because each functional department handles various projects, each department can coordinate at the level of technologies or components for which it is responsible. Fourth, is direct mutual coordination among the individual engineers working on each separate project. (We only observed this type of coordination within the functional areas.)

In our survey of project managers, we asked which approach seemed more effective as an organizational mechanism when they needed technical coordination with another project. Respondents had a choice of the four approaches described above. Figure 7–3 illustrates the results. By far, more respondents (49 percent) rated direct coordination among the project managers as the most effective mechanism, followed by coordination through supervision of the project managers (35 percent). Respondents generally did not view coordination through functional department managers (12 percent) or individual engineers (4 percent) as effective. Of course, there

FIGURE 7–3

Inter-Project Coordination Mechanisms

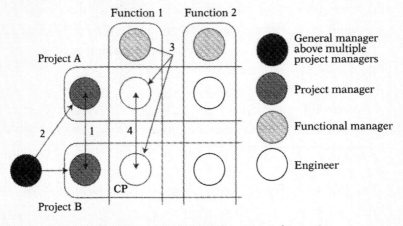

What was the most effective inter-project coordination mechanism?
1. Direct coordination between project managers (49%).
2. Coordination by general manager above project managers (35%).
3. Coordination by functional manager (12%).
4. Direct coordination between engineers (4%).

Source: The data is from our questionnaire survey to vehicle product managers in the United States and Japan. See Chapter 5 for a discussion of the sample and methodology.

may be a bias in this data since we surveyed project managers. Nonetheless, the strong results seem to confirm our earlier argument, namely, that managers and engineers from functional departments cannot effectively coordinate multiple projects because of their relatively narrow perspectives.

Because of the limitations of a survey, we used interviews to explore in more depth some of the key organizational structure and process issues involved in effective multi-project management. The next section discusses some of our major findings.

MULTI-PROJECT MANAGEMENT THROUGH MATRIX MANAGEMENT

The use of simple matrix organizations that increase the authority of project managers makes it difficult for functional department managers and engineers to coordinate multiple projects. Nevertheless, since the early 1990s, various companies have modified traditional matrix organizations to make multi-project coordination more effective. We were especially impressed by two types of organizational innovations: the differentiated matrix and the dual responsibility system for engineers, which we introduced in Chapter 3 as part of the discussion of Mitsubishi (see Figure 3–4 in Chapter 3).

The Differentiated Matrix and Component Characteristics

As we noted earlier, most auto manufacturers use some sort of project matrix structure to combine functional departments with product teams, although they continue to debate how much authority to give project managers as opposed to functional managers. Coordination or integration across multiple projects has generally been less of an issue. Nevertheless, some auto companies have found ways to coordinate multiple projects within a matrix structure.

The differentiated matrix provides a balance that minimizes the conventional trade-offs between a functional versus a project-oriented structure. It allows functional groups to focus on components that management wants to standardize across multiple projects, which a functional structure would easily do. But it also allows projects to create distinctive products by creating separate groups for those components that truly differentiate products, such as exterior and interior parts that are directly visible to the customer. To make the differentiated matrix structure work, however, a company needs to have a strategy for creating sub-systems or common components and then for sharing these across products. It also needs to organize and coordinate these different groups and project teams.

Figure 7–4 presents a framework for analyzing technical requirements and then creating different types of component groups. The first step implied in this analysis is to clarify what is necessary to coordinate among functional departments as well as among projects. The next step is to form different component development groups, which we have divided into four types: different individual components, different sub-systems, common sub-systems, and standard components.

For example, in an automobile, interior and exterior components generally differ for each product. Moreover, engineers must develop

FIGURE 7–4

Impact of Component Characteristics on the Differential Matrix Organization

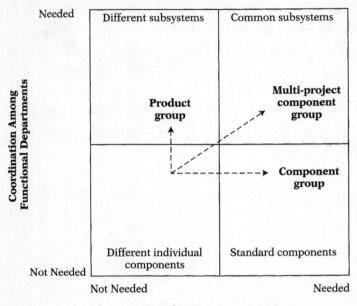

Coordination Among Projects

most of these parts as different sub-systems. As a result, it appears better to develop these components in product groups that differ for each product. In contrast, standard sub-systems such as audio equipment can be common across multiple products. They do not require much coordination across different functional groups since they are more-or-less self-contained components. Engineers can build (or buy) these parts through basic specifications. Separate component groups can easily develop these kinds of parts.

Then there are sub-systems that require high levels of coordination among different engineering groups but management wants different projects to share them. In this case, multi-project groups are a reasonable solution. Examples include automobile platforms as well as braking systems. There also may be parts that differ for each product but require low levels of coordination among different functional groups or projects. These are rare in complex systems products like automobiles, although engineers should develop these as well in individual component groups.

We have seen applications of the differential matrix in other industries. In personal computer software, for example, Microsoft uses multiple projects and concurrent technology transfer to develop products such as Office.[8] It forms different product groups (Microsoft calls them "product units") for the three major subsystems of the standard Office product—Excel (for spreadsheets), Word (for word-processing), and PowerPoint (for graphical presentations). The product groups design the basic menu and toolbar layout as well as the overall feature set for the Office product as a whole and for the sub-systems that Microsoft also ships as separate products—Excel, Word, and PowerPoint. (Though 90 percent or so of all customers now buy the Office suite, this was not true several years ago, and Microsoft continues to sell the products separately.)

The product groups ensure that Microsoft will have four separate products to sell with some distinctive characteristics. These product groups share about half of their components, however, so Microsoft also forms different kinds of component groups to build common sub-systems and coordinate requirements, if necessary, across the multiple projects. For example, all the products in the Office suite do text processing, printing, cut-and-paste, file management, and some mathematical calculations. Individual product groups build these shared components, but the team activities vary depending on how much they need to coordinate requirements with the other product units and other functional groups.

Because the Word group has the most experience with text processing, file management, and printing, Microsoft management has decided that the Word group should build these modules for all the applications groups. The Excel group has the most experience with mathematical calculations and charts, so it builds these modules for itself and the other groups. One group takes charge of building the common component not only because it has more expertise, however. Microsoft also found that if too many groups are involved in deciding the design requirements for the common component, then the design task becomes too complex to manage. Therefore, one group always takes the lead. The lead group is then responsible for consulting the other groups. If there are disagreements on the requirements, then the three most important groups—Word, Excel, and Office—each cast a vote to decide.

For components that other product groups can reuse with no special attention to their requirements, such as the printing module or file management module, Microsoft simply uses what we would refer to as component groups—they need little or no coordination with other functional (component) departments. For components that require special features or changes for other product groups to reuse them properly, Microsoft uses what we would call multi-project component groups. Again, an example is the text-processing module. Users write text in Excel and PowerPoint, but they do not need all the rich features available in Word. Microsoft needs to design the text-processing module so that different product groups can cut features to meet their user needs better. Consequently, the Word group has to consult carefully with the other product groups before completing the design of the text-processing component.

Each product in the Office suite has some unique components that other product groups do not share but which have major interdependencies with other subsystems in the product. An example in PowerPoint is the presentation wizard. Word and Excel do not contain this feature. The PowerPoint product team can build this module on its own, but the feature still has to work with modules such as text-processing and file management, which the Word group builds. Each product also may have some unique components that have few or no interdependencies with other sub-systems in the product. As in an automobile, however, these kinds of components are very rare because software is also a systems product. Nearly every component has some interdependency or coordination requirements with at least one other component. If truly independent components exist, however, then separate component teams can build them with no worries about coordinating with other component teams or projects.

As in automobiles, moreover, we also can see the value of concurrent technology transfer as opposed to sequential technology transfer. If projects are not overlapping chronologically, then Microsoft teams cannot consult each other, mutually adjust their designs, or jointly design components. Of course, product units also reuse some components with no changes. In these cases, sequential technology transfer works fine for one or two new product generations. These kinds of components are relatively rare, however, given the fast pace of change in the personal computer market.

We must note that flexibility is an important feature of the differentiated matrix and our framework for forming component groups. Companies can and should change their organizational structures as products, customers, technologies, and strategies change. They may want to switch emphases, for example, from new components to common components, or to more distinctive designs, and thus move from independent component or product teams to multi-project component teams, or vice-versa.

Dual Responsibility System for Engineers

The differentiated matrix addresses the issue of coordination among different functions or component groups, but it does not address the issue of coordinating engineers across different functional departments and projects. Some companies have introduced various mechanisms to tackle this problem. In a simple matrix organization, there is the dilemma of whether to control engineers through the functional department structure or through the project structure. Managers must balance these two structures to make the organization work or they must accept specific trade-offs. For example, a company might choose to place more emphasis on the project structure. Then, functional departments probably cannot do as good a job of coordinating across projects (such as looking for opportunities to standardize components). If a company places more emphasis on functional departments and cost reduction, then engineers may not pay enough attention to the needs of individual projects.

Rather than accepting these trade-offs or seeking a simple balance, some automobile companies have introduced mechanisms within project-oriented organizations that allow engineers to coordinate their work across multiple projects. Figure 7–5 presents a simplified model that illustrates this "dual responsibility system for engineers." We based this diagram on our interviews at Mitsubishi, though several other companies have similar practices.

As seen in this figure, there are four vehicle projects (A through D) and 20 vehicle engineers. All the engineers work on the four projects, each of which contains 20 components (*a* through *t*). In this system, however, individual engineers take on coordination responsibilities for specific components. For example, engineer #3 has two separate responsibilities. First, he is a member of a five-person engineering team working on components *a* through *t* used in project A. Second, he is individually responsible for coordination related to component *c* among the four vehicle projects. Engineer #3 must make sure that the different groups share the appropriate information regarding component *c*. He also checks whether the different projects are sharing component *c*. In turn, engineers working on the other projects are responsible for giving technical information and specifications to engineer #3. At the same time, they can also receive information on

FIGURE 7–5

Dual Responsibility System for Engineers

Components or Subsystem Development

Project	Engineer	a	b	c	d	e	f	g	h	i	j	k	l	m	n	o	p	q	r	s	t
Project A	1	X																			
	2		X																		
	3	←		X																	→
	4				X																
	5					X															
Project B	6								X												
	7									X											
	8										X										
	9											X									
	10												X								
Project C	11					X															
	12						X														
	13							X													
	14								X												
	15									X											
Project D	16															X					
	17																X				
	18																	X			
	19																		X		
	20																				X

component *c* from engineer #3. This system of dual responsibility for engineers thus combines the good points of both project-oriented and functional structures, even within a conventional matrix.

KNOWLEDGE RETENTION AND TRANSFER MECHANISMS

In addition to overlapping projects and using cross-functional teams, companies have various organizational and technological mechanisms to help them capture knowledge about designs or manufacturing processes and then transfer this knowledge across different projects or different generations of products. One of the researchers in our group, Yaichi Aoshima, focused on this topic. He surveyed 229 project members from 25 Japanese automobile projects conducted during the 1990s and came to several conclusions that we summarize here.[9]

First, Aoshima examined two types of knowledge. One related to the development of specific components, such as an engine or a body shell or a brake; he called this "local" knowledge. The other related to integration of different components; he called this "system" or "integrative" knowledge. Second, he measured the effectiveness of different types of mechanisms for retaining knowledge on the ability to transfer knowledge effectively from one project to another. To measure performance, he asked survey respondents to evaluate how satisfied they were with costs, schedules, manufacturability, technical novelty, technical performance, and sales levels of the components or products they developed.

For component knowledge, Aoshima found that archival-based mechanisms, such as documents, reports, written engineering standards, and computerized tools, were more effective in promoting knowledge retention than individual-based mechanisms such as transfer of people or direct communication between members of different projects. This seems to be because component-level knowledge is rather specialized and possible to write down.

For system or integrative knowledge, however, Aoshima found that companies did better if they relied more on individual-based mechanisms, primarily face-to-face communication and transfer of people from one project to another. This is probably because this kind of knowledge is difficult to communicate and write down. For example, car engineers try to integrate components such as the engine and transmission with the body shell and platform in a way that minimizes vibrations and noise. This integration requires knowledge of many different areas, both in design and manufacturing. Engineers need to learn how to do this kind of design work through experience, and what they need to do may vary widely from project to project. It is difficult to write down or codify this type of knowledge.

These findings support our arguments for multi-project management. For example, to implement concurrent technology transfer, firms should overlap projects so that engineers can communicate and solve design problems face-to-face, rather than only through written documents. Transferring major subsystems such as a platform clearly requires integrative knowledge that is difficult to write down. In addition, from Aoshima's findings, we also can see why sequential technology transfer may not result in high-quality designs. On these types of projects, engineers must rely on archival forms of knowledge to transfer technology, whether for components or sub-systems that require more complex integrative knowledge. Aoshima's study also suggests the importance of keeping people together for more than one product generation precisely because complex products such as automobiles require different types of knowledge, some of which is hard to learn and transfer to new people.

Aoshima found that companies which placed a lot of emphasis on mechanisms to retain prior knowledge had special problems introducing very new designs. They were not as innovative as firms that paid less attention to knowledge retention. We see a similar potential danger if firms rely too much on concurrent technology transfer, sequential technology transfer, or design modification. Firms need to place an equal emphasis on creating new technologies. To do this effectively, as we discussed in prior chapters, relatively independent product teams that focus on new designs seem to be the best approach. Once companies make these investments, however, the data we presented in Chapters 5 and 6 indicate that transferring technologies and other knowledge quickly to other projects has a positive impact on market performance as well as development costs and lead time for follow-on projects. Again, what seems to be important is *strategy:* To achieve optimal performance, firms need specific programs to invest in new technology as well as to retain and transfer technology and other forms of knowledge.

PRODUCT VARIETY AND MANUFACTURING

Finally, we need to address the issue of manufacturing flexibility at least briefly. This is another organizational capability that is useful to support platform families and product variations. It is especially important to multi-project management because this capability encourages firms to create different products. Accordingly, factories need to be able to handle the increasing product variations that come with a multi-project strategy such as concurrent technology transfer, which also demands new designs to be effective. Various researchers have examined the impact of product variations on manufacturing performance, using interviews as well as statistical analysis of assembly plant data (including both automotive assembly and printed circuit board factories). Although the subject is complicated, our research and that of others associated with our research program at MIT point to several conclusions.[10]

First, there is the issue of how much and what kind of product variety do firms need to compete effectively. We talked to some companies that are expanding model lines and body style variations, such as convertibles, sports cars, and recreational vehicles. Some companies also let customers combine different options or equipment offerings to "semi-customize" their purchases. We see this kind of "peripheral" or superficial variety continuing to increase at some auto makers. Concurrent technology transfer facilitates this type of variety at minimal engineering and manufacturing costs because companies can reuse major components such as platforms.

At the same time, however, many auto makers and other companies are trying to reduce uneconomical variety—low-volume models, redundant platforms, non-standardized components that provide little added value, and low-demand options. Toyota managers, for example, told us that they are trying to get down to the elusive "20 percent of model and option variations that bring in 80 percent of sales." We see many other companies moving in the same direction. Shifting in emphasis from new designs to concurrent technology transfer and sequential technology transfer should help firms reduce this type of low-payoff product variety.

Second, our interviews and plant data indicate quite clearly that factory managers need not worry too much about variety once their factories are operating. In the automobile industry, neither fundamental nor peripheral variety seems to have a measurable impact on assembly-plant productivity. Both kinds of variety also have little impact on manufacturing quality (although we did find an association between lots of body styles and engine combinations with slightly more defects reported by customers).[11] In printed circuit board assembly, we did not find any connection between high levels of product variety and defects or manufacturing costs.[12] Some assembly plants even combined high levels of product variety with high levels of productivity and quality. This is because companies that have a lot of different products generally design plants and train workers to handle large amounts of variety (such as platforms of different sizes, different model and option variations) or to handle new product introductions easily.

In fact, companies have a wide range of strategies to counteract the potential negative impact of product variety on manufacturing performance (Table 7–2). Engineers can design products to share platforms and other major sub-systems. They also can design sub-systems such as platforms and engines with reusable modules. In the auto industry, for example, engines contain blocks (which determine the number of cylinders), heads (camshaft and valves), fuel delivery systems (electronic fuel injection, carburetor, diesel), and displacement specifications (cylinder and piston diameters). Companies mix and match these modules to produce different types of engines for different products.[13] In printed circuit board assembly,

TABLE 7–2

Strategies to Minimize the Impact of Product Variety on Manufacturing

Strategy	Functional Area of Responsibility
Products designed to share subsystems	Design engineering
Subsystems designed to share modules	Design engineering
Flexible manufacturing techniques	Manufacturing
Low-inventory production techniques	Manufacturing and procurement
Parallel assembly or production lines	Manufacturing
Computerized scheduling and planning systems	Production planning and manufacturing
Flexible automation	Manufacturing
Fast set-up equipment	Manufacturing
Broader worker training	Personnel, manufacturing

companies that designed products from reusable modules were also much more flexible in handling variety in manufacturing.[14]

To handle variety on the manufacturing end rather than in design, companies in different industries have introduced flexible manufacturing and low-inventory production techniques as well as new computerized systems such as flexible scheduling and materials planning programs. Some companies use parallel assembly lines to accommodate very different models simultaneously. In addition, programmable robots and other types of flexible automation have very fast set-up times. These are useful to accommodate different model lines and variations in the mix of products being produced (although many companies that we surveyed did not take full advantage of flexible automation). In Japan, several companies have very flexible systems for body welding that enable them to produce different kinds of products with the same equipment: Toyota's FBL (Flexible Body Line), Nissan's IBAS (Intelligent Body Assembly System), and Mazda's C-BAL (Circulation Body Assembly Line) are good examples. In addition, companies are increasing their manufacturing flexibility by providing workers with broader and sometimes deeper training to handle multiple jobs as well as new computerized equipment.[15]

Improving flexibility is more than a technical issue at the plant level. The data indicates that plants differ in their levels of flexibility, so companies need to link product portfolio plans and production plans with manufacturing investments. In addition, flexible factories often require more up-front capital and training costs. For example, companies need to buy programmable robots and flexible automation systems, hire computer technicians to write and rewrite computer programs, or retrain workers to use the new equipment. Companies that produce a lot of different models also have to deal with a more complex supply chain for materials and components.

As our colleagues at the Wharton School also noted, U.S. companies generally fund new equipment purchases for individual projects. Many do not have accounting systems that make it easy to invest in equipment flexible enough for multiple models. This means that many U.S. companies will find it difficult to share manufacturing investments across multiple projects unless they modify their accounting practices.[16] At most Japanese firms, in contrast, they found that process engineering divisions, rather than individual projects, have their own budgets for new equipment at plants. The Japanese accounting systems generally have facilitated investment in expensive flexible equipment such as Nissan's IBAS. Nonetheless, problems still exist in Japan. Nissan, for example, seems to need better coordination between its product strategy (which is complicated in itself) and equipment investment strategy. Other companies have similar problems.

COMMENTS

We reemphasize our belief that simply creating a balance between a project-oriented versus a functional structure is not enough to implement effective multi-project management. In particular, we talked about the inherent limitations of trying to improve multi-project management by giving more authority to functional departments. Multi-project management, as the name implies, is essentially *project-based* management. In this sense, it builds on as well as goes beyond lean thinking as applied to product development. Companies that follow a multi-project strategy must simultaneously coordinate both functional areas and projects.

On the other hand, we discussed two mechanisms that companies are using to move beyond simply trying to balance a functional and a project-oriented structure: the differentiated matrix and the dual responsibility system for engineers. These organizational innovations have become more common since the early 1990s. We also reviewed different mechanisms that firms can use to capture component-level as well as integrative or cross-functional knowledge, and the importance of balancing initiatives to create new knowledge or designs with efforts to take advantage of new designs quickly in other projects.

We also can say that there is a "bottom line" conclusion from research on product variety and manufacturing. Companies do not have to increase the more expensive "fundamental variety"—different platforms, in the case of the automobile—to provide customers with more product alternatives. Factory managers do not have to worry too much if they have prepared for variety in advance. But managers and engineering teams do need to plan and invest in accommodating product variety, both in the product design stage and in manufacturing preparations. This is another reason why portfolio planning, as well as communication, coordination, and integration within and across projects and across different functions in the firm (such as marketing, product engineering, process engineering, and procurement) are so important.

Chapter 8

Implications and Lessons
for Managers

T he *Machine That Changed the World* and *Lean Thinking*
stated that it took auto companies about half a century to
move from mass production to lean production in manufacturing operations.[1] As we have seen in product development, however, companies have advanced beyond conventional functional
approaches to lean thinking for single projects much faster—within
a decade or less. We also have seen several firms, led by Japanese
companies such as Toyota, move beyond the management of individual projects to strategies and structures for multi-project product development. This latter move may be less revolutionary than the
transition from functional to lean. But if multi-project management
and particular strategies such as concurrent technology transfer
were easy to implement, then surely many more firms would try
them. Not every company does, and we need to consider why before
closing this book.

This final chapter focuses on the implications and lessons for
managers of what we have presented. First, we point out what we

183

think managers should learn from the Toyota case and our sketches of other companies. Second, we summarize some of the arguments for and against concurrent technology transfer and multi-project management more generally. Finally, we propose a simple framework for deciding when it is appropriate to adopt a multi-project strategy for product development.

All of our findings point to a simple but powerful conclusion: Managers are better off if they leverage investments in new technology (such as through multi-project management) as opposed to not leveraging these investments at all. And they are better off if they leverage these investments *quickly across markets* (as in concurrent technology transfer) rather than *slowly across time* (as in sequential technology transfer).

LESSONS FROM TOYOTA AND OTHER COMPANIES

When it comes to managing manufacturing or product development, Toyota has been one of the most important companies to learn from in this century. We would like to point out a few lessons we believe are most important from Toyota's experience with multi-project management.

First, Toyota, as well as most of the companies we discussed in this book, demonstrate that firms can evolve beyond traditional functional, matrix, or single-project organizations. In other words, *Toyota and other firms have explicitly adopted multi-project management systems that work*. Figure 8–1 illustrates this evolutionary pattern in product development. As we described earlier, Toyota shifted from a functional to a stronger project-oriented matrix in the 1950s and 1960s.[2] Most other Japanese auto makers followed Toyota by the late 1970s or early 1980s.[3] U.S. and European companies followed in the late 1980s and 1990s. During 1992–1993, Toyota shifted again, this time from single-project management to multi-project management.

Second, the discussions of various companies suggest that *it is important to improve integration across different engineering functions as*

FIGURE 8–1

Evolutionary Pattern to Multi-Project Management in Product Development

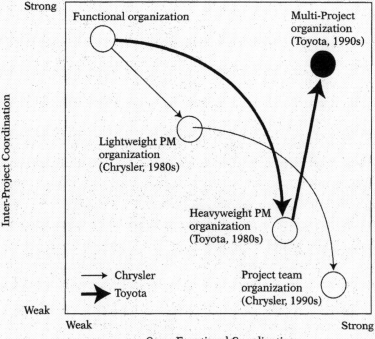

well as across different projects simultaneously. Again, Toyota provides an excellent example of how to do this. Its center organization facilitates coordination among technically related projects. At the same time, Toyota has improved integration across functions by strengthening the authority of project managers over functional managers. Toyota also streamlined tasks for integrating across functional groups in order to make it easier to integrate multiple projects.

Chrysler, another company that has recently done well in product development, provides a useful contrast to Toyota. A primary issue for the American company in the 1980s was a lack of cross-functional coordination and product integrity, in addition to old technology. Chrysler executives wanted to improve project integration as well as stimulate creativity. Therefore, in 1989, they changed from a matrix organization with lightweight product managers to a product team organization. The new organization has minimal barriers between engineering functions. It worked effectively to develop individual products such as the LH and the Neon. Because platform teams stay together, they also have been able to leverage their experience and success with particular design concepts in multiple projects. Toyota was already relatively efficient at managing individual projects and aimed at better multi-project management through the center organization.

There are similarities, though, between the organizations at Toyota and Chrysler. Neither is a traditional matrix; both are *project-centered* organizations. And neither disperses engineers after completing a project; people stay together for multiple product generations, which allows them to learn and carry forward a consistent design philosophy from project to project. Chrysler focuses more on individual projects, directed by heavyweight project managers. Toyota focuses more on coordinating multiple projects, directed together by project managers and the center manager—a heavyweight multi-project manager. Toyota retains some aspects of a matrix organization within each center. But because the center managers play active management roles and officially supervise all functional engineers, the center organization is really a project organization covering multiple products.

Third, Toyota and other cases suggest that *simply grouping related projects is not so effective without introducing a logic for grouping projects and then supporting mechanisms and processes for multi-project management.* Other automobile firms in Japan and elsewhere also employ some type of product clustering. But firms need to decide whether this grouping should be by market similarities or technical similarities in the products themselves. Creating groups of projects around common platforms seems far more effective for promoting technology sharing than other schemes. But creating centers for technically related projects still does not necessarily lead to effective multi-project management. Other companies with platform groups or development centers or semi-centers, for example, do not seem to work as effectively as Toyota.[4]

Toyota seems to work so well because of how managers and engineers deal with the *details* of implementing multi-project management. For example, not only did Toyota executives bring technically similar projects together but they also maintained a consistent design philosophy for their products and reduced the number of engineering functions in the three vehicle development centers. In addition, Toyota added a fourth center for common component and subsystem development. Now, the management scope of the center heads and planning division managers is small enough to allow them to effectively oversee all activities within a center. In addition, Toyota added a powerful planning division of more than 150 people to each center to support the work of the center head. Furthermore, Toyota created specific development goals or themes for each center, which appear to help managers and engineers focus their efforts. Finally, Toyota executives have encouraged the centers to compete in performance and then share what they learn. This sharing promotes company-wide improvement, efficiency, and innovation.

Other firms that want to introduce multi-project management systems need not copy Toyota exactly. Mazda, for example, was really too small to introduce separate development centers. Nevertheless, the general principle is that companies must create supporting mechanisms and processes to facilitate a multi-project strategy and organization. Companies also need to solve a delicate strategic and organizational dilemma: how to integrate different engineering functions to create distinctive individual products while sharing technologies and coordinating multiple projects. Again, we think Toyota's center structure and management techniques provide excellent suggestions on how to do this.

Strategy should drive the decisions that managers make on how to organize product development. When considering whether to establish centers for product development, companies need to determine how much they want to pursue efficiency as opposed to simplification in project management. If they opt for centers, then companies need to figure out how to group products and how many groupings to establish. In the case of semi-center structures, they need to decide which functions to put inside the centers and which to keep centralized. In all cases when they mix projects with functional departments, companies must deal with conflicts among managers that share authority and responsibility.

It is also important to recognize that even a multi-project management structure still requires creative engineers and "product champions" to produce successful projects, although companies may use these kinds of special people in different ways. For example, in multi-project management, executives might encourage engineers to channel their creativity toward thinking about how to design components that more than one product can use effectively. And product champions may want to focus on imparting their design philosophy to a family of products that share key technologies or designs.

The examples we discussed in this book should help company executives analyze these issues before they make decisions about stronger project-management systems, product teams, or center approaches. It seems critical to determine beforehand, for example, the relative authority of multi-project executives, project managers, and functional department managers. We also believe that companies should explicitly establish positions for multi-project managers, such as center heads, platform directors, or other senior executives who take on a leadership role for technically related product lines. These kinds of executives are necessary to implement multi-project portfolio strategies as well as to mediate disputes between projects and functional departments.

Insufficient thought and analysis of their goals and problems before a fundamental reorganization can lead firms to make too frequent organizational changes. Engineering organizations for complex products such as automobiles need stability and focus as well as flexibility because product development for them is especially difficult, expensive, and time-consuming. Nissan, Mazda, and GM, for example, tend to reorganize so frequently that engineers and managers often are uncertain what their roles are or will be in the near future. We noticed that people at these companies seem to waste a lot of time drawing and redrawing organization charts and trying to figure out who is responsible for what activity. Toyota, again, presents an instructive contrast. Before they reorganized, executives seemed to give extremely careful thought to what structure would be most useful given the company circumstances. Their decision to operate with four centers seems to have been a good one because the new organization has worked well for several years.

WHY CONCURRENT TECHNOLOGY TRANSFER?

Development centers such as Toyota's should make it easier to create new platforms and leverage these new designs quickly and effectively in overlapping projects. More importantly, firms that follow concurrent technology transfer appear to grow more quickly than competitors who develop new products one at a time or sequentially transfer platforms to other projects. This conclusion is consistent with at least one other study.[5] A unique contribution of our research, however, is the finding that firms do better if they leverage key components across multiple product lines *while the technology is still relatively new.* In other words, not only the *decision* to leverage technology but also the *speed* with which firms transfer key components across projects seems to have an impact on corporate-level performance.

Most managers we interviewed wanted to coordinate multiple projects and share components and technologies, formally or informally. But relatively few companies took advantage of concurrent technology transfer. The followers of this strategy during the period of our study were mostly in Japan, and only occasionally in Europe and the United States. Our interviews with managers suggested several *strategic* reasons why firms might not try concurrent technology transfers, although we would like to suggest some counterarguments.

First, some firms want to maximize product innovation or product integrity in *every* project. There are managers who believe that relying on the transfer of technologies from other projects may compromise these goals, and that heavyweight project managers and isolated project teams are better for fostering innovation. In the auto industry, we have seen companies compete on innovations in areas such as body design, engine technology, suspension systems, safety systems, and automotive electronics, to name a few. We argue, however, that concurrent technology transfer does not prevent firms from innovating with new designs and technologies. Rather, this strategy *depends* on firms developing new technologies first! The objective of concurrent technology transfer is to take advantage of new platforms and other components in more than one product as effectively and as quickly as possible. True, this strategy does create linkages and interdependencies among projects, and it may constrain innovation in some new design projects or follow-on projects. But most firms need to have a portfolio of products and projects. When managers want to maximize innovation for a particular market segment, then they can organize a separate project with no constraints imposed from other projects.

Second, we heard the argument that firms relying on concurrent technology transfer undertake some risks in addition to possibly constraining the base project. In particular, there is some danger in transferring technologies not proven in the marketplace or in transferring designs that may have some technical flaws. We argue, however, that firms can reduce these risks by taking extra care in analyzing market requirements and specifying designs for base projects. They also can make sure to test the quality of the shared components with extra thoroughness.

Third, some managers feel that concurrent technology transfer places too heavy a burden on company planners for new products. In particular, concurrent technology transfer requires long-term plans that map out a portfolio of new products over several years. This plan needs to clarify design goals as well as interdependencies and sources of components (such as in-house versus from suppliers) among the different projects. Not all firms do this kind of detailed planning as well as others. In fast-paced markets, moreover, such long-term planning may not be wise. We argue, however, that all firms need to do some type of long-term strategic and product-portfolio planning. It is a good exercise. For fast-paced industries, companies should review and adjust these plans frequently. But companies still need to plan, otherwise they cannot make long-term investments and strategic commitments.

Managers also suggested several *organizational* reasons why firms might not adopt concurrent technology transfer. First, some people believe that concurrent technology transfer overly complicates project management due to increased interdependencies among projects. In particular, concurrent technology transfer projects need especially good communication and coordination in design and scheduling. This is necessary to ensure the timely delivery of shared components that meet the objectives of both the base project and the follow-on project. We argue that, although managing interrelated projects is difficult, our data and case studies indicate that it is possible and provides clear benefits when done well.[6]

Second, some managers fear that companies relying heavily on suppliers could face an additional complicating factor in coordinating multiple projects. This could clearly be a problem in the automobile industry, where Japanese companies and Chrysler buy as much as 70 percent of their components from suppliers and outsource as much as 50 percent of their design and engineering work.[7] We argue, however, that in-house engineers in well-managed companies usually have good control over development processes as well as functional specifications of all components. They should be close to suppliers and manage them as they would any other development group. (In Chapter 5, we actually tested this idea by adjusting our results for the degree of supplier involvement. We found that the difficulties but also the benefits of concurrent technology transfer apply equally to components designed and manufactured in-house as well as by suppliers.)

Third, it seems that some managers and engineers prefer to invent their own technologies rather than rely on outside sources, even within the same company. People often refer to this as the "Not

Invented Here" or "NIH" syndrome. We argue, however, that the overlapping nature of concurrent technology transfer should give engineers some sense of control over the technologies they import.

Fourth, some managers simply want to expand the size of a single project to accommodate multiple distinct products, rather than have a separate base project and a follow-on project relying on concurrent technology transfer. Renault and Chrysler tend to do this, for example, and so does GM on occasion. We argue, however, that an expanded project can contain too many people to operate effectively. Also, a team may lose its focus and not be able to create distinctive products if it has to develop more than one product in a single project.

We agree as well that concurrent technology transfer between autonomous project teams may require those project teams to make unwise compromises in their designs or cause too much additional time for coordination activities. Therefore, in order to benefit from concurrent technology transfer, a firm needs to manage multiple projects at the same time and avoid accommodations that sacrifice product quality and uniqueness.

This observation brings us back to the subject of organizational requirements for multi-project management. We admitted earlier that this demands some capabilities, including particular organizational structures and processes, that differ from those useful for managing single projects. For example, heavyweight project managers and relatively autonomous project teams are important to optimize individual project performance. What is optimal for one project, however, may not be optimal for the firm that wants to develop and leverage new technologies across many projects.

In short, multi-project management requires *strategic portfolio planning* and *organizational capabilities* that are more difficult to nurture and implement than single-project management. Unfortunately, we do not think that firms can acquire the necessary organizational and personal skills overnight. It should not take fifty years, however. We have seen firms do it within a decade or less. In particular, firms that succeed in introducing concurrent technology transfer as a regular development strategy should see a long-term benefit in addition to introducing more new products and growing faster than competitors following other strategies. They may create a powerful competitive advantage precisely because concurrent technology transfer is relatively difficult for competitors to introduce—or imitate.

THE APPLICABILITY OF MULTI-PROJECT MANAGEMENT

We recognize that we are advocates of multi-project management and that not all firms should attach equal weight to this idea. How important this concept is depends on a company's strategy and range of product offerings. Even firms with several products and opportunities to transfer technology *across markets* may want to manage a particular project independently. For example, there clearly are cases when managers want to encourage innovation and "do something different." Managers also have to worry that some engineers will not want to work on projects where they are borrowing key technologies from other projects. Furthermore, in the opposite case of the multi-product or multi-market firm—a company that has only one product—managers may seem to have very little need for multi-project management. Nonetheless, we think that managers and engineers even in these firms should still think about transferring technology or specific components across different product generations. This sequential transfer *over time* is also a form of multi-project management. Therefore, even in the case of single-product firms, we think multi-project management is still appropriate in many cases.

More important, multi-project management addresses *the future*. Nearly every firm, if it is successful, wants to expand product lines as well as remain competitive by frequently introducing new technologies into existing products. How strategically a company creates new products and replaces old ones depends on its portfolio strategy, financial and human resources, and organizational capabilities. There are very few cases where internal technology transfer and multi-project strategies have no application. In the auto indus-

FIGURE 8–2

The Applicability of Multi-Project Management

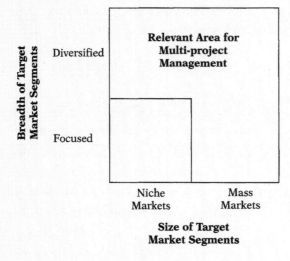

try, in fact, *every* company has multiple products. *Most* companies also try to share at least some components and thus need to coordinate, at some level, multiple projects.

Figure 8–2 provides a framework for thinking about when it is appropriate to adopt multi-project management. The vertical axis indicates the breadth of a firm's target market segments—whether it focuses on a few segments or diversifies across many segments. The horizontal axis indicates the size of the target segments—ranging from niche to mass markets. As illustrated in this figure, we think a multi-project approach to product development does not apply only for a focused niche strategy. For example, a company that only produces luxury sports cars—such as Lamborghini—has little need for a multi-project system. It has very few products, and the company should try to make each product distinctive and state of the art in its class. There are other niche producers in the auto industry, such as Rolls-Royce and Ferrari. But the examples are few, and their percentage of total output in the industry is extremely small.

On the other hand, some specialized companies focus on mass-market segments. For them, multi-project management should be *very* important. For example, Suzuki is a highly focused producer of small or lightweight vehicles. But this is a global mass market (more so in Japan, Asia, and Europe than the United States), and there are many opportunities for Suzuki to share technologies in its different product lines. Furthermore, even apart from mass markets, there are cases where firms might target more than one niche segment with different products and still find opportunities to share technologies. Around 1990, for example, Nissan utilized the platform from a lightweight car (called the March in Japan) to create two other niche products, the lightweight Be-1 and the Figaro.

Most of the world's auto makers actually target multiple mass-market and niche-market segments and have many opportunities for multi-project coordination of product development. Scale economies in design and manufacturing alone push auto makers to seek common components. Many companies also find it difficult to remain competitive over long periods of time simply with one niche product because user needs, market structures, and industry competition change. Companies tend to have more diversified product strategies, and eventually try to move toward multiple mass-market segments.

We also described how some companies deliberately decide to manage a project in isolation, rather than incorporate it into a multi-project strategy. Again, a good example of this approach is Chrysler, whose independent product teams during the early 1990s created the very successful LH and Neon projects. But Chrysler built only one new car platform in the early 1980s and reached a crisis a decade later when customers reacted negatively to its old product lines. The LH and Neon projects were really life or death situations for the company. Management chose to focus engineering resources on getting two new quality products out the door as quickly as possible.[8]

Chrysler would have wasted the extra investment to design common components for future products if the company had failed to deliver the LH and Neon. There would have been no future! Chrysler also probably did not have the financial or engineering resources to launch more than these two projects. At the time and in its dire circumstances, therefore, a single-project focus worked for Chrysler. But the company has dispersed its engineers and eliminated centralized R&D. It also relies very heavily on suppliers for design and engineering work. Technological innovation as well as cost reductions in engineering and manufacturing may become more important in the future. If this is the case, then separate product teams, Tech Clubs, and task forces for special research projects may not be adequate to maintain a competitive product-development organization, unless Chrysler is especially good at leveraging its supplier contributions to design and engineering.

Other auto companies have had occasions to launch "guerrilla-type" product teams as special projects. Mazda, for example, did this with the highly successful Miata sports car.[9] As a relatively small auto maker, Mazda has tried to maintain a distinctive image based on its engineering skills. In prior decades, it used the Wankel rotary engine in some of its products to do this. In the late 1980s, despite severe economic pressures, Mazda management decided that it needed a distinctive new product that would again establish the company as a technical leader. Management organized a special team and placed it in a different building from the main engineering organization. The team created a new platform even though it also decided to focus on a low-volume niche product—a 1960s style European roadster. Thus, even though the company had a multiproject strategy and management system, Mazda still was able to create a highly successful independent project.

Similarly, companies that change their emphasis from a functional to a project organization need not change their development organizations completely. We observed earlier that, with few exceptions, project structures are not particularly good at fostering radical innovation in particular areas because they do not promote deep technical excellence or specialization. If companies want to promote radical innovation in particular technologies, such as in suspension system design or engines, then they may be better off managing these technologies through permanent functional departments. Companies seeking deep technical expertise should avoid repeatedly forming and disbanding projects because they lose continuity in department membership and technical knowledge.

One problem with mixing projects and functional departments, even in a project-oriented structure, is that this requires cooperative people and relatively sophisticated organizational processes. It is difficult to manage projects well and coordinate across both multiple projects and different functional departments. The strategic and organizational requirements are particularly demanding in concurrent technology transfer, the multi-project strategy with the highest potential payoff.

We can make similar arguments for multi-firm multi-project management. As we saw in Chapter 4 with the brief examples of Ford and Mazda, Mitsubishi and Volvo, Mazda and Suzuki, and Fiat and Peugeot, companies can work with partners to share platforms and other technologies, and do this in overlapping or sequential projects. The coordination needed for technology transfer is difficult enough within one firm because of potentially conflicting objectives among executives, project managers, functional department managers, and engineers. There are likely to be similar and probably more serious conflicts in multi-firm sharing, although it is becoming a more popular strategy in automobiles as well as other industries.

FINAL THOUGHTS

We have argued in this book that companies have a clear choice in product development: They can manage projects one at a time, or they can manage projects as part of a portfolio. Managers can bet on producing hit products one at a time, or they can try to make the most of their investments by leveraging the development of new technologies across a stream of new products in rapid succession.

There are organizational costs, of course, to multi-project management as we have described it. This mode of thinking requires integrating across engineering functions that cut across multiple projects. Integrating functions within one project at a time is difficult enough for many firms. Integrating functions across projects requires more long-term planning and more frequent communication among project members, as well as managers and engineers willing to cooperate on product goals and project work. It also requires companies that can make smart decisions on how much to overlap projects and how much authority to give functional department managers versus project managers. In addition, companies need to be smart in how they group projects and to what extent they tolerate redundancies in development to simplify project management and encourage specialization.

But these are details, however important ones. More fundamentally, companies need to decide if they want to think and manage in a *multi-project* mode. We think the evidence is clear. Lean thinking provided a wonderful set of principles that companies have used to manage single projects more efficiently than was possible in traditional functional or matrix approaches. But the efficient management of one project at a time is no longer adequate for companies to succeed in highly competitive global markets. The demands on product development organizations have changed, and so must the concepts that define best practice. The pressure is likely to increase on companies to introduce even more products at lower costs. As a result, we expect the concept of multi-project management to become even more important to managers because of the gains in efficiency and flexibility that it provides—for auto makers as well as firms in other industries.

Appendix 1

Change Index of Platform Design

Floor Panels

Points	Description
0	*Same*. Both wheelbase and track are unchanged except for variations of tire size and wheel off-set.
1	*Partially new*. Only either wheelbase or track are new with considerations of tire size and wheel off-set.
2	*New*. Both wheelbase and track are new with considerations of tire size and wheel off-set.

Suspension Technology and Design

Points	Description
0	*Same*. Suspension system and design are unchanged.
1	*Partially new*. Suspension system is bascially the same, but design is modified such as changing the shape of arms. Small modifications made only for the sake of *multi-product line* applications are not considered as changes.
2	*New*. Suspension system is completely new. (See variations of suspension types described below.)

Source: Nobeoka and Cusumano, 1997, p. 186.

199

If the sum of the points from both areas is three or more, the platform design is defined as new. These points were reviewed based on interviews with about 45 engineers at Toyota, Nissan, Mazda, Mitsubishi, Honda, Ford, GM, Chrysler, Fiat, Renault, and VAG regarding the actual design changes made on the specific platform designs.

Appendix 2

Definitions and Measurements
of Lead Time and Engineering Hours

Lead Time

The questionnaire asked program managers to estimate the lead time from the beginning of concept and product planning to job #1. This period includes primary development tasks including "concept and product planning," "product engineering and testing," "process engineering," and "pilot production."

Engineering Hours

Engineering hours (*EH*) for each project are estimated as follows:

$$EH = (FS + PS*PR)*LT*WH/2$$

FS: The number of engineers who worked on the project (full time).
PS: The number of engineers who worked on the project (part time).
PR: Average percentage of time part-time engineers spent on one project.*
LT: Lead time (months)
WH: Average monthly working hours per engineer.*

This estimation scheme is based on our interviews and discussions with engineers primarily at five Japanese firms. In this equation, the number is divided by two based on the assumption with respect to a typical pattern of changes in engineering hours throughout each project, as shown in the figure in the previous page.

Adjustments for Supplier Contribution

The data on average supplier contribution in component design for each manufacturer was obtained from the questionnaire survey of design engineers.

$$EHA = EH/(1-SC)$$

EHA: Adjusted engineering hours by supplier's contribution.
 EH: Engineering hours explained above.
 SC: Average supplier's contribution at the corporate level.*

* The corporate-level average was obtained from the questionnaire survey of design engineers, which was conducted in the same research project. The method of this survey is described in Nobeoka, 1993.

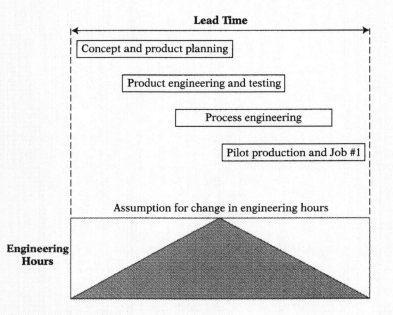

Source: Nobeoka and Cusumano, 1995, pp. 406, 408.

Differences in Time Lag with Base Project Between Concurrent Technology Transfer and Sequential Technology Transfer (N = 103)

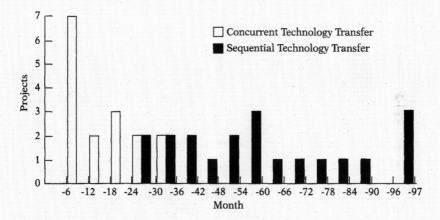

Source: Nobeoka and Cusumano, 1995, p. 407.

Appendix 4

Data on Project Content and Project Performance (N = 76)

		Platform Design			
	New Design	**Concurrent Technology Transfer**	**Sequential Technology Transfer**	**Design Modification**	**Total**
Projects	18	18	16	24	76
Japanese	11	15	9	17	52
United States	7	3	7	7	24
Price ($) (8,000)	21,390 (8,680)	16,390 (7,920)	15,160 (7,040)	16,350 (7,590)	17,30
Body types	1.7 (0.6)	1.7 (0.5)	1.6 (0.8)	2.0 (0.9)	1.8 (0.7)
Truck/van	4	4	2	4	14
New design ratio (%)					
Engine/transmission	69 (34)	63 (39)	64 (37)	54 (36)	62 (37)
Body/interior	98 (7)	89 (22)	94 (13)	83 (31)	90 (22)
Innovativeness index (0–1)	0.33 (0.30)	0.33 (0.38)	0.22 (0.32)	0.08 (0.19)	0.23 (0.31)
Lead time (months)	57.9 (14.0)	49.7 (11.1)	49.0 (13.3)	50.1 (15.2)	51.6 (13.8)
Engineering hours (million)	1.89 (1.60)	0.72 (0.48)	2.02 (2.55)	1.95 (2.03)	1.66 (1.87)

Source: Nobeoka and Cusumano, 1995, p. 408.
Standard deviations are in parentheses.

Appendix 5

Company Interviews, 1992–1997

Company	People Interviewed
1. Chrysler	11
2. Daihatsu	7
3. Fiat	33
4. Ford	16
5. Fuji	1
6. GM	13
7. Honda	36
8. Isuzu	5
9. Mazda	40
10. Mercedes	4
11. Mitsubishi	19
12. Nissan	44
13. Renault	6
14. Suzuki	3
15. Toyota	72
16. VW-Audi	19
17. Volvo	6
Total	335

Note: The list below includes all individuals that we interviewed or exchanged information with during our research for this book. We met a few of these individuals in off-the-record informal settings or advisory meetings where we had promised not to use any specific information or data that they provided. In these cases, we have not used any specific information or data. We list these individuals here, however, because we want to acknowledge their assistance in helping us understand organizational structures at these companies as well as product development processes and management problems in general. Firms and names of interviewees are in alphabetical order, with positions at the time of the interview.

Chrysler

Ronald R. Boltz, Vice-President, Product Strategy and Regulatory Affairs
Joseph Caddel, General Product Manager–Small Car
Roger P. Lundburg, Exective Engineer, Jeep Program Management
James Rickert, Director, Product Strategy and Cycle Planning
P. Jeffrey Trimmer, General Product Manager, Jeep/Dodge Truck Business
    Operations
Six other LH project members

Daihatsu

Shinsuke Hori, Manager, Body Design Division
Takashi Kohukada, Project Manager, Corporate Planning Division
Tsuneo Morita, Manager, Test & Experiment Division
Takashi Namekawa, Chief Coordinator, Management Planning Division
Shotaro Nishino, Project Manager, Management Planning Division
Yukitoshi Ono, General Manager, Product Planning Center
Etsuo Usui, Project Manager, Product Planning Division

Fiat

Andrea Aparo, Corporate Development and Control
Dunia Astrologo, Information Manager
Antonio Bene, Direzione Tecnica, Direttore di Piattaforma
Giovanni Biaggini, Truck Technical Operations, Iveco
Lauretta Borsero, Director, Studies and Research
Pier Luigi Bottero, Plant Manager, Arese Carrozzeria Assembly Plant
Alessandro Cannavacciuolo, Human Resources, Research and Innovation
    Director
Luca Chevallard, Director, Body and Trim Purchasing
Marcello Cucchi, Production Department, Strategic Planning
Nevio Di Giusto, Director, Design Engineering
Roberto Faldella, Direzione Progettazione e Sviluppo Industriale,
    Ingegneria Motopropulsori, Transmissione del Moto—Capo Progetto
Willy Fant, Direttore Coordinamento Iniziative Sviluppo Prodotto
Pier Renato Franzero, Direzione Tecnica, Ingegneria Velicoli Fiat,
    Finizioni—II Responsabile Abbigliamento

Giorgio Guelfi, Direzione Tecnica, Direttore di Piattaforma
Stefano Iacoponi, Vice President, Product Engineering
Alfredo Melloni, Director, Organization and Management Development
Lidia Montebruno, Central Development, Coordination and Control
    Department Sector Analysis, Plans and Strategies Competitive Analysis
    and Scenarios
Lorenzo Morello, Director, Vehicle Engineering
Guiseppe Perlo, Vice President, Product/Market Strategies
Renato Pettarini, Development, Coordination and Control Central
    Management Strategic Coordination and Planning Scenarios and
    Demand
Giuseppe Piritore, Director, Platform Engineering
Claudio Poli, Amministratore Delegato
Giuseppe Ragni, General Manager, Power Train Operations
Roberto Romani, New Model Project Manager, Product Engineering
Flavio Rossi, Direzione Strategie Prodotto/Mercato—Prodotto
Luigi Sburlati, Platform Engineering Commercial Vehicles and
    International Products
Paolo Scolari, Vice President, Product Engineering & Industrial
    Development
Carlo Serrati, Direzione Acquisti, Pianificazione e Qualita Fornitori, Piani
    Integrazione e Crescita Sistema Fornitori
Antony M. Sheriff, Direzione Prodotto, Sviluppo Prodotto Briefing e
    Segmentazione
Giancarlo Spelta, Direzione Produzione Veicolo, Stabilimento Di Rivalta,
    II Direttore
Marco Antonio Barros Teixeira, Cerente—Familia 178
Giorgio Trebbi, Product Engineering, Planning and Control Director
Renato Zambrano, Director, Platform Engineering

Ford

Peter Abowd, Product Design Engineer, Audio Software Section,
    Electronics Division
A. Andrade, Manager, Chassis Engineering
Richard Billington, Cross Carline Planning Manager, Car Programs
    Management, Car Product Development
Thomas Burke, Product Design Engineer, Electronic Instrumentation
Michael Carty, Product Development Process Benchmarking, Product
    Design Engineer
Peter Coote, Manager, Competitive Analysis, Finance Staff, Ford of Europe
Brent Egleston, Car Strategy & Product Planning Manager, Worldwide
    Technical Strategy & Planning
Taras Fedak, Product Design Engineer, Integrated Vehicle Controls
Chuck Feltner, Director, Manufacturing Planning and Information
    Systems Office
Richard Greene, World Class Process
Dennis Henderson, Team Leader, Automotive Components Group,
    Underhood Team

William Kath, Manager, Technology Implementation, Technical Strategy
Office
John Krafcik, Manager, VE160 Chassis Engineering, Transit Program
Center
Louis Miller, Supervisor, Software Section, Integrated Vehicle Controls
Arthur Pope, Advanced Large Car Programs Manager, Planning and
Control, Engineering and Manufacturing Staff
Craig Schmatz, Supervisor, Technology Planning /Breakthrough Projects,
L.T. Business & Cycle Planning, Truck Operations

Fuji (Subaru)

Yasunori Yoshinaga, Project Manager, Corporate Planning Division

General Motors

Andrew Brown, GM Research, Director, Research and Administration
Services
Steve Carlisle, Vehicle Systems Manager, Mid-size Car Division
Jerry Collins, Executive-in-Charge, Vehicle Launch Center
Bob deKruyff, Executive Engineer, Vehicle Integration
Jamal El-Hout, Vehicle Systems Integration Manager, Vehicle Launch
Center
John Fickes, Vehicle Systems Manager, Vehicle Launch Center
John Gaydash, Group Manager, North American Truck Platforms
Michael Kusnic, General Director, Business Decision Center
David Levering, Director, Technology/Marketing Planning, Automotive
Components
Inaki Lopez de Arriortua, Vice-President, Worldwide Purchasing
Dantar Oosterwal, Project Engineer
Juliane Parks, Vehicle Systems Analyst, Vehicle Launch Center
Tom Wallace, Executive Director, Quality NAO Technical Center

Honda

Morishi Horiuchi, Chief Engineer, Chief Project Leaders Office
Takehumi Hosaka, Director, Automotive Planning Division
Hirohide Ikeno, Chief Engineer, Engineering Design Division 7
Masahiro Ishiwada, Deputy General Manager, Technical Administration
Division
Kiyoshi Ito, Europe Division (Automobile)
Akio Kazama, Chief Engineer, Engineering Design Division 1
Masaaki Kato, Director, Deputy General Manager, Tochigi R&D Center
Shuichi Kato, Chief Engineer, Automotive Design Division
Tadataka Kobayashi, Chief Engineer, General Manager, Computer
Integrated Systems
Akihiro Kubo, Chief Engineer, Engineering Design Division 7
Hiroshi Kuroda, Chief Engineer, Chief Project Leaders Office
Sadao Makiguchi, Chief Engineer, Automotive Planning Division
Hideki Maru, Chief Engineer, Engineering Design Division 6

Norio Miyashita, Chief Engineer, Engineering Research Division 12
Rokuro Nakaji, Deputy General Manager, Administrative & Legal Affairs
	Division
Shigeru Nakamura, Manager, Europe Division (Automobile)
Terumasa Ohsawa, Chief Engineer, Automobile Production Planning Office
Masaru Okada, Engineer, Suzuka Factory
Yutaka Ooyama, Engineering Research Division 9
Hirofumi Otsuka, Assistant Chief Engineer, Engineering Research Division 8
Takehiko Sayama, Assistant Chief Engineer, Engineering Design Division 1
Motoatsu Shiraishi, Director, Production Planning Division
Tadao Sugiura, General Manager, Administration Office, Suzuka Factory
Tomoyuki Sugiyama, Executive Chief Engineer, Representative of
	Automotive Development (RAD), Automobile Planning Board
Hiroshi Suzuki, Chief Engineer, Automotive Planning Division
Shinichi Takahashi, Chief Engineer, Engineering Design Division 6
Kazuhiro Takizawa, Europe Division (Automobile)
Shinichi Tanaka, Assistant Manager, Public Relations Division
Yoshikazu Tateno, Engineering Design Division 2
Masato Tezuka, Executive Chief Engineer, Representative of Automotive
	Development (RAD), Automobile Planning Board
Gen Tsujii, Chief Engineer & Leader, R&D 8K
Shigeru Uehara, Executive Chief Engineer, Representative of Automotive
	Development (RAD), Automobile Planning Board
Mitsuhiro Ueno, Chief Engineer, Automotive Design Division
Takashi Umemoto, Chief Engineer, Engineering Design Division 1
Tetsuji Yamakawa, Manager, Technical Administration Division
Kuniaki Yanagiuchi, Chief Engineer, Engineering Design Division 6

Isuzu

Kazuyuki Amada, Product Manager, Product Planning Office
Shoichi Imaizumi, General Manager, F.S. Planning
Kenji Shimohara, Manager, Product Development Administration Division
Hiromi Suzuki, Manager, Product Planning Office
Yasushi Tanabe, Senior Planner, F.S. Planning

Mazda

Atsushi Edahiro, Assistant Manager, Vehicle Designing Division 1, Product
	Center I
Tadayuki Hayashi, Product Program Manager, Product Center II
Ryuji Ikeda, Deputy General Manager, Vehicle Designing Division 1,
	Product Center I
Fumiaki Inami, Senior Manager, Product Planning and Control Division
Kimihaku Kamigasa, Manager, Corporate Planning Division
Masaharu Kanaoka, General Manager, Development Administration
	Division
Hirotaka Kanazawa, Deputy General Manager, Vehicle Designing Division
	2, Product Center II
Shuichi Katamura, Assistant Manager, Information Systems Division

Noriyuki Kawaichi, Manager, Vehicle Designing Division
Reiji Kikuchi, Assistant Manager, Product Planning & Development
  Division
Hidenori Kita, General Manager, Development Administration Division
Toichiro Kurata, Product Program Manager, Product Center I
Koji Kurimoto, Executive Vice-President, Mazda R&D of North America
Kenji Kuwaki, Senior Staff Manager, Product Planning and Control
  Division
Jiro Maebayashi, Senior Manager, Product Planning & Development
  Division
Hideichi Miyamoto, Staff General Manager, Corporate Planning Division
Shunichiro Miyawaki, Assistant Manager, Vehicle Designing Division 2,
  Product Center II
Masao Morioka, Manager, Product Center II
Hiroshi Motonaga, Manager, Product Planning Group, Mazda R&D of
  North America
Nobuyuki Nakanishi, Assistant Program Manager, Product Center II
Mitsuhiro Niimi, Chief Project Manager, Office of Management Innovation
  Projects
Hidenori Ohta, Manager, Vehicle Designing Division 2, Product Center II
Yoshimi Okada, General Manager, Information Systems Division
Ittoku Okamura, Assistant Manager, Information Systems Division
Sadao Ozeki, Assistant Program Manager, Vehicle Designing Division 1,
  Product Center I
Shinji Saeki, Assistant Manager, Vehicle Designing Division 1, Product
  Center I
Naoshige Saito, Manager, Product Planning and Control Division
Yoshio Sekine, Assistant Manager, VA Division
Akio Suzuki, Deputy General Manager, Corporate Planning Division
Tetsukan Takasue, Assistant Manager, Vehicle Engineering Division 1
Hitoshi Takeshita, Assistant Manager, Vehicle Engineering Division 1
Takeshi Tatsuta, General Manager, Marketing Division
Yutaka Toi, Senior Managing Director, Mazda Engineering Corp.
Akio Uchiyama, Product Program Manager, Product Center I
Shigemi Uotani, Deputy Program Manager, Marketing Division
Naotada Utsunomiya, Assistant Program Manager, Vehicle Testing &
  Research Division 1, Product Center I
Kiyoshi Yagi, Manager, Product Planning and Control Division
Tatsuya Yamamoto, Assistant Manager, Development Administration
  Division Product Development Management Center
Kaoru Yamane, Manager, Vehicle Designing Division 2, Product Center II
Ikuhiro Yoshinaga, Assistant Manager, Product Planning and Control
  Division

Mercedes Benz

Herbert Gzik, Hauptreferent, Zentrale Arbeitsgertaltung
Peter Laur, Leiter der Projekmanagermentunterstutzung, Strategic
  Planning Project Management

Jorg Prigl, Leiter der Hauptabteilung, Organisation, Datenverabeitung PKW-Entwicklung

Heinrich Reidelbach, Leiter der Uternehmensplanung der Mercedes-Benz AG

Mitsubishi

Hiroyuki Hosono, General Manager, Product Development Office

Yoshihisa Iba, Deputy Senior General Manager, Product Development Office

Atsuo Iida, Deputy General Manager, Nagoya Production Engineering Division

Masaki Kawaguchi, Manager, Chassis Designing Division

Akira Kawanobe, Deputy General Manager, Nagoya Production Engineering Division

Mitsunori Kitao, Assistant Manager, Production Engineering Division

Junichi Nagano, Assistant Manager, Body Designing Division

Shoji Nakatani, Manager, Corporate Planning Division

Shiro Niki, Deputy General Manager, Nagoya Production Engineering Division

Tetsuo Ozaki, Manager, Engineering Administration Division

Hideo Sano, Manager, Product Development Systems Division

Junji Suzuki, Manager, Nagoya Production Engineering Division

Kiyoshi Takahashi, Deputy General Manager, Body Engineering Division

Norio Takehara, Fellow, Corporate General Manager, Office of Overseas Production Engineering and Control

Tomonori Tanaka, Deputy Manager, Corporate Planning Division

Haruo Teraoka, Assistant Engineering Manager, Equipment Designing Division

Masahiro Terazono, Deputy General Manager, Okazaki Plant

Naomitsu Tomitani, Manager, Electronics Engineering Division

Akio Watanuki, Project Manager, Corporate Planning Division

Nissan

Hiromi Aihara, Engineer, Production Engineering Division No. 3

Yutaka Aoyama, Manager, Product Planning and Development Division No. 2

Toshihiro Araki, Engineer (High Rank), Body Engineering Division

Yoshio Fukai, General Manager, Product Planning & Development Division

Koji Hamanaka, Product & Marketing Strategy Office

Hiroshi Hashimoto, Manager, Powertrain Engineering Division

Shinsuke Hisamitsu, Manager, Product Planning & Development Division No. 1

Hidetoshi Imazu, Senior Manager, Production Control & Engineering Division, Oppama Plant

Yasuaki Inari, Manager, Engineering Systems Division

Toyokazu Ishida, Manager, Corporate Communications Division

Hisashi Ishikawa, Chassis Design Division

Takeo Ishikawa, General Manager, External & Government Affairs
  Division
Koichiro Kawamura, General Manager, Product Planning & Marketing
  Division
Nobu Komatsu, External & Government Affairs Division
Hisashi Komine, Manager, External & Government Affairs Division
Yuki Kuma, External & Government Affairs Division
Kensho Kusumi, Director, Public Affairs
Kiichi Kusunoki, Engineer, Electronics Engineering Division
Naohisa Mamiya, Engineer, Power Train Designing Division 2
Shigesada Masaaki, Engineer, Interior Design Division
Kenichi Moki, Product Planning and Development Division No. 2
Makoto Murata, Senior Engineer, Chassis Engineering Division
Mitsuhiro Nakamuki, Engineer (High Rank), Body Design Division
Sadao Namioka, Senior Engineer, Power Train Engineering Division
Hiroyuki Nomura, Manager, Electronics Engineering Division
Hiroaki Obayashi, Manager, Electronics Engineering Division
Hiroo Ogino, Advisor, Administration, Nissan Research & Development,
  USA
Yasuhiro Saitoh, Manager, Vehicle Designing Division 1, Product Planning
  and Development Division No. 1
Kenichi Sasabe, Manager, Design Administration Division
Akihiro Sato, Engineer (High Rank), Engineering Management Division,
  Oppama Plant
Sadaharu Sato, Senior Engineer, Vehicle Engineering Division
Sadao Sekiyama, Manager, Design for Manufacturing Division
Tsutomu Shikata, Manager, Product Planning and Development Division
  No. 2
Mitsuhiro Sonomura, Engineer (High Rank), Body Engineering Division
Masaaki Suga, Manager, Technology Planning, Nissan Research &
  Development, USA
Masaki Sugisawa, General Manager, Product Planning & Development
  Division No. 1
Ken Suzuki, Manager, Product Planning and Development Division No. 2
Isao Suzuki, Manager, Product Design Administration Division
Akira Takahashi, General Manager, Purchasing Engineering Support
  Division
Yoshisada Takamatsu, Manager, Engineering Systems Division
Masayoshi Takano, Manager, Production Engineering Division 3
Shuji Takata, Production Engineering Division 3
Jitsuo Tomii, Manager, Technology Engineering Division 1
Kimio Tomita, Manager, Engine Design Division

Renault

Pierre Amouyel, Vice-President, Strategy and Corporate Planning
Yves Boccadoro, Chief Engineer, Advanced Engine Engineering, Direction
  des Etudes
Jacques Lacambre, Executive Director, Vehicle Product and Process
  Engineering, Architecture and Advanced Engineering

Dominique Piednoir, Groupe Delta
Michel Rousseau, Groupe Delta, Direction Technique
Raymond Savoye, Project General Manager, Direction de Project

Suzuki

Norio Hamahata, General Manager, Corporate Planning Division
Takeo Hattori, Deputy General Manager, Marketing Promotion Division
Junzo Sugimori, General Manager, North and Latin America Automobile
  Division

Toyota

Takami Aoyama, Planning Division 1, Vehicle Development Center I
Norimasa Arakawa, Public Communications
Tamio Arakawa, Manager, Technology Management Division
Kozo Ezaki, Deputy General Manager, Body Designing Division 1
Susumu Fukazawa, Manager, Power Train Division 1, Vehicle
  Development Center I
Toshiro Furuta, Manager, Industrial Affairs Division
Shigeru Handa, Deputy General Manager, Industrial Affairs Division
Takeshi Hashimoto, Chassis Engineering Division 1, Vehicle Development
  Center I
Tetsuo Hattori, General Manager, Product Planning and Management
  Division
Kazunori Hayashi, Project General Manager, International Purchasing
  Division
Ryoichi Hibio, Staff Leader, Purchasing Division 1
Masahide Hisayama, Manager, Body Designing Division 2
Mitsuyuki Horie, Project General Manager, Technical Administration
  Division
Yoichi Hyodo, Chassis Designing Division 1
Kazuo Igarashi, Deputy General Manager, Technical Administration
  Division
Hiromi Ikehata, Vice-President, Toyota Technical Center, USA
Masamitsu Isaka, Assistant Manager, Purchasing Planning Division
Takashi Ishidera, Chief Engineer, Product Planning Division
Kunihiro Iwatsuki, Manager, Drivetrain Engineering Division, Component
  & System Development Center
Hidenori Kashima, Purchasing Planning Division
Shigeo Kato, Assistant Manager, International Purchasing Division
Toru Kato, Project General Manager, Electronic Commerce Promotion
  Division
Yuji Kawaguchi, Deputy General Manager, Purchasing Planning Division
Toyoaki Kawaji, Assistant Manager, Accounting Division
Masaharu Kawakami, Deputy General Manager, Accounting Division
Siichiro Kitahashi, Design Division
Akira Kodera, Manager, Technical Administration Division
Yutaka Kondo, General Manager, Vehicle Engineering Division, Vehicle
  Development Center IV

Kunihiro Masaki, Executive Vice-President, Toyota Technical Center, USA
Akio Matsubara, Director, Technical Administration Division
Takaaki Matsumoto, Deputy General Manager, Public Communications
Kenji Miura, Manager, Operations Management Consulting Division
Takashi Miura, Deputy General Manager, Production Engineering
    Planning Division
Naoki Miyazaki, Assistant Manager, Industrial Affairs Division
Akihiko Morikawa, Assistant Manager, Purchasing Division 1
Masaaki Morikawa, Assistant Manager, Body Designing Division 1, Vehicle
    Development Center I
Tadashi Nakagawa, Chief Engineer, Vehicle Development Center II
Katsumi Nakajima, Manager, Design Division
Yoichi Nakamura, Manager, Overseas Planning Division
Chisato Niki, Assistant Manager, Technical Administration Division
Toshihide Ninomiya, Assistant Manager, Planning Division I, Vehicle
    Development Center I
Yasushi Nohno, Manager, Power Train Division 2
Hiroshi Nokura, Manager, International Purchasing Division
Masakatsu Nonaka, Chief Engineer, Vehicle Development Center III
Yuichiro Obu, General Manager, Development Planning & Operations,
    Toyota Technical Center, USA
Yoshinori Ogata, Project General Manager, Information Systems Division I
Hiroshi Ohira, Assistant Manager, Information Systems Division I
Eiji Ohno, Project General Manager, Technical Administration Division
Shu Otobe, Product Testing Division
Hidesoto Ozaki, General Manager, Accounting Division
Shigeki Sakurai, Manager, Industrial Affairs Division
Katsuyuki Sano, Chassis System Development Division, Component &
    System Development Center
Ikuo Sengoku, General Manager, Planning Division II, Vehicle
    Development Center II
Takunori Shibahara, Technical Administration Division
Hiroaki Shinto, Manager, Chassis System Development Division,
    Component & System Development Center
Hiroshi Shirasawa, Project Manager, Chassis Engineering Division 1,
    Vehicle Development Center I
Mikiya Soyama, Deputy General Manager, Industrial Affairs Division
Toshihiro Sugai, General Manager, Quality Assurance Division
Nobuhiko Suzuki, Project General Manager, International Purchasing
    Division
Masanori Takahashi, Manager, Overseas Production Planning Division
Seihachi Takahashi, General Manager, Planning Division 2, Vehicle
    Development Center II
Eiji Takeichi, Assistant Manager, Government & Industrial Affairs Division
Yasushi Tanaka, Chief Engineer, Vehicle Development Center I
Michiro Tanaka, Deputy General Manager, International Purchasing
    Division
Misao Tsutsuki, Project Manager, Technical Administration Division
Takeshi Umehara, Assistant Manager, Purchasing Division 1

Masatoshi Uramoto, Manager, Purchasing Planning Division
Takuji Yatagai, Project General Manager, Government & Industrial Affairs
  Division
Yoichi Yokohori, Manager, Equipment Management Division Tahara Plant
Hiroyuki Watanabe, Chief Engineer, Vehicle Development Center I
Taminori Yanagisawa, General Manager, Production Engineering Planning
  Division
Jun Yasumatsu, General Manager, Planning Division II, Vehicle
  Development Center II

Volkswagen

Hans-Jurgen Bartels, Leiter Geschaftsprozesse
Wolfgang Beese, Executive Director, Strategy and Development Projects
Winfried Bernhardt, R&D, Head of Research Project Steering
Hauke Bruhn, Executive Representative, Technical Representative, Tokyo
Gernot Dollner, Research and Development
Hans-Dieter Fischer, General Manager, Design Management
Klaus V. Holleben, Corporate Counsel, Goverment Relations, Foreign
  Legal Department
Hans-Heinrich Sander, Forschung und Entwicklung, Fahrzeug-
  Entwicklung
Gerald Klier, Group Purchasing Strategy
Udo-Willi Kogler, Executive Managing Director, Research and
  Development
Hans Markgraf, Strategy Development and Product Planning
Jurgen Raschke, Manager, Technical Representative, Tokyo
Hans-Henrich Sander, Forschung und Entwicklung, Fahrzeug-
  Entwicklung
Setsuo Takasaki, Senior Manager, Research Division, Technical
  Representative, Tokyo
Trac Tang, Corporate Director, Information Systems for Product
  Development
Oliver Tegel, R&D, Information Processes
Peter Walzer, Forschung Antriebstechnik
Bernd Wilhelm, Group Production Strategy
Rudiger Weisner, Forschung und Entwicklung, Leiter Pkw-Konstruktion,
  Ausstattung

Volvo

Kristrau Abel, Corporate Strategy
Sven Bildtsen, Manager, Cost Engineering, Product & Process
  Engineering Department
Haus Cawlstedt, Large Platform Leader
Dennis Langervik, Chief Engineer, Engine Development
Mats Mobery, Manager, Chassis Engineering
Stephen Wallman, Director, Strategy & Business Development

Endnotes

Chapter 1. Introduction: Beyond "Lean" in Product Development

1. Clark, Chew, and Fujimoto, 1987 Clark and Fujimoto, 1991.

2. Krafcik had worked at NUMMI, the Toyota-GM joint manufacturing venture, and now works at Ford. See Krafcik, 1988, and Womack, Jones, and Roos, 1990.

3. Womack and Jones, 1996.

4. Sheriff, 1988; Womack, Jones, and Roos, 1990; Cusumano and Nobeoka, 1992.

5. Ellison, Clark, Fujimoto, and Hyun, 1995.

6. Fujimoto, 1997b; and Cusumano, 1994.

7. Dewar and Dutton, 1986; Ettlie, et al., 1984; Kleinschmidt and Cooper, 1991.

8. This discussion of differences between concurrent and sequential transfer is partially based on Thompson's distinction between "long-linked technology" and "intensive technology," where the latter also enables mutual adjustments. See Thompson, 1967.

9. This was the strategy according to managers at Renault that we interviewed. See Appendix 5 for a list of interviewees.

10. Aoshima, 1996.

11. Kotler, 1989; Pine, 1993; Kotha, 1995.

12. Meyer and Utterback, 1993; Sanderson and Uzumeri, 1996.

13. Meyer and Lehnerd, 1997.

14. Cusumano, 1991, 1992; Cusumano and Selby, 1995.

15. Prahalad and Hamel, 1990.

Chapter 2. The Toyota Benchmark: Multi-Project Development Centers

1. This chapter is based mainly on interviews at Toyota with 3 general managers, 4 product managers, 15 engineers, and 3 cost management planners between 1992 and 1994. We also visited the company several times during 1995–1997. See Appendix 5 for a complete list of interviewees.

2. Schonberger, 1982; Cusumano, 1985; Womack, Jones, and Roos, 1990.

3. Ikari, 1985; Womack, Jones, and Roos, 1990.

4. See Womack, Jones, and Roos, 1990; and Womack and Jones, 1996, as well as Cusumano, 1985.

5. We used Ikari, 1985, as a reference for the shusa organization during the 1950s and 1960s.

6. Each of the 10 shusas was responsible for the Crown, Mark II, Publica, Century, Celica/Carina, Toyota 200GT, Corona, Corolla/Sprinter, Toyoace, and Mini-Ace.

7. The 7,000 people in the 16 engineering divisions and the 2,000 people in the RAD group added up to 9,000. There were, in total, about 11,500 people working on product development. The rest of the people were engaged in support activities such as patent management, certification process management, CAD system development, and prototype development.

8. Even though there were 16 engineering divisions, a chief engineer for a particular project did not necessarily need to manage all of these. This data was based on Toyota's internal measurements. The company did not explain in detail its methodology for determining these metrics, however.

9. There were a few exceptions. For example, as of 1991, there were already two separate body engineering divisions, each of which was responsible for front-wheel-drive and rear-wheel-drive vehicles, respectively. Therefore, each functional manager was in charge of about half of all the vehicle projects.

10. Because the Research and Advanced Development Group was mainly located in the Higashi-Fuji Technical Center, these two names often are used interchangeably. Higashi-Fuji is located about 150 miles east of Toyota headquarters, where most product development engineers are located. This chapter uses a shorter name, the RAD Group, which is not used at Toyota.

11. We rely on data from an internal Toyota document. The manager that provided us with this document claimed that these numbers are based on a comparison of similar projects, although we did not receive a more detailed explanation of the measurement methodology. The numbers in this table include not only direct outcomes of the change in the organization structure but also those of accompanying process changes. In addition, some factors not directly related to the reorganization, such as an increase in the use of computer-aided engineering (CAE) tools, are also included.

Chapter 3. Organizing Product Development in the World Auto Industry

1. This discussion is based on interviews we conducted between 1994 and 1997, as well as working papers from another member of our research group, Gregory Scott, on Chrysler, GM, and Ford (Scott 1994a, 1994b, 1995). For a list of interviews, see Appendix 5.

2. Some of the historical background on the evolution of project management in Renault comes from Midler, 1995.

3. Also see Midler for an analysis of the Twingo case.

4. For a description of the NedCar joint venture, see Fourin, No. 139 (March 1997), pp. 26–27, as well as Laage-Hellman, 1996.

5. This discussion of Fiat relies on Calabrese, 1994, as well as our own interviews in 1993 and 1996.

6. Clark and Fujimoto, 1991.

7. Imai, Nonaka, and Takeuchi, 1985.

8. Doi, 1992.

9. IRC, 1995c.

10. IRC, 1995c.

11. For a discussion of Honda's early history in English, see Sakiya, 1982.

12. For a historical comparison of Nissan and Toyota, see Cusumano, 1985.

13. For a brief discussion of Nissan's changes in product development during the late 1980s, see Iansiti and Clark, 1994.

14. "Nissan to Reduce Car Platform Types," *New York Times*, 26 June 1997, p. D19; and "Cost Reduction through Platform Integration," *Nihon Keizai Shimbun*, 24 June 1997, p. 1.

15. Scott, 1995.

16. Micheline Maynard, "Saab 9⁵: New car drives strategy," *USA Today*, 31 July 1997, p. 7B.

17. Scott, 1994b.

18. Robyn Meredith, "Ford to Revive Dying Mercury Cougar as Small Coupe," *New York Times*, 30 July 1997, p. C1 (national edition).

19. Tagliabue, 1996.

20. Womack, Jones, and Roos, 1990; Clark and Fujimoto, 1991.

Chapter 4. Strategies for Product Development and Mutiple Projects

1. See Cooper, 1987, and Roberts, 1988.

2. Ansoff and Stewart, 1967.

3. Lieberman and Montgomery, 1988; Kerin, Varadarajan, and Peterson, 1992.

4. Porter, 1980, 1985.

5. Johnson and Jones, 1957.

6. For example, Abernathy and Clark, 1985; Clark, 1989; Meyer and Roberts, 1986; Hayes, Wheelwright, and Clark, 1988; Adler, Riggs, and Wheelwright, 1989; Roberts and Meyer, 1991.

7. For examples, see Wernerfelt, 1984; Aaker, 1989; Diercks and Cool, 1989; Prahalad and Hamel, 1990; Itami and Numagami, 1992; Amit and Schoemaker, 1993; Meyer and Utterback, 1993.

8. Ettlie, Bridges, and O'Keefe, 1984; Dewar and Dutton, 1986; Tushman and Anderson, 1986; Kleinschmidt and Cooper, 1991; Achilladelis, 1993.

9. Dosi, 1988; Pavitt, 1990.

10. Arrow, 1962; Reinganum, 1983.

11. Tushman and Anderson, 1986.

12. Banbury and Mitchell, 1995.

13. Adler et al., 1989.

14. Enos, 1962; Hollander, 1965; Cohen et al., 1984; Banbury and Mitchell, 1995.

15. See Cringely, 1993.

16. See Cusumano and Selby, 1995.

17. Rosenbloom and Cusumano, 1987.

18. See Rumelt, 1974, Yoshihara, 1986, and Datta et al., 1991 on diversification at the firm level and Meyer and Roberts, 1986, and Tallman and Li, 1996 for product-level studies.

19. Norman, 1971; Cooper and Schendel, 1976; Duncan, 1976; Daft, 1982; Tushman and Anderson, 1986; Kagano, 1988; Vincenti, 1994.

20. Burns and Stalker, 1961; Arrow, 1974; Daft and Weick, 1984; Nelson and Winter, 1982.

21. Garud and Nayyar, 1994; Garud and Kumaraswamy, 1995.

22. Prahalad and Hamel, 1990.

23. Henderson and Clark, 1990.

24. Dougherty, 1992; Iansiti, 1995; Kusunoki, Nonaka, and Nagata, 1995.

25. Wheelright and Sasser, 1989.

26. Wheelright and Clark, 1992; Meyer and Utterback, 1993.

27. Prahalad and Hamel, 1994.

28. Meyer and Lehnerd, 1997.

29. Sanderson and Uzmeri, 1996.

30. This discussion is also based on interviews with managers and engineers from various companies. See Appendix 5.

31. Scott, 1995.

32. Scott, 1994b, 1995.

33. *Automotive News*, May 20, 1996, p. 6.

34. Sanchez, 1995.

35. Teece, 1980; Goldhar and Jelinek, 1983; Clark, 1989.

36. Markides and Williamson, 1994.

37. Sanchez, 1995; Garud and Kumaraswamy, 1995.

38. Nobeoka, 1995.

39. Leonard-Barton, 1988; Clark and Fujimoto, 1991.

Chapter 5. Multi-Project Strategies and Project Performance

1. The discussion in this chapter largely follows Nobeoka and Cusumano, 1995.

2. Clark and Fujimoto, 1991.

3. Rosenberg, 1982; Henderson and Clark, 1991; Iansiti, 1995.

4. For example, Cohen, et al., 1979; Quinn and Mueller, 1982; Imai, et al., 1985; Leonard-Barton, 1988; Gomory, 1989; Leonard-Barton and Sinha, 1991; Tyre, 1991; Clark and Fujimoto, 1991.

5. Cusumano, 1991.

6. See Appendix 3 for complete distributions of the time lag associated with each strategy.

7. Engineering hours are converted using a natural logarithm. We obtained a residual plot for predicted values from a trial regression analysis using unadjusted engineering hours as a dependent variable and independent variables. The plot indicated that the engineering hours should be adjusted by logarithm. Specifically, many residuals showed minuses in the middle of the predicted values and large positive numbers for the high predicted values. The standard deviation for engineering hours, which is even bigger than the average, is also a crude indicator of the need for adjustments.

8. These are: product price = $17,300, number of body types = 1.8, engine/transmission new component ratio = 62 percent, body/interior new component ratio = 90 percent, innovation index = 0.23, except for the country and vehicle-type dummy variables (= U.S. passenger car projects).

9. See Nobeoka, 1993 for the actual data and analysis.

10. See Nobeoka, 1993 for the actual data and analysis.

11. The difference was statistically significant at the 0.001 level.

12. Program managers and engineers we interviewed basically agreed with our interpretations. However, some of the following interpretations are still only hypotheses that should be studied further in detail.

13. Aoshima, 1996.

14. For related discussions of tacit knowledge as well as "sticky" knowledge that does not transfer easily, see Nonaka, 1990; von Hippel, 1990; Nonaka and Takeuchi, 1995; and Aoshima, 1996.

15. See Cusumano, 1991, 1992.

16. A similar argument could be made not only for general managers but also for other key functional engineering personnel responsible for component engineering on multiple projects.

17. See Ulrich and Eppinger, 1995, on this subject, as well as for techniques to group tasks more effectively.

18. See Cusumano and Selby, 1995, for a discussion of how Microsoft manages late design changes in software projects through daily integration techniques.

19. For a discussion of interdependencies, see Staudenmayer, 1997. Also see Eppinger et al., 1994.

Chapter 6. Multi-Project Strategies and Company Performance

1. The discussion in this chapter largely follows Nobeoka and Cusumano, 1997.

2. Miller, 1988; Fujimoto and Sheriff, 1989; Kekre and Srinivasan, 1990; Sanchez, 1995.

3. Bagozzi, 1986; Kotler, 1986; Bower and Hout, 1988.

4. Clark and Fujimoto, 1991.

5. Clark and Fujimoto, 1991; Nobeoka and Cusumano, 1995.

6. von Braun, 1991.

7. Clark, 1989; Clark and Fujimoto, 1991.

8. Garud and Kumaraswamy, 1995.

9. Cusumano, 1991, 1992.

10. Prahalad and Hamel, 1990.

11. Meyer and Roberts, 1986.

12. Clark and Fujimoto, 1991.

13. Nobeoka, 1995a.

14. VAG: VW and Audi; PSA: Peugeot and Citroen; Fiat Group: Fiat and Lancia. Data for Alfa Romeo is not included in the Fiat Group because it became a part of the Fiat Group in November 1986, the middle of the period that our database covers.

15. We do not count special "off-line" products such as the Toyota Sera, the Dodge Viper, the Honda NSX, the Nissan PAO, or the BMW Z1, whose production volume is approximately 0.5 percent or less of a firm's total car production volume. These products usually are not developed with the same level of production preparation or development standards as mass-production models. New products whose platforms are primarily developed externally also are excluded. For example, we excluded the 1989 Mazda Carol and the 1987 Ford Probe from this study because Suzuki developed the platform for the 1989 Mazda Carol and Mazda developed the platform for the 1987 Ford Probe. Including products developed or sold through alliances would have added only about 10 products to the sample of 210. In addition, more than half of these products are nearly identical to other products covered in our sample and are sold under a different company label on an OEM basis.

16. We chose the scheme of four three-year periods because we believe that longer or shorter periods both present problems. For example, a longer interval, such as two six-year periods, may create a causality problem because six years is enough time for firms to choose a product strategy for the later years that directly reflects their market performance within the earlier years of the same period. On the other hand, we believe that a shorter period, such as two years, is not long enough to

capture the effects of a dynamic multi-project strategy. In contrast, three-year periods are long enough for the influence of company strategies to appear in the market because the sales peak for new car products usually is recorded within the first year after introduction. Thereafter, sales usually decline gradually. (We also calculated the timing of new product introductions in the analysis from six months after the official introduction of the products to the market because it often takes several months for the production, distribution, and sale of new products to reach target levels.) Nevertheless, in order to detect any serious bias resulting from the three-year period scheme, we conducted sensitivity tests using other time periods, and found no significant changes in the results.

17. We used average sales prices for the U.S. market, adjusted to 1991 levels. For products not available for purchase in the U.S. market, we estimated prices from equivalent products in the U.S. market with respect to size and equipment. This methodology is similar to using purchasing power parity rather than exchange rates and minimizes the impact of changing exchange rates.

18. Major components for exterior styling include doors, fenders, pillars, roofs, bumpers, windshields, hoods, trunk lids, hatchback doors, front grilles, and exterior moldings. A new exterior styling means that all of these components are new. The same idea applies to changes in interior stylings. In the automobile industry, particularly in Japan and Europe, it is usually clear whether a new product is actually a "new product" or a "face-lift product." For example, Japanese industry people (and customers) clearly distinguish these two by referring to them as a "major-change" projects and "minor-change" projects, respectively.

19. We assigned points according to changes in platform design between the new product and related preceding products, based primarily on the wheelbase, tracks, and suspension. These measurements cover the extent of changes to the platform (primarily the floor panels, the under-body structure, and the suspension system).

20. We believe that analyzing all new products introduced during this time period using a systematic methodology based on public data was better than relying on the subjective opinions of engineers involved in a sample of projects. We did not consider it practical or necessary to interview engineers for the entire set of 210 projects. Some projects had ended more than 10 years ago, and most products were relatively easy to classify. Nonetheless, during the course of our research, we relied on interviews with approximately 45 engineers and program managers to help us validate our point scheme as well as check the specific points we assigned to particular products. We also made a list of the half-dozen or so products that were difficult to classify from the public data and directly asked company engineers and program managers to help us categorize them.

21. According to our survey data, platform technology transfer between multiple projects within 2.0 years always came with on-going interactions between a base project and a new project. Those projects with a transfer lag between 2.0 years and 3.0 years show mixed results: Some projects have interactions with a base project and some do not. No project derived from a base project with delays of 3.0 years or longer had any interactions with the base project. These data included projects both in the United States and in Japan, and there was no regional difference evident. Nevertheless, we also tested the sensitivity of the 2.0-year division by using 1.5 years and 2.5 years as cutoff points, with no changes in the results.

22. See *Car Styling*, 61, November 1987, p. 78.

23. *Automobil Revue*, 1984, p. 300.

24. *Automobil Revue*, 1989, p. 313.

25. *Automobil Revue*, 1990.

26. *Automobil Revue*, 1982, p. 274.

27. *Automobil Revue*, 1987, p. 462.

28. *Automobil Revue*, 1989, p. 554.

29. Hartigan and Wong, 1979; SYSTAT, 1992.

30. As in the cluster analysis, the data set included both cross-sectional (17 firms) and time-series (4 periods) components. Pooling observations for each firm violates the assumption of independence required for ordinary least squares regression. In order to rule out the effects of unmeasured firm differences in the analysis of the panel data, we estimated fixed-effects models, introducing one dummy variable for each firm and eliminating the constant. In these models, all cross-firm variation is captured in the estimates of the dummy variables. The fixed effects model assumes that each firm has its own intercept, and firm-specific effects are fixed over time. We also estimated an alternative model, the random effects model, which assumes that firm-specific effects are random variables. Because there are no significant differences in results between these two models, we report those from the fixed effects model. In addition, we computed the heteroskedasticity-consistent standard errors for the regression coefficients, using procedures discussed by White (1980). This test computes standard errors that are consistent even in the existence of unknown heteroskedasticity.

We also designed the fixed effects model to correct for autocorrelation of errors for individual firms over time. First, the dependent variable was assessed as the percentage change. Second, dependent variables in a prior period ($t-1$) was added as an independent variable. Third, we added three dummy variables to represent three of the four periods to control for time effects. These treatments usually ease autocorrelation problems. As a result, residuals for each firm in our regression models did not show any signs of autocorrelation in our visual observation of a residual plot for predicted values. Consequently, in addition to firm dummy variables in the fixed effects model, we also introduced some other control variables including market coverage, sales growth in a prior period, and four different time periods. We measured market coverage by the number of product offerings throughout world markets for each firm at the beginning of each period primarily to control for firm size.

31. We conducted various tests to examine the sensitivity of our data and analysis schemes. First, we conducted two additional analyses using samples separately excluding the second and then the third periods. This analysis also tried to detect any autocorrelation problems. Second, we ran sensitivity tests for different data-processing schemes, using two other alternative methods for period divisions: three four-year periods and two six-year periods. Finally, we tested two alternative cut-off points between the concurrent technology transfer strategy and the sequential technology transfer strategy: 1.5 years and 2.5 years. There are no major differences in the results using these alternative methods.

32. The adjusted R-squared is 0.510 for the full-variable model in Table 6-4, as compared to 0.312 for the model without the multi-project strategy variables.

33. In order to obtain these numbers, we used an OLS regression model that includes similar variables as in Table 6-4. In the calculation, we used average numbers for control variables such as new product introduction rate, dummies for regional areas of firms (not individual firms), market coverage, and sales growth change ($t-1$). We assumed, however, the last period for period dummy variables.

Chapter 7. Organizational Requirements for Effective Multi-Project Management

1. Clark and Fujimoto, 1991; Wheelright and Clark, 1992; Ulrich and Eppinger, 1995; and others.

2. Marquis and Straight, 1965; Galbraith, 1974; Davis and Lawrence, 1977; Galbraith and Nathanson, 1978; Allen, Lee, and Tushman, 1980; Katz and Allen, 1985; Allen, 1986; Larson and Gobelli, 1988.

3. Yanagida, 1986.

4. Allen, 1977.

5. Lawrence and Lorsch, 1967.

6. Nobeoka, 1993.

7. See Staudenmayer, 1997, for a discussion of different types of interdependencies and strategies to deal with these.

8. For a more complete discussion, see Cusumano and Selby, 1995, as well as Staudenmayer, 1997.

9. This section is based on Aoshima, 1996.

10. This section relies primarily on Fisher, Jain, and MacDuffie, 1995; Boon, 1992; and Suarez, Cusumano, and Fine, 1996.

11. Boon, 1992, p. 23.

12. Suarez, Cusumano, and Fine, 1996.

13. For a discussion of these modules and the hierarchy in engine design, see Doi, 1992.

14. Suarez, Cusumano, and Fine, 1996.

15. Fisher, Jain, and MacDuffie, 1995, p. 140.

16. Fisher, Jain, and MacDuffie, 1995, pp. 117–118.

Chapter 8. Implications and Lessons for Managers

1. Womack, Jones, and Roos, 1990, p. 256; Womack and Jones, 1996, pp. 22–23.

2. Ikari, 1985.

3. Clark and Fujimoto, 1991.

4. This statement is based on interviews and company visits. At Japanese firms such as Nissan, Mitsubishi, and Mazda, for example, one of the differences with Toyota is that some key functions such as planning, chassis/engine engineering, and cost management are not divided into centers. In this sense, it seems that these firms have been evolving organizationally in the same direction as Toyota, but have adopted only partial or incomplete multi-project organizations.

5. Meyer and Roberts, 1986.

6. See also Nobeoka, 1995.

7. Cusumano, 1985; Clark and Fujimoto, 1991; Cusumano and Takeishi, 1991.

8. Scott, 1994a.

9. Matano and Nobeoka, 1992.

References

Aaker, D. A. (1989). "Managing Assets and Skills: The Key to Sustainable Competitive Advantage," *California Management Review*, 31, 2 (Winter), pp. 91–106.

Abegglen, J., and G. Stalk, Jr. (1985). *Kaisha: The Japanese Corporation*, New York, Basic Books.

Abernathy, W. (1978). *The Productivity Dilemma: Roadblock to Innovation in the Automobile Industry*, Baltimore, Johns Hopkins University Press.

Abernathy, W., and K. Clark (1985). "Innovation: Mapping the Winds of Creative Destruction," *Research Policy*, 14, pp. 3–22.

Abernathy, W., K. Clark, and A. Kantrow (1983). *Industrial Renaissance*, New York, Basic Books.

Abernathy, W., and J. Utterback (1978). "Patterns of Industrial Innovation," *Technology Review*, 80, 7 (June–July), pp. 40–47.

Achilladelis, B. (1993). "The Dynamics of Technological Innovation: The Sector of Antibacterial Medicines," *Research Policy*, 22, pp. 279–308.

Adler, P., H. Riggs, and S. Wheelright (1989). "Product Development Know-How: Trading Tactics for Strategy," *Sloan Management Review*, 30 (Fall), pp. 7–17.

Aizcorbe, A., C. Winston, and A. Friedlaender (1987). "Cost Competitiveness of the U.S. Automobile Industry," from *Blind Intersection: Policy and the Automobile Industry*, edited by C. Winston, Brookings Institution, Washington, D.C.

Allen, T. J., and S. I. Cohen (1969). "Information Flow in R&D Labs," *Administrative Science Quarterly*, 14, pp. 12–19.

Allen, T. J. (1977). *Managing the Flow of Technology*, Cambridge, MIT Press.

Allen, T. J. (1986). "Organizational Structure, Information Technology, and R&D Productivity," *IEEE Transactions on Engineering Management*, EM–33, 4, pp. 212–217.

Allen, T. J., D. Lee, and M. Tushman (1980). "R&D Performance as a Function of Internal Communication, Project Management, and the Nature of the Work," *IEEE Transactions on Engineering Management*, EM-27, 1, pp. 2–12.

Amit, P., and P. J. H. Schoemaker (1993). "Strategic Asset and Organizational Rent," *Strategic Management Journal*, 14 (January), pp. 33–46.

Ansoff, H. I. (1965). *Corporate Strategy*, New York, McGraw-Hill.

Ansoff, H. I., and J. M. Stewart (1967). "Strategies for a Technology-Based Business," *Harvard Business Review*, 45, 6 (November–December), pp. 71–83.

Aoshima, Y. (1996). "Knowledge Transfer Across Generations: The Impact on Product Development Performance in the Automobile Industry," Ph.D. diss., MIT Sloan School of Management, Cambridge, MA.

Arrow, K. J. (1962). "Economic Welfare and the Allocation of Resources to Innovation," in *The Rate and Direction of Inventive Activity*, edited by R. Nelson, University National Bureau Conference Series, 14, New York, Arnold Press, pp. 609–626.

Arrow, K. J. (1974). *The Limits of Organization*, New York, W.W. Norton.

Automobil Revue. Bern, Switzerland, Hallwag Ag., Annual.

Automotive News. Detroit, MI, Crain Communications, Inc., Weekly.

Automotive News, 1997 Market Data Book. Detroit, MI, Crain Communications, Inc., Annual.

Bagozzi, R. (1986). *Principles of Marketing Management*. Chicago, Science Research Associates.

Banbury, M., and W. Mitchell (1995). "The Effect of Introducing Important Incremental Innovations on Market Share and Business Survival," *Strategic Management Journal*, 16 (Summer Special Issue), pp. 161–182.

Bettis, R. A., and M. A. Hitt (1995). "The New Competitive Landscape," *Strategic Management Journal*, 16 (Summer Special Issue), pp. 7–19.

Boon, Jane (1992). "Product Variations, Quality, and Productivity: A Cost-Benefit Analysis," Master's thesis, MIT Department of Mechanical Engineering and Technology and Policy Program, Cambridge, MA.

Bower, J., and T. Hout (1988). "Fast-Cycle Capability for Competitive Power," *Harvard Business Review*, November–December, pp. 110–118.

Brown, Shona. L., and Kathleen M. Eisenhardt (1995). "Product Development: Past Research, Present Findings, and Future Directions," *Academy of Management Review*, 20, 2, pp. 343–378.

Burns, T., and G. M. Stalker (1961). *The Management of Innovation*, New York, The Free Press.

Calabrese, Giuseppe (1994). "Fiat Auto: A Simultaneous Engineering Experience," Instituto de Ricerca sull'Impreso e lo Sviluppo, Consiglio Nazionale della Ricerche, Turino, Italy.

Car & Driver. Diamandis Communications, New York, Monthly.

Car Graphic. Nigensha, Tokyo, Monthly.

Car Styling. Saneisha, Tokyo, Bimonthly.

Cater, D. E., and B. S. Baker (1992). *Concurrent Engineering: The Product Development Environment for the 1990s*, Reading, MA, Addison-Wesley.

Child, J. (1972). "Organization Structure, Environment and Performance: the Role of Strategic Choice," *Sociology*, 6, 1, pp.1–22.

Clark, K. (1989). "Project Scope and Project Performance: The Effect of Parts Strategy and Supplier Involvement on Product Development," *Management Science*, 35, pp. 1247–1263.

Clark, Kim B., W. Bruce Chew, and Takahiro Fujimoto (1987). "Product Development in the World Auto Industry," *Brookings Papers on Economic Activity*, 3, pp. 729–781.

Clark, K., and T. Fujimoto (1991). *Product Development Performance: Strategy, Organization, and Management in the World Auto Industry*, Boston, Harvard Business School Press.

Cohen, H., S. Keller, and D. Streeter (1979). "The Transfer of Technology from Research to Development." *Research Management* (May), pp. 11–16.

Cohen, S., D. J. Teece, L. Tyson, and J. Zysman (1984). *Global Competition: The New*

Reality, Vol. III, Washington D.C., President's Commission on Industrial Competitiveness, Government Printing Office.

Cooper, A. C., and D. Schendel (1976). "Strategic Response to Technological Threats," *Business Horizons*, 19, pp. 61–69.

Cooper, A. C. (1987). "Defining the New Product Strategy," *IEEE Transactions on Engineering Management*, EM–34, 3, pp. 184–193.

Cooper, R. G., and E. J. Kleinschmidt (1987). "New Products: What Separates Winners and Losers?" *Journal of New Product Management*, 4, 3, pp. 169–184.

Cordero, R. (1991). "Managing for Speed to Avoid Product Obsolescence: A Survey of Techniques," *Journal of Product Innovation Management*, 8, pp. 283–294.

Cravens, D. W. (1986). "Strategic Forces Affecting Marketing Strategy," *Business Horizons*, 21, 5, pp. 77–86.

Crawford, C. Merle (1992). "The Hidden Costs of Accelerated Product Development," *Journal of Product Innovation Management*, 9, pp. 188–199.

Cringely, Robert (1993). *Accidental Empires*, New York, Harper Business.

Cusumano, Michael A. (1985). *The Japanese Automobile Industry: Technology and Management at Nissan and Toyota*, Cambridge, Harvard University Press.

Cusumano, Michael A. (1991). *Japan's Software Factories: A Challenge to U.S. Management*, New York, Oxford University Press.

Cusumano, Michael A. (1992). "Shifting Economies: From Craft Production to Flexible Systems and Software Factories," *Research Policy*, 21, 5, pp. 453–480.

Cusumano, Michael A. (1994). "The Limits of Lean," *Sloan Management Review*, 35, 4, Summer 1994, pp. 27–32.

Cusumano, Michael A., and Kentaro Nobeoka (1992). "Strategy, Structure, and Performance in Product Development: Observations from the Auto Industry," *Research Policy*, 21, pp. 265–293.

Cusumano, Michael A., and Richard W. Selby (1995). *Microsoft Secrets*, New York, The Free Press.

Cusumano, Michael A., and Akira Takeishi (1991). "Supplier Relations and Management: A Survey of Japanese, Japanese-Transplant, and U.S. Auto Plants," *Strategic Management Journal*, 12, pp. 563–588.

Daft, R. L. (1982). *Bureaucratic versus Nonbureaucratic Structure and the Process of Innovation and Change*, Greenwich, CT, JAI Press.

Daft, R., and E. Weick (1984). "Toward a Model of Organizations as Interpretation Systems," *Academy of Management Review*, 9, pp. 284–295.

Daft, R. L., and R. H. Lengel (1986). "Organizational Information Requirement, Media Richness, and Structural Design," *Management Science*, 32, 5, pp. 554–571.

Datta, D. K., N. Rajagopalan, and A. M. A. Rasheed (1991). "Diversification and Performance: Critical Review and Future Directions," *Journal of Management Studies*, 28, pp. 529–558.

Davis, S. M., and P. R. Lawrence (1977). *Matrix*, Reading, MA, Addison-Wesley.

Dertouzos, M. L., R. K. Lester, and R. M. Solow (1988). *Made in America*, Cambridge, MA, MIT Press.

Dewar, R., and J. Dutton (1986). "The Adoption of Radical and Incremental Innovations: An Empirical Analysis," *Management Science*, 32, pp. 1422–1433.

Diercks, I., and K. Cool (1989). "Asset Stock Accumulation and Sustainability of Competitive Advantage," *Management Science*, 35, 12, December, pp. 1504–1511.

Doi, Douglas Alan (1992). "Major Automotive Firms' Engine Technology Development (1980–1990), Master's thesis, MIT Sloan School of Management, Cambridge.

Dougherty, D. (1992). "Interpretive Barriers to Successful Product Innovation in Large Firms," *Organization Science*, 3, pp. 179–202.

Dosi, G. (1982). "Technological Paradigms and Technological Trajectories," *Research Policy*, 11, 3, pp. 147–162.

Dosi, G. (1988). "Sources, Procedures, and Microeconomic Effects of Innovation," *Journal of Economic Literature*, 26, pp. 1120–1171.

Duncan, R. B. (1976). "The Ambidextrous Organization: Designing Dual Structures for Innovation," in *The Management of Organization Design: Strategies and Implementation*, edited by I. Duncan and B. Robert, New York, North-Holland.

Ellison, D., K. Clark, T. Fujimoto, and Y. Hyun (1995). "Product Development Performance in the Auto Industry: 1990s Update." Working paper, Harvard Business School and MIT International Motor Vehicle Program, Boston and Cambridge.

Enos, J. L. (1962). *Petroleum Progress and Profits: A History of Process Innovation*, Cambridge, MIT Press.

Eppinger, S., D. Whitney, R. Smith, and D. Gebala (1994). "A Model-Based Method for Organizing Tasks in Product Development," *Research in Engineering Design*, 6, pp. 1–13.

Ettlie, J., W. Bridges, and R. O'Keefe (1984). "Organization Strategy and Structural Differences for Radical Versus Incremental Innovation," *Management Science*, 30, pp. 682–695.

Fisher, Marshall, Anjani Jain, and John Paul MacDuffie (1995). "Strategies for Product Variety," in *Redesigning the Firm*, edited by E. Bowman and B. Kogut, New York, Oxford University Press.

Fourin jidosha chosa geppo [Fourin's Monthly Report on the Global Automotive Industry], Monthly.

Fujimoto, Takahiro (1997a). "Capability Building and Over-Adaptation—A Case of 'Fat Design' in the Japanese Auto Industry," *Actes du GERPISA*, 19 (February), pp. 9–23.

Fujimoto, Takahiro (1997b). "Shortening Lead Time through Early Problem Solving—A New Round of Capability-Building Competition in the Auto Industry," University of Tokyo, Faculty of Economics, Research Institute for the Japanese Economy, Discussion Paper 97–F–12 (March).

Fujimoto, Takahiro, Kim B. Clark, and Yaichi Aoshima (1992). "Managing the Product Line: A Case of the Automobile Industry," working paper 92–067, Harvard Business School, Boston.

Fujimoto, T., and A. Sheriff (1989). "Consistent Patterns in Automotive Product Strategy, Product Development, and Manufacturing Performance—Road Map for the 1990s," working paper, MIT International Motor Vehicle Program, International Policy Forum, Cambridge.

Fujimoto, T., and A. Takeishi (1994). *Jidosha sangyo 21-seiki heno senario* [Scenario for the automotive industry toward the 21st century], Tokyo, Seisansei Shuppan.

Galbraith, J. R. (1974). "Organization Design: An Information Processing View," *Interfaces*, 4 (May), pp. 28–36.

Galbraith, J., and D. A. Nathanson (1978). *Strategy Implementation: The Role of Structure and Process*, St. Paul, MN, West Publishing Co.

Garvin, D. (1993). "Building a Learning Organization," *Harvard Business Review*, 71, 4, pp. 78–92.

Garud, R., and A. Kumaraswamy (1995). "Technological and Organizational Designs for Economies of Substitution," *Strategic Management Journal,* 16 (Summer Special Issue), pp. 93–109.

Garud, R., and P. R. Nayyar (1994). "Transformative Capacity: Continual Structuring by Intertemporal Technology Transfer," *Strategic Management Journal,* 15, pp. 365–385.

Ghemawat, P. (1986). "Sustainable Advantage," *Harvard Business Review,* 64, 5 (September–October), pp. 53–58.

Gold, Bella (1987). "Approaches to Accelerating Product and Process Development," *Journal of Product Innovation Management,* 4, 8, pp. 1–8.

Goldhar, J., and M. Jelinek (1983). "Plan for Economies of Scope," *Harvard Business Review,* 61, 6, pp. 141–148.

Gomory, R. E. (1989). "Moving IBM's Technology from Research to Development." *Research/Technology Management,* 32, 6 (November–December), pp. 27–32.

Grant, R. M. (1991). "The Resource-Based Theory of Competitive Advantage: Implications for Strategy Formulation," *California Management Review,* 33, 3 (Spring), pp. 114–135.

Gupta, Ashok K., and David L. Wilemon (1990). "Accelerating the Development of Technology-Based New Products," *California Management Review,* 32, 2 (Winter), pp. 24–44.

Hall, B. (1995). *Times Series Processor, Version 4.3, User's Guide,* Palo Alto, CA, TSP International.

Hartigan, J. A., and M. A. Wong (1979). "A K-Means Cluster Algorithm: Algorithm AS 136," *Applied Statistics,* 28, pp. 126–130.

Hartley, J. R. (1992). *Concurrent Engineering,* Cambridge, MA, Productivity Press.

Hayes, R. H., and G. P. Pisano (1994). "Beyond World Class Manufacturing: The New Manufacturing Strategy," *Harvard Business Review,* 71, 2, pp. 77–87.

Hayes, Robert H., Steven C. Wheelwright, and Kim B. Clark (1988). *Dynamic Manufacturing,* New York, The Free Press.

Henderson, Rebecca M., and Kim B. Clark (1990). "Architectural Innovation: The Reconfiguration of Existing Product Technologies and the Failure of Established Firms," *Administrative Science Quarterly,* 35, 1, pp. 9–30.

Hollander, S. (1965). *The Sources of Increased Efficiency: A Study of du Pont Rayon Plants,* Cambridge, MIT Press.

Iansiti, Marco, and Kim B. Clark (1994). "Integration and Dynamic Capability: Evidence from Product Development in Automobiles and Mainframe Computers," *Industrial and Corporate Change,* 3, 3, pp. 557–605.

Iansiti, Marco (1995). "Technology Integration: Managing Technological Evolution in a Complex Environment," *Research Policy,* 24, pp. 521–542.

Ikari, Yoshiro (1985). *Toyota tai Nissan: shinsha kaihatsu no saizensen* [Toyota versus Nissan: the front line of new car development], Tokyo, Diamond.

Imai, K., I. Nonaka, and H. Takeuchi (1985). "Managing the New Product Development Process: How Japanese Learn and Unlearn," in *The Uneasy Alliance: Managing the Productivity-Technology Dilemma,* edited by K. B. Clark et al., Boston, Harvard Business School Press.

IRC (1992). *Toyota Jidosha Gurupu no jittai 92 nenban* [Report on Toyota Motor Group '92], IRC, Nagoya, Japan.

IRC (1994a). *Toyota Jidosha Gurupu no jittai 94 nenban* [Report on Toyota Motor Group '94], IRC, Nagoya, Japan.

IRC (1994b). *Nissan Gurupu no jittai 94 nenban* [Report on Nissan Group '94], IRC, Nagoya, Japan.

IRC (1995a). *Mazda Gurupu no jittai 95 nenban* [Report on Mazda Group '95], IRC, Nagoya, Japan.

IRC (1995b). *Mitsubishi Jidosha Gurupu no jittai 95 nenban* [Report on Mitsubishi Motor Group '95], IRC, Nagoya, Japan.

IRC (1995c). *Honda Giken-Honda Gijutsu Kenkyusho Gurupu no jittai 95 nenban* [Report on Honda Motor-Honda R&D Group '95], IRC, Nagoya, Japan.

Itami, H. (1987). *Mobilizing Invisible Assets*, Cambridge, Harvard University Press.

Itami, H., and T. Numagami (1992). "Dynamic Interaction between Strategy and Technology," *Strategic Management Journal*, 13, pp. 119–135.

Jidosha nenkan 1996 [Automotive yearbook 1996], Tokyo, Nikkan Jidosha Shinbunsha, 1996.

Johnson, S., and C. Jones (1957). "How to Organize for New Products," *Harvard Business Review*, May–June, pp. 49–62.

Kagono, Tadao (1988). *Kigyo no paradaimu henkan* [Paradigm change at companies], Tokyo, Kodansha Gakujutsu Bunko.

Kamimoto, H., and H. Hashimoto (1995). "Richo Gazo Shisutemu Jigyobu no TP manejimento" [TP Management at the Richo Picture System Division], *TP Manejimento no Gijutsu Jireishu 5* [TP Management Technology Case Studies 5], Nihon Noritsu Kyokai, pp. 60–73.

Katz, R., and T. J. Allen (1985). "Project Performance and the Locus of Influence in the R&D Matrix," *Academy of Management Journal*, 28, 1, pp. 67–87.

Kekre, S., and K. Srinivasan (1990). "Broader Product Line: A Necessity to Achieve Success," *Management Science*, 36, pp. 1216–1231.

Kerin, R. A., R. P. Varadarajan, and R. Peterson (1992). "First-Mover Advantages: A Synthesis, Conceptual Framework, and Research Propositions," *Journal of Marketing*, 53, pp. 80–91.

Kleinschmidt, E., and R. Cooper (1991). "The Impact of Product Innovativeness on Performance," *Journal of Product Innovation Management*, 8, pp. 240–251.

Kogut, B., and U. Zander (1992). "Knowledge of the Firm, Combinative Capability, and the Replication of Technology," *Organization Science*, 3, 1, pp. 383–397.

Konno, N., and I. Nonaka (1995). *Chiryoku keiei* [Management by knowledge power], Tokyo, Nihonkeizai Shinbunsha.

Kotler, P. (1986). *Principles of Marketing*, Englewood Cliffs, NJ, Prentice Hall.

Kotler, P. (1989). "From Mass Marketing to Mass Customization," *Planning Review*, 17, pp. 10–13.

Kotha, S. (1995). "Mass Customization: Implementing the Emerging Paradigm for Competitive Advantage," *Strategic Management Journal*, 16 (Summer Special Issue), pp. 21–42.

Krafcik, John (1988). "Triumph of the Lean Production System," *Sloan Management Review*, 30, 1 (Fall), pp. 41–52.

Kusunoki, K., I. Nonaka, and A. Nagata (1995). "Nihonkigyo no seihin kaihatsu ni okeru soshiki noryoku" [Organizational capabilities of Japanese firms in product development], *Soshiki kagaku* [Organizational science], 29, 1, pp. 92–108.

Kvanli, A., C. S. Guynes, R. Pavur (1986). *Introduction to Business Statistics*, St. Paul, MN, West Publishing Company.

Laage-Hellman, Jens (1996). "NedCar: A Joint Venture Between Volvo Car, Mitsubishi Motors, and the Dutch State," in *International Technology Cooperation:*

The Case of Sweden-Japan. Working draft, Chalmers Institute of Technology, Gothenburg, Sweden (September).

Larson, E. W., and D. H. Gobeli (1988). "Organizing for Product Development Projects," *Journal of Product Innovation Management*, 5, pp. 180–190.

Lawrence, P. R., and J. W. Lorsch (1967). *Organization and Environments: Managing Differentiation and Integration*, Homewood, IL, Irwin.

Leonard-Barton, D. (1988). "Implementation as Mutual Adaptation of Technology and Organization," *Research Policy*, 17, pp. 251–267.

Leonard-Barton, D., and D. K. Sinha (1991). "Exploring Development-User Interaction in Internal Technology Transfer." Working paper 91–029, Boston, Harvard Business School.

Leonard-Barton, D. (1992). "Core Capabilities and Core Rigidities: A Paradox in Managing New Product Development," *Strategic Management Journal*, 13, pp. 111–125.

Lieberman, M., and D. Montgomery (1988). "First Mover Advantage," *Strategic Management Journal*, 9 (Summer Special Issue), pp. 41–58.

Lind, M. R., and R. W. Znud (1991). "The Influence of a Convergence in Understanding between Technology Providers and Users on Information Technology Innovativeness," *Organization Science*, 2, pp. 195–217.

McDonough III, Edward F., and Gloria Barczak (1991). "Speeding Up New Product Development: The Effects of Leadership Style and Source of Technology," *Journal of Product Innovation Management*, 8, pp. 203–211.

Maidique, M. A. (1984). "A Study of Success and Failure in Product Innovation: The Case of the U.S. Electronics Industry," *IEEE Transactions on Engineering Management*, EM–31, 4, pp. 192–203.

Mansfield, E. (1985). "How Rapidly Do New Industrial Technologies Leak Out?" *The Journal of Industrial Economics*, 34, pp. 217–223.

Markides, C., and P. Williamson (1994). "Related Diversification, Core Competencies and Corporate Performance," *Strategic Management Journal*, 15 (Summer Special Issue), pp. 149–165.

Markides, C., and P. Williamson (1996). "Corporate Diversification and Organizational Structure: A Resource-Based View," *Strategic Management Journal*, 15 (Summer Special Issue), pp. 149–165.

Marquis, D. G., and D. L. Straight (1965). "Organizational Factors in Project Performance." Working paper, Cambridge, MIT Sloan School of Management.

Matano, T., and K. Nobeoka (1992). "The Design Strategy Behind the Mazda Miata," *Journal of Business Strategy*, 13, p. 35.

Meyer, M., and A. Lehnerd (1997). *The Power of Product Platforms*, New York, Free Press.

Meyer, M., and E. Roberts (1986). "New Product Strategy in Small Technology-Based Firms: A Pilot Study," *Management Science*, 32, pp. 806–821.

Meyer, M., and J. Utterback (1993). "The Product Family and the Dynamics of Core Capability," *Sloan Management Review*, 34 (Spring), pp. 29–47.

Midler, Christophe (1995). "Organisational Innovation in Project Management: The Renault Twingo Case," in Lars Erik Andreasen et al., *Europe's Next Step: Organisational Innovation, Competition, and Employment*, London, Frank Cass.

Miles, R. E., and C. C. Snow (1994). *Fit, Failure & The Hall of Fame*, New York, The Free Press.

Miller, A. (1988). "A Taxonomy of Technological Settings, with Related Strategies and Performance Levels," *Strategic Management Journal*, 9, pp. 239–254.

Moenaert, R. K., D. Deschoolmeester, A. D. Meyer, and W. E. Souder (1992). "Information Styles of Marketing and R&D Personnel During Technological Product Innovation," *R&D Management*, 22, pp. 21–39.

Motor Trend, Petersen Publishing Company, Los Angeles, Monthly.

Motor Vehicle Statistics of Major Countries. Japan Automobile Manufacturers Association, Tokyo, Annual.

Myers, S., and D. Marquis (1969). *Successful Industrial Innovation*, National Science Foundation, Washington, D.C.

NAVI, Nigensha, Tokyo, Monthly.

Nelson, R., and S. Winter (1982). *An Evolutionary Theory of Economic Change*, Cambridge, Harvard University Press.

New York Times, daily.

Nihon keizai shimbun [Japan economic newspaper], daily.

Nobeoka, K. (1993). "Multi-Project Management: Strategy and Organization in Automobile Product Development," Ph.D. diss. MIT Sloan School of Management, Cambridge.

Nobeoka, K. (1995). "Inter-Project Learning in New Product Development," *Academy of Management Best Papers Proceedings '95*, pp. 432–436.

Nobeoka, Kentaro (1996). *Maruchi-purojiekuto senryaku: posuto-riin no seihin kaihatsu manejimento* [Multi-project strategies: post-lean product development management], Tokyo, Yuhikaku.

Nobeoka, K., and M. Cusumano (1995). "Multi-Project Strategy, Design Transfer, and Project Performance: A Survey of Automobile Development Projects in the U.S. and Japan," *IEEE Transactions on Engineering Management*, 42, 4 (November), pp. 397–409.

Nobeoka, Kentaro, and Michael A. Cusumano (1997). "Multi-Project Strategy and Sales Growth: The Benefits of Rapid Design Transfer in New Product Development," *Strategic Management Journal*, 18, 3, pp. 169–186.

Nonaka, I. (1990). *Chishiki sozo no keiei* [Management by knowledge creation], Tokyo, Nihonkeizai Shinbunsha.

Nonaka, Ikujiro, and Hirotaka Takeuchi (1995). *The Knowledge Creating Company*, New York, Oxford University Press.

Normann, R. (1971). "Organizational Innovativeness: Product Variation and Reorientation," *Administrative Science Quarterly*, 16, pp. 203–215.

Pavitt, K. (1990). "What We Know About the Strategic Management of Technology," *California Management Journal*, 32, pp. 17–26.

Penrose, E.T. (1959). *The Theory of the Growth of the Firm*, New York, Basil Blackwell.

Perrow, C. (1967). "A Framework for Comparative Organizational Analysis," *American Sociological Review*, 32, 2 (April), pp. 194–208.

Peters, T. (1992). *Liberation Management*, New York, Alfred A. Knopf.

Pine, J. (1993). *Mass Customization: The New Frontier in Business Competition*, Harvard Business School Press, Boston.

Porter, M. E. (1980). *Competitive Strategy*, New York, Free Press.

Porter, M. E. (1985). *Competitive Advantage*, New York, Free Press.

Prahalad, C., and G. Hamel (1990). "The Core Competence of the Corporation," *Harvard Business Review*, 68, 3, pp. 79–91.

Prahalad, C. K., and G. Hamel (1994). *Competing for the Future*, Boston, Harvard Business School Press.

Quinn, J. B., and J. A. Mueller (1982). "Transferring Research Results to Operations," in *Readings in the Management of Innovation*, edited by M. L. Tushman and W. L. Moore, Cambridge, MA, Ballinger, 1982, pp. 60–83.

Reed, R., and R. J. DeFilippi (1990). "Causal Ambiguity, Barriers to Imitation, and Sustainable Competitive Advantage," *Academy of Management Review*, January, pp. 88–102.

Reinganum, J. F. (1983). "Innovation and Industry Evolution," *Quarterly Journal of Economics*, 100, 1, pp. 81–99.

Roberts, E. B. (1988). "What We've Learned: Managing Invention and Innovation," *Research Technology Management*, 31, 1, pp. 11–29.

Roberts, E. B., and M. H. Meyer (1991). "Product Strategy and Corporate Success," *Engineering Management Review*, 19, 1 (Spring), pp. 4–18.

Rosenberg, Nathan (1982). *Inside the Black Box: Technology and Economics*, Cambridge, Cambridge University Press.

Rosenbloom, R., and M. Cusumano (1987). "Technological Pioneering: The Birth of the VCR Industry," *California Management Review*, 24, 4 (Summer), pp. 51–76.

Rothwell, R., C. Freeman, A. Horlsey, V. Jervis, A. Robertson, and J. Townsend (1974). "SAPPHO Updated—Project SAPPHO Phase II," *Research Policy*, 3, pp. 258–291.

Rothwell, R. (1992). "Successful Industrial Innovation: Critical Factors for the 1990s," *R&D Management*, 22, 3, pp. 221–239.

Rousenau, M. D. (1988). "Speeding Your New Product to Market," *Journal of Consumer Marketing*, 5, 2, pp. 27–40.

Rumelt, R. P. (1974). *Strategy, Structure and Economic Performance*, Cambridge, Harvard University Press.

Sahal, D. (1985). "Technological Guideposts and Innovation Avenues," *Research Policy*, 14, 2, pp. 61–82.

Sakiya, Tetsuo (1982). *Honda Motor: The Men, the Management, the Machines*, Tokyo, Kodansha International.

Sanchez, R. (1995). "Strategic Flexibility in Product Competition," *Strategic Management Journal*, 16 (Summer Special Issue), pp. 135–159.

Sanderson, Susan, and Mustafa Uzumeri (1996). *Innovation Imperative*. Burr Ridge, IL, Irwin.

Schonberger, Richard (1982). *Japanese Manufacturing Techniques*, New York, Free Press.

Scott, G. (1994a). "IMVP New Product Development Series: The Chrysler Corporation." Working paper, International Motor Vehicle Program, Cambridge, MIT.

Scott, G. (1994b). "IMVP New Product Development Series: The Ford Motor Company." Working paper, International Motor Vehicle Program, Cambridge, MIT.

Scott, G. (1995). "IMVP New Product Development Series: The General Motors Corporation." Working paper, International Motor Vehicle Program, Cambridge, MIT.

Selznick, P. (1957). *Leadership in Administration*, New York, Harper & Row.

Sheriff, Antony (1988). "Product Development in the Automobile Industry: Corporate Strategies and Project Performance," Master's thesis, MIT Sloan School of Management, Cambridge.

Shintaku, J. (1994). *Nihon kigyo no kyoso senryaku* [The competitive strategy of Japanese firms], Tokyo, Yuhikaku.

Shiosawa, Shigeru (1987). *Toyota no shusa purojekuto chiimu* [The chief engineer: Toyota project teams], Tokyo, Kodansha.

Smith, P. G., and D. G. Reinertsen (1991). *Developing Products in Half the Time*, New York, Van Nostrand Reinhold.

Song, X. M., and M. E. Parry (1992). "The R&D-Marketing Interface in Japanese High-Technology Firms," *Journal of Product Innovation Management*, 9, pp. 91–112.

Stalk, G., and T. Hout (1990). *Competing Against Time*, New York, The Free Press.

Staudenmayer, Nancy (1997). "Managing Interdependencies in Large-Scale Software Development." Ph.D. diss., MIT Sloan School of Management, Cambridge.

Suarez, Fernando F., Michael A. Cusumano, and Charles H. Fine (1996). "An Empirical Study of Manufacturing Flexibility in Printed-Circuit Board Assembly," *Operations Research*, 44, 1 (January–February), pp. 223–240.

SYSTAT (1992). *SYSTAT Statistics, Version 5.2 Edition*, Evanston, IL, SYSTAT, Inc.

Tagliabue, John (1996). "A European Model-T for the '90s," *The New York Times*, 19 July 1996, p. D1.

Tallman, S., and J. Li (1996). "Effects of International Diversity and Product Diversity on the Performance of Multinational Firms," *Academy of Management Journal*, 39, 1, pp. 179–196.

Teece, D. (1980). "Economies of Scope and the Scope of the Enterprise," *Journal of Economic Behavior and Organization*, 1, pp. 223–247.

Teece, D. J., G. Pisano, and A. Shuen (1994). "Dynamic Capabilities and Strategic Management." Working paper, Consortium on Competitiveness and Cooperation at University of California, Berkeley.

Thompson, J. (1967). *Organizations in Action*, New York, McGraw-Hill.

Toyota Motor Corporation, "Outline of Toyota Technical Center," Toyoda, Japan. Various years.

Tushman, M. L. (1978). "Technical Communication in R&D Laboratories: The Impact of Project Work Characteristics," *Academy of Management Journal*, 21, 4, pp. 624–645.

Tushman, M. L., and P. Anderson (1986). "Technological Discontinuities and Organizational Environments," *Administrative Science Quarterly*, 31, pp. 439–465.

Tushman, M. L., and D. Nadler (1986). "Organizing for Innovation," *California Management Review*, 28, 3 (Spring), pp. 74–92.

Tyre, M. J. (1991). "Managing the Introduction of New Process Technology: International Differences in a Multi-Plant Network," *Research Policy*, 22, pp. 57–76.

Ulrich, Karl, and Steven Eppinger (1995). *Product Design and Development*, New York, McGraw-Hill.

USA Today. Daily.

Utterback, J. M., and W. J. Abernathy (1975). "A Dynamic Model of Product and Process Innovation," *Omega*, 3, 6, pp. 639–656.

Utterback, J. M., and F. Suarez (1993). "Innovation, Competition, and Industry Structure," *Research Policy*, 22, pp. 1–21.

Vincenti, W. G. (1994). "Variation-Selection in the Innovation of the Retractable Airplane Landing Gear: The Northrup 'Anamoly,'" *Research Policy*, 23, pp. 575–582.

von Braun, C. (1991). "The Acceleration Trap in the Real World," *Sloan Management Review*, 32 (Summer), pp. 43–52.

von Hippel, Eric (1990). "Sticky Information and the Locus of Problem Solving: Implications for Innovation," *Management Science*, 36, 4, pp. 429–439.

Wernerfelt, B. (1984). "A Resource-Based View of the Firm," *Strategic Management Journal*, 5, pp. 171–180.

Wheelwright, S., and E. Sasser (1989). "The New Product Development Map," *Harvard Business Review*, May–June, pp. 112–125.

Wheelwright, S., and K. Clark (1992). *Revolutionizing Product Development*, New York, The Free Press.

Wheelwright, S. C., and K. B. Clark (1995). *Leading Product Development*, New York, The Free Press.

White, H. (1980). "A Heteroskedasticity-Consistent Covariance Matrix Estimator and a Direct Test for Heteroskedasticity," *Econometrica*, 48, pp. 817–838.

Winter, S. (1987). "Knowledge and Competence as Strategic Assets," in *The Competitive Challenge: Strategies for Industrial Innovation and Renewal*, edited by D. J. Teece, Cambridge, MA, Ballinger, pp. 159–184.

Womack, J., and D. Jones (1996). *Lean Thinking*, New York, Simon & Schuster.

Womack, J., D. Jones, and D. Roos (1990). *The Machine That Changed the World*, Rawson Associates, New York.

Yanagida, K. (1986). *Katsuryoku no kozo kaihatsuhen* [Structure of dynamics in the case of product development], Tokyo, Kodansha.

Yoshihara, H. (1986). *Senryakuteki kigyo kakushin* [Strategic corporate innovation], Tokyo, Toyo Keizai Shinposha.

Zirger, B., and M. Maidique (1990). "A Model of New Product Development: An Empirical Test," *Management Science*, 36, pp. 867–883.

Index

Italic page numbers refer to illustrations/tables

Ansoff, H. I., 102
Aoshima, Yaichi, 175–176
Architectural innovation, 105

BMW, 14
  matrix organization at, 57–58

Center organizations. *See* Development
  center organizations
Central Research & Development Labo-
  ratories, Inc., 40
Chrysler Corp.
  Aries/Reliant, 14, 146
  brands, 109
  component sharing, 77
  Concord, 76
  Dynasty, 147
  Eagle Vision, 77
  Intrepid, 76
  K-cars, 14, 146–147
  Lancer/LeBaron, 147
  lessons from 185–186
  LH, 77, 195
  management structure, 75–76
  Mitsubishi and, 68
  Neon, 77, 195
  New Yorker, 77, 147
  product development at, *12*, 13, 14
  product/platform team organization
    at, 75–78, *76*
  Shadow/Sundance, 147
  Tech Clubs, 77
Chrysler Technology Center (CTC), 77
Clark, Kim B., 4, 140, 165
Communication and coordination of
  projects, 164–168, *166*, *168*
Concurrent technology transfer, *10*, 11
  See also Performance (company);
    Performance (project)
  at Honda, 14

at Mitsubishi, 66
  reasons for, 189–193
Core competence, 17
Cross-functional versus strong managers, 4–5, 158

Daihatsu
  Move (Mira), 108
  Pizer (Charade), 108
Design modification, *10*, 11–12
  See also Performance (company);
    Performance (project)
Development center organizations
  See also Semi-center organizations
  defined, 3, *53*, 54
  examples of, 54
  at Ford, 95–98, *96*
Development centers at Toyota
  benefits of, 42–48
  center 4, role of, 38–40, *39*
  center heads, roles of, 35–36, 43–44
  Center Management Meeting, 43
  centers, role of, 45
  chief engineers, hierarchical organi-
    zation of, 37–38, *37*
  comparison of old/new body engi-
    neering division, *32*
  competition between centers, 47–48
  component sharing, 46–47
  cost management, 45–46
  creation of, 29–31, *30*
  cross-area system project, 39
  functional engineering divisions, re-
    duction of, 31–34
  functional managers, reductions of
    projects for, 34–35
  performance improvements as a re-
    sult of, 44–45, *44*, 220n.11
  planning divisions in each center,
    36–37

Development centers at Toyota *(Cont.)*
  problems with, 48–49
Differentiated matrix, 52, 169–173, *170*
  at Mitsubishi, 66, *67*
  at Renault, 60

Engineering hours. *See* Lead times and
    engineering hours
Engineers
  coordination of, 173–175, *174*
  information/knowledge transfer be-
    tween, problems with, 133–134

Fiat
  Alfa Romeo, 69, *71*, 108, 109
  brands, 108, 109
  component sharing, 73–74
  functions outside the platform teams,
    71–72
  Lancia, 69, *71*, 108, 109
  management structure, 69–70, 72–73
  matrix organization at, 57, 68–74,
    70, 71
  platform teams, 69, *70, 71*
  product planning, 73
  quality teams, 73
  simultaneous engineering (SE)
    teams, 72
  Ulysse, 111
Ford Motor Co.
  brands, 109
  component sharing, 97
  Contour, 97, 111
  development center organization at,
    95–98, *96*
  Escort, 111
  global platform integration, 97
  international platform sharing,
    110–111
  Mercury Cougar, 97
  Mercury Mystique, 97, 111
  Mercury Topaz, 97, 110
  Mondeo, 97, 111
  Probe, 111
  Sierra, 97, 110
  Tempo, 97, 110
  Thunderbird, 97
Ford 2000, 95
Fujimoto, Takahiro, 4, 140, 165
Functional engineering divisions at Toy-
    ota, reduction of, 31–34
Functional management
  comparison with other strategies, *16*

at Toyota, reductions of projects for,
    34–35
  versus project-centered, 158–161
Future Project 21 (FP21), 21

General Motors (GM)
  bill of materials process, 94–95
  brands, 108–109, 110
  component sharing, 90
  international operations, 91, 93, 111
  management structure, 93
  Opel, 91, 111
  Saab, 91
  semi-center organization at, 90–95,
    92
  Technical Center, 91
  Vehicle Development and Technical
    Operations (VDTO) Group, 91,
    93, 94
  Vehicle Launch Center (VLC), 91,
    93–94

Hamel, G., 106
Heavyweight project management sys-
    tem, at Toyota
  chief engineer term replaced shusa,
    21
  competition, impact of, 26–29
  defined, 19
  functional managers, problems for,
    24, 220n.9
  growth of staff, 23, 220nn.7,8
  narrow specialization, problems
    with, 24–25
  organizational problems, 22–26, *22*
  problems with, 20–29
  product teams, problems with, 25
  Research and Advanced Develop-
    ment (RAD) Group, 25–26,
    220n.10
Higashi-Fuji Technical Center, 26,
    220n.10
Honda
  Accord, 80, 108
  Acura Integra, 14, 80
  Civic, 14, 80, 108, 145–146
  component sharing, 80–81
  Concerto, 14, 80, 146
  CR-V, 108
  Domani, 80
  Inspire, 80
  Large Project Leaders (LPLs), 78
  management structure, 78–79

Odyssey, 80, 108
Orthea, 108
product development at, *12*, 13, 14
product/platform team organization
at, 78–81
Representative of Automotive Development (RAD), 79–81
SMX, 80
Stepwagon, 80

Incremental product development, radical versus, 103–106
Information/knowledge transfer
between engineers, problems with, 133–134
mechanisms, 175–177

Johnson, S., 102
Jones, C., 102
Jones, D., 4
Just-in-time (JIT) technologies, 19

Kinbara, Yoshiro, 21
Krafcik, John, 4
Kume, Yutaka, 86

Lead times and engineering hours
average lead times, *119*
comparison between Japan, U.S., and Europe, 5–7, *5*
definitions and measurements, 201–202
performance and, 116–118, 120–126, *121, 124, 125*
regression analysis of, 123, *124, 125*, 222nn.7,8
Lean
use of term, 4
versus single product development, 4–7, *5*
Lean Thinking (Womack and Jones), 4, 183

Machine That Changed the World, The (Womack, Jones, and Roos), 4, 183
Managers
communication and coordination by, 164–168, *166, 168*
cross-functional versus strong, 4–5, 158
lessons for, from Toyota, 184–189
Market share and sales growth *See* Performance, company

Mass customization, 17
Matrix organizations
at BMW, 57–58
defined, 52–53, *53*
differentiated, 52, 60, 66, 169–173, *170*
examples of, 53
at Fiat, 57, 68–74, *70, 71*
at Mercedes, 57–58
at Mitsubishi, 57, 63–68, *64*
multi-project management and, 57–74, 168–173, *170, 174*
at Renault, 57, 58–63, *58*
at Volkswagen-Audi, 57–58
at Volvo, 57–58
Mazda
Capella, 111
Carrol, 111
Demio (Revue), 108
development centers at, 82
Familia, 111
Miata, 196
semi-center organization at, 82–86, *83*
Mercedes, 14
matrix organization at, 57–58
Microsoft Corp., 104, 171–173
Mitsubishi
Charisma, 68, 111
Colt (Mirage), 65
concurrent technology transfer at, 66
development with other firms, 68
Diamante, 66
differentiated matrix at, 66, *67*
dual responsibility system, 67
Eclipse, 66
Galant, 66
GTO, 66
management structure, 64–65
matrix organization at, 57, 63–68, *64*
MPV, 68
platform sharing, 65–66
product planning, 65–66
Space Runner, 65
Multi-project/product development
applicability of, 193–197, *194*
comparison with other strategies, *16*
defined, 56
evolutionary pattern to, *185*
key factors to consider, 2–4
matrix organizations and, 57–74, 168–173, *170, 174*
at multi-firms, 16–17

Multi-project/product development
(Cont.)
product/platform team organizations
and, 74–81
purpose of, 2
semi-center organizations and,
82–95
shift from single product development to, 7–9
similar ideas, 17
simple model of, *2*
strategies and organizations for,
9–17, *10, 12, 16*
Multi-project strategy maps
applications, 112
common platforms, role of, 107
examples, 106–107
impact of recreational vehicle market expansion, 107–108
international platform sharing,
110–111
intra-company platform standardization, 108–110
platform sharing through alliances,
111
purpose of, 106
strategic portfolio planning, 114
timing of technology leveraging,
112–113
typology, 112–113

Nakamura, Kenya, 20
NedCar (Netherlands Car), 68
New design, 10–11, *10*
See also Performance (company);
Performance (project)
Renault as an example, 14
New product introduction rate, 138
Nissan
Be-1, 195
Bluebird, 87, 90
development centers (kaihatsu
honbu) at, 87
Figaro, 195
Laurel/Skyline, 108
management structure, 86–87, 89
Maxima, 87
Pulsar, 87, 108
Rasheen, 108
semi-center organization at, 86–90,
88
Sentra, 14, 87, 90, 108
Stagea, 108

240SX, 87
300ZX, 87
Nomura Research Institute, 21

Organizational requirements
communication and coordination of
projects, 164–168, *166, 168*
coordination of engineers, 173–175,
174
cross-functional versus strong management, 4–5, 158
functional versus project-centered,
158–161
information/knowledge transfer
mechanisms, 175–177
matrix management of multiple projects, 168–173, *170, 174*
for multiple projects, 161–164, *164, 165*
product variations, controlling,
177–180, *179*

Performance, concurrent technology
transfer and statistics on, 15, *15*
Performance (company)
analysis and key findings, 149–156,
150, 153, 154, 155
data used to study, 141–144,
223nn.14–16, 224nn.17–21
market share and sales growth calculations, 142–143, 224n.17
new products defined and introduction rates calculated, 143,
224n.18
project content and, 205
relationship of product introductions
to, 138–141
strategy types used, 143–144,
224nn.19–21
time to market issues, 140–141
Performance (company), concurrent
technology transfer and
best strategy for, 137–138, 155
cluster analysis, 149–152, *150*
descriptive data/correlation matrix,
152, *153*, 225n.30
identification of, 146
new products introduced, 148, *148*
regression results, 153, *154*
225n.31
relative sales growth, 155, *155*,
225n.33
Performance (company), design modification and

cluster analysis, 148–152, *149*
descriptive data/correlation matrix, 152, *153*, 225n.30
identification of, 146–147
new products introduced, 147–148, *148*
regression results, 153–*154*, 225n.31
relative sales growth, 155, *155*, 225n.33
Performance (company), new design and
  cluster analysis, 149–152, *150*
  descriptive data/correlation matrix, 152,153, *152*, 225n.30
  identification of, 145–146
  new products introduced, 148, *148*
  regression results, 153, *154* 225n.31
  relative sales growth, 155, *155*, 223n.33
Performance (company), sequential technology transfer and
  cluster analysis, 149–152, *150*
  descriptive data/correlation matrix, 152, *153*, 225n.30
  identification of, 146–147
  new products introduced, 148, *148*
  regression results, 153, *154*, 225n.31
  relative sales growth, 155, *155*, 225n.33
Performance (project)
  advance planning for transfers, 130–131
  analysis and key findings, 120–129, *121*, *124*, *125*, *128*
  comparison of strategic types, 127–129, *128*
  complexity issues, impact of, 126–127
  data used to study, 118–120
  existing designs versus new designs, 132–134
  general managers, role of, 134–135
  information/knowledge transfer between engineers, problems with, 133–134
  lead time and engineering hours, 116–118, 120–126, *121*, *124*, *125*
  mutual adjustments, task sharing, and joint design, 131–132, *132*
  regression analysis of lead time and engineering hours, 123, *124*, *125*,

222nn.7,8
reusing designs/components, problems with, 116–117
Performance (project), concurrent technology transfer and
  average lead times, *119*
  best strategy for, 115, *117*, 129–135
  project content and performance data, *121*, 205
  project priorities, *128*
Performance (project), design modification and
  average lead times, *119*
  project content and performance data, *121*, 205
  project priorities, *128*
Performance (project), new design and
  average lead times, *119*
  project content and performance data, *121*, 205
  project priorities, *128*
Performance (project), sequential technology transfer and
  average lead times, *119*
  project content and performance data, *121*, 205
  project priorities, *128*
Peugeot
  -Citroen, 62, 69, 108, 109
  806, 111
Platform design, 199–200
  See also Multi-project strategy maps
Platform management/teams, 17, 52
  at Chrysler, 75–78, *76*
  at Fiat, 69–74, *70*, *71*
Porsche, 14
Porter, M. E., 102
Power of Product Platforms, The, 107
Prahalad, C. K., 106
Product development organizations
  See also under type of
  company size and type of, 55–56, *55*
  development center organizations, *53*, 54
  matrix organizations, 52–53, *53*
  product/platform team organizations, 53–54, *53*
  semi-center organizations, *53*, 54
  types of, 53
Product Development Performance (Clark and Fujimoto), 4
Product development strategies
  See also Multi-project strategy maps

Product development strategies *(Cont.)*
  categories of, 102–103
  leaders, 102
  low-cost/follower approach, 102
  radical versus incremental, 103–106
  rapid followers, 102
  technological/market newness, 102
Product families, 17
Product/platform team organizations
  at Chrysler, 75–78, *76*
  defined, 53–54, *53*, 74–75
  examples of, 54
  at Honda, 78–81
  multi-project management and,
    74–81
Project-centered organization, func-
    tional versus, 158–161
Project managers
  cross-functional versus strong, 4–5,
    158
  communication and coordination by,
    164–168, *166*, *168*
PSA Group, 108, 109, 111

Radical versus incremental product de-
    velopment, 103–106
Renault
  Clio, 60
  company size and competitive strat-
    egy, problem with, 62–63
  complexity of projects, problem
    with, 62
  differentiated matrix at, 60
  Director of Product Planning and
    Projects (DPPP), 59
  Groupe Delta, 61
  layout section, 60
  management structure, 59–60
  matrix organization at, 57, 58–63, *58*
  Megane project, 62
  product development at, *12*, 13, 14
  Twingo project, 60–61
Research and Advanced Development
    (RAD) Group, 25–26, 29, 220n.10
Reuse technologies, 17
Roos, D., 4

Sales growth. *See* Performance, com-
    pany
Semi-center organizations
  defined, *53*, 54
  examples of, 54
  at General Motors, 90–95, *92*

  at Mazda, 82–86, *83*
  multi-project management and,
    82–95
  at Nissan, 86–90, *88*
Sequential technology transfer, *10*, 11,
    219n.8
  See also Performance (company);
    Performance (project)
  at Chrysler, 14, 76
Shusa system. *See* Heavyweight project
    management system
Single product/project development
  comparison with other strategies, *16*
  lean versus, 4–7, *5*
  shift from, to multi-product develop-
    ment, 7–9
Sony, CD Walkman, 159
Stewart, J. M., 102
Strategic architecture, 106
Strategic portfolio planning, 114
Suzuki, 195
  Wagon R (Alto/Cervo), 108, 111

Time lag differences, 203
Toyota
  brands, 110
  Camry, 28
  Celica/Carina ED, 28
  Central Research & Development
    Laboratories, Inc., 40
  Corolla, 14, 147–148
  Corona/Carina, 28, 108
  Crown, 20–21
  ES 300, 37–38
  Future Project 21 (FP21), 21
  Ipsum, 108
  just-in-time (JIT) technologies, 19
  lessons from, 184–189
  organizational changes, outcomes of,
    42–48, *42*, *44*
  organizational changes, summary of,
    40–42, *41*
  organizational problems, 22–26, *22*
  performance and, 15–16, 19–20
  Raum, 108
  Starlet, 38
  Supra, 37–38
  Tercel, 38, 108
Toyota, development centers at
  benefits of, 42–48
  center 4, role of, 38–40, *39*
  center heads, roles of, 35–36, 43–44
  Center Management Meeting, 43

centers, role of, 45
chief engineers, hierarchical organization of, 37–38, *37*
  comparison of old/new body engineering division, *32*
  competition between centers, 47–48
  component sharing, 46–47
  cost management, 45–46
  creation of, 29–31, *30*
  cross-area system project, 39
  functional engineering divisions, reduction of, 31–34
  functional managers, reductions of projects for, 34–35
  performance improvements as a result of, 44–45, *44*, 220n.11
  planning divisions in each center, 36–37
  problems with, 48–49
Toyota, heavyweight project management system at
  chief engineer term replaced shusa, 21
  competition, impact of, 26–29

defined, 19
  functional managers, problems for, 24, 220n.9
  growth of staff, 23, 220nn.7,8
  narrow specialization, problems with, 24–25
  organizational problems, 22–26, *22*
  problems with, 20–29
  product teams, problems with, 25
  Research and Advanced Development (RAD) Group, 25–26, 29, 220n.10

Volkswagen-Audi
  brands, 108, 109
  matrix organization at, 57–58
Volvo
  matrix organization at, 57–58
  Mitsubishi and, 68, 111

Womack, J., 4

Xerox, 104

About the Authors

MICHAEL A. CUSUMANO is the Sloan Distinguished Professor of Management at the MIT Sloan School of Management. He was educated at Princeton University (A.B.) and Harvard University (Ph.D.) and has been a Fulbright Fellow at the University of Tokyo, a postdoctoral fellow at the Harvard Business School, and a visiting professor and researcher at Hitotsubashi University, the University of Tokyo, and the University of Maryland. He specializes in product development management and competitive strategy in the computer software and automobile industries, and often writes on Japanese and U.S. comparisons. He consults widely with major corporations around the world in the area of software development and technology strategy. His books include *The Japanese Automobile Industry* (1985), *Japan's Software Factories* (1991), and international bestseller *Microsoft Secrets* (1995, with Richard Selby), which has been translated into fourteen foreign languages. He is currently writing another book on flexible and rapid strategic planning and product development at Netscape and other Internet software companies.

KENTARO NOBEOKA is Associate Professor of Business at Kobe University, where he teaches management of technology and corporate strategy. His current research interests are in the management of new product development, supplier network, and the effective usage of CAD tools. He is the author of *Multi-Project Strategy* (in Japanese), which won the Nikkei Prize for Excellent Books in Economic Science in 1997. He has seven years of experience as a product planner with Mazda Motor Corp., where he was involved in project management teams for the RX-7, Miata, and 929. He received his B.S. degree in mechanical engineering from Osaka University, and M.S. and Ph.D. degrees in management from the Massachusetts Institute of Technology.

Made in the USA
Lexington, KY
30 September 2010